t
5.4.07

MUSLIMS AND THE NEWS MEDIA

MUSLIMS AND THE NEWS MEDIA

Edited by

Elizabeth Poole

and

John E. Richardson

I.B. TAURIS

LONDON · NEW YORK

Published in 2006 by I.B.Tauris & Co Ltd
6 Salem Road, London W2 4BU
175 Fifth Avenue, New York, NY 10010
www.ibtauris.com

In the United States of America and Canada distributed by Palgrave Macmillan,
a division of St. Martin's Press, 154 Fifth Avenue, New York, NY 10010

ISBN 1 84511 171 0   (hardback)
EAN 978 1 84511 171 7   (hardback)
ISBN 1 84511 172 9   (paperback)
EAN 978 1 84511 172 4   (paperback)

A full CIP record for this book is available from the British Library
A full CIP record for this book is available from the Library of Congress

Library of Congress catalog card: available

Project management by M&M Publishing Services
Typeset in 10/12pt Times by FiSH Books, Enfield, Middx.
Printed and bound in Great Britain by MPG Books Ltd, Bodmin

For Jude

Contents

List of Figures

List of Tables

Acknowledgements

This book could not have been completed without the support and assistance of many people. We would like to thank Philippa Brewster at I.B. Tauris for initially asking Liz to put together an edited book on this subject.

We are very grateful for the collaboration from the contributors to this volume – the authors included and those whose chapters unfortunately did not make the final cut. Not only did they submit fascinating and valuable chapters, they sent them on time (for the most part!) and accepted our suggested edits and alterations with understanding and generosity of spirit. Our thanks to Lee Armstrong at Design Mule for his help in sourcing the cover image and to our students, colleagues and friends who have read and commented on draft versions of the chapters in this book or otherwise supported its development. In particular, we would like to thank Daphna Baram and Simon Cottle for endorsing the manuscript with enthusiasm.

On a more personal note, this book was put together during difficult times for both of us, for different reasons. The love and support of our families and friends has been indispensable in helping us get through. Thank you all.

Elizabeth Poole, Staffordshire University
John E. Richardson, Loughborough University
September 2005

List of Contributors

Sameera Ahmed has conducted a longitudinal study about the connection between media representation and Muslim women's identity. She is currently teaching Islamic Studies at the University of Manchester.

Mike Berry is currently working as a researcher at the University of Glasgow on an ESRC financed project examining political communication strategies in the run up to the 2005 British general election. Previously he worked on a three year study that examined the reporting of the Israel–Palestine conflict and its impact on public knowledge, the results of which were published as 'Bad News from Israel' (2004, Pluto Press). He has also worked as a researcher at the University of California on projects looking at international patterns of media censorship. His research interests include political communication, economic and development journalism, the Israel–Palestine conflict and audience research methodologies.

Gary R. Bunt is a lecturer in Islamic Studies at University of Wales, Lampeter. Having a special research interest in religion on the Internet, he has written *Virtually Islamic,* and *Islam in the Digital Age.* Gary instigated and coordinated the TRIS Interactive Widening Access research project (1999) for Lampeter, funded by HEFCW, and aimed at school leavers in underrepresented groups. He is currently researching open and distance learning for the LTSN, with a particular emphasis on accessibility issues, pedagogy and technological solutions for distance learning. Gary has first-hand experience of using video conferencing technology to teach, actively encouraging the integration of the Web as a teaching tool within his own modules. Prior to entering academia, he worked in production and research for the BBC and other broadcasters.

Professor Peter Cole is head of the department of Journalism Studies at the University of Sheffield. Before joining the academy Cole worked as a national newspaper journalist. He was a reporter, news editor and deputy editor on the *Guardian*. He was founder editor of *The Sunday Correspondent*, editor of the News Review section of *The Sunday Times*, Londoner's Diary editor on the *Evening Standard* and reporter, diary writer and New York correspondent on the *London Evening News*. He is on the board of the National Council for the Training of Journalists and the Society of Editors. He chairs the Society's training committee, where he has been responsible for reports on training and newsroom diversity. He writes a weekly column on media affairs for the *Independent on Sunday*.

Liz Fekete is Deputy Director of the Institute of Race Relations and senior researcher on the IRR's European Race Audit. Her most recent publications include *Racism: the Hidden Cost of September 11* and *Anti-Muslim Racism in the European Security State*.

Fred Halliday is Professor of International Relations at the London School of Economics. He has travelled widely and written extensively on the Middle East, international relations and politics in the contemporary climate. He is author of *Two Hours that Shook the World. September 11, 2001: Causes and Consequences* (Saqi Books 2001) and *Islam and the Myth of Confrontation: Religion and Politics in the Middle East* (I.B. Tauris 1996).

Siobhan Holohan is an independent scholar specialising in race, representation and power. A social and cultural theorist and a qualitative researcher she has studied the representation of crime and major trials such as that of O.J. Simpson and that of Stephen Lawrence. She has published widely in this area and is the author of *The Search for Justice in a Media Age* (Ashgate 2005).

Karim H. Karim is an assistant professor at the School of Journalism and Communication, Carleton University in Ottawa. Prior to teaching, he worked as a journalist for the Rome-based Inter Press Service and the Luxemburg-based Compass News Features. He has published on the social aspects of traditional and new media, diasporic communication, transnational news flows, and the depiction of various peoples.

Alina Korn is assistant lecturer in the department of Criminology at Bar-Ilan University, Israel. Her research interests include social control, sociology of law, and the links between crime, politics and the media. Her current research is concerned with the ghettoisation of Palestine.

Peter Manning is Adjunct Professor of Journalism and Senior Lecturer at the University of Technology, Sydney, and is currently completing a doctorate on media representations of Arabic and Muslim people in Australia. He is a former head of Current Affairs at the commercial Seven Network, a former head of News and Current Affairs at the Australian Broadcasting Corporation, a former executive producer and producer of the investigative programme on ABC TV, 'Four Corners', and a print journalist at the *Sydney Morning Herald*.

David Miller is Professor of Sociology in the Department of Geography and Sociology. He is also co-founder of Spinwatch (http://www. spinwatch.org) which monitors corporate spin and government propaganda. His recent books include *Arguments against G8* (Pluto 2005, co-editor); *Tell Me Lies: Propaganda and Media Distortion in the Attack on Iraq* (Pluto 2004, editor); *Open Scotland? Journalists, Spin Doctors and Lobbyists* (Polygon 2001, co-author); and *Market Killing: What Capitalism does and what Social Scientists can do about it* (Longman 2001, co-author).

Julian Petley is Professor of Film and Television Studies in the School of Arts at Brunel University, joint chair of the Campaign for Press and Broadcasting Freedom and a trustee of MediaWise. His most recent book, co-written with James Curran and Ivor Gaber, is *Culture Wars: the Media and the British Left* (Edinburgh University Press 2005). He is a member of the board of the *British Journalism Review* and principal editor of the *Journal of British Cinema and Television*. He is currently writing *The Censorious Press* for Routledge.

Greg Philo is the research director of the Glasgow University Media Group. His latest book is *Bad News From Israel* (Pluto 2004).

Lawrence Pintak is director of the Adham Center for Television Journalism at the American University in Cairo. A veteran of thirty years in journalism on four continents, Pintak has contributed to many of the world's leading news organizations. He has also served as Howard R. Marsh Visiting Professor of Journalism and Public Policy at the University of Michigan. Pintak covered the birth of suicide bombing as CBS News Middle East correspondent in the 1980s and more recently reported on the overthrow of Indonesian President Suharto for *The San Francisco Chronicle* and ABC News. He won two Overseas Press Club awards for his Middle East coverage and was twice nominated for Emmys. His books include *Beirut Outtakes: A TV Correspondent's Portrait of America's Encounter with*

Terror (Lexington 1988); *Seeds of Hate: How America's flawed Middle East policy ignited the jihad* (Pluto 2003); and *Reflections in a Bloodshot Lens: America, Islam & the War of Ideas* (Pluto/Univ of Michigan 2006).

Elizabeth Poole is a lecturer in Media Studies at Staffordshire University and a specialist in the representation of Islam and the media. Having published widely in the area of representation, media audiences and new technologies, she has also worked with the Muslim community to bring awareness of their marginalization to the public sphere. She is the author of *Reporting Islam: Media Representations of British Muslims* (I.B. Tauris 2002).

John E. Richardson is a lecturer in the Department of Social Sciences, Loughborough University. His research interests include racism in journalism, readers' letters, (critical) discourse analysis and argumentation. His recent publications include the book *(Mis)Representing Islam* (2004 John Benjamins), the co-authored book *Key Concepts in Journalism* (2005 Sage) and articles on argumentation and prejudice in readers' letters.

Isabelle Rigoni holds a Ph.D. from the University Paris 8, France. She completed post-doctoral research on minority ethnic media as an EU Marie Curie Research Fellow at the Centre for Research in Ethnic Relations (University of Warwick, 2001–03), and at the Centre Marc Bloch (Berlin 2004–05). She has been teaching for several years in sociology and political science in the universities of Paris 8 and Evry-Val d'Essonne. Her books include *Faire figure d'étranger: regards croisés sur la production de l'altérité* (2004, edited with C. Cossée and E. Lada); *Mobilisations et enjeux des migrations turques en Europe de l'Ouest* (2001); and *Turquie, les mille visages. Politique, religion, femmes, immigration* (2000, ed.) and has written numerous articles on migration (identity, media, transnational association networks, citizenship) and political violence through the Kurdish and Tamil cases. She is currently working on the minority ethnic media in Europe.

Mohamed Zayani is Associate Professor of Critical Theory at the American University of Sharjah, UAE. He received his Ph.D. from Indiana University in Bloomington. He is the author of *Arab Satellite Television and Politics in the Middle East* (ECSSR 2004) and *The Al Jazeera Phenomenon: Critical Perspectives on New Arab Media* (Pluto Press 2005). Currently, he is working on a collaborative Social Science Research Council research project on media in the Arab world.

Introduction

This book examines the role and representation of Muslims in the news media in both British and international contexts. The collection includes sections explaining the circumstances and the politics surrounding the representation of Muslims, the presence and influence of Muslims in the processes of news production, studies of outputs from a range of journalistic genres, media and national contexts, and media uses and practices of audiences, both Muslim and non-Muslim. Drawing on the critical insights and research of academics and the experiences of professional journalists, this book discusses a range of noteworthy issues and themes, draws on a variety of research methods and analyses diverse national and international media to make more general comments on the manner in which Islam and Muslims are represented, and *mis*represented, in the news media.

There were three principal motivations for putting this edited book together. First, the book answers a theoretical desire to demonstrate, in as full a way as possible, the constituted and creative nature of journalism. In other words, we attempt to 'square the circle' of journalism studies and show how social ideas shape the way in which Islam and Muslims are reported and, in turn, the way that journalism helps shape the ideas that the general public hold about Islam and Muslims. It goes without saying that Islam and the activities of certain Muslims are very newsworthy subjects. Indeed, very few of the more significant news stories of the past few years have not included Muslims in some form or other while very few of the stories 'about Muslims' over this same period have been about anything other than 'the War on Terror'. It is in this climate of threat, fear and misunderstanding that the reporting of Islam and Muslims is currently situated – circumstances that, we feel, not only influence the content of journalism but also can be reproduced in and through the news media.

Second, there remains an empirical need to situate and study journalistic discourse in its social, cultural and national contexts of production. News about Muslims is partly the result of international 'flashbulb' events – such as 9/11 (the terrorist attack on the World Trade Center in New York, 2001), the invasion of Iraq, the Beslan hostage massacre and others – but it is also affected by local histories, local concerns and local agendas. Such local concerns will typically and principally revolve around particular colonial histories; patterns of migration and settlement (e.g. 'Pakistani Muslims in Bradford', 'Moroccan Muslims in Amsterdam'); secularism and/vs. multiculturalism (e.g. Muslim schools, French laïcité and the ban on hijab); and the actions and interests of prominent neighbouring Muslim countries. That said, due to the centralisation and intensification of political and economic globalisation, the increasing standardisation of journalism due to the (often ideological) norms of the profession and the widespread and continuing influence of Orientalist imagery and scholarship (particularly post-9/11 and in relation to the 'War on Terror'), news about Muslims displays certain consistencies from country to country. Thus, this book examines both the specific features of certain national reporting concerns and their similarities with prominent themes of other national contexts.

Further, the particular production requirements of the different news media exert an unquestionable influence on the content of the journalistic texts they produce. For example, the absence of newspaper regulation compared to broadcast news media allows newspapers to print the often extreme views of columnists and letter writers. Similarly, the need for pictures exerts a particularly strong influence on television media, wherein stories can be ignored due to boring pictures or else not included because pictures could not be obtained. Hence, this book analyses journalistic texts taken from a range of news media, and produced and disseminated a range of national contexts.

Third, we feel there is a pressing ethical and political obligation to criticise and counteract the distorted reporting that so often characterises the coverage of Islam and Muslims. It goes without saying that the potential effects of negative reporting patterns – from encouraging acts of individual street racism and giving succour to extreme right-wing political parties to encouraging discriminatory political policies such as racial profiling and the detention of Muslims without trial, validating the current 'imperialist adventures' of the US–UK and further excluding and disenfranchising Muslim communities – are issues of great social consequence. However, we feel that any critique of journalism should be made from a frame of reference that understands the pressures that journalists are faced with, respects good journalism and, where applicable, commends good journalistic practice. Hence, the selected contributors include a range of critical, reflective practitioners and production-minded academics.

The book in outline

This book aims to examine and elucidate the links between social and political contexts, institutional and professional production practices, the content of media outputs and the perceptions and responses of audiences in relation to the reporting of Islam and Muslims. The book is structured over three sections: Context, Politics and Production; Media Outputs; and Audience Practices – in order to attempt to reflect the whole cycle of the journalistic communication process and the reproduction of social meanings on this most important and timely subject. Opening our collection is a chapter by Siobhan Holohan that provides essential background to the rhetoric and reality of multiculturalism in Britain, and specifically the successive responses of governments to the 'problems' assumedly caused by the presence of Britain's ethnic minority communities. Her discussion takes us as far as David Blunkett's reactionary and (some would argue *racist*) White Paper *Secure Borders, Safe Haven* (2002), with its emphasis on patriotism, requiring immigrants to prove their loyalty to the UK and associating Muslims with the 'terror threat'. In conclusion, Holohan suggests that New Labour's approach to multiculturalism seems to be regressing 'towards a strong idea of national identity evocative of Powell and the theory of ethnic assimilationism' (p.22).

Following this historic and theoretical contextualisation, the next chapters study aspects of the contemporary position of Muslims in Britain and Europe. In the first, Fred Halliday writes about the BBC's dismissal of presenter Robert Kilroy-Silk, following a particularly vitriolic attack on 'Arabs' that he wrote for the *Express on Sunday* newspaper. As a consequence of this dismissal, a 'debate' raged for some weeks in newspaper letters pages and elsewhere on the limits of free speech. In this chapter, Halliday offers four observations on anti-Arab prejudice as a contribution to this debate. Next, Liz Fekete describes the techniques of racial profiling currently being used by European security services and illustrates their racist consequences, particularly for Muslims. Using 9/11 as a pretext, European security services have extended surveillance structures to profile any groups perceived to constitute a 'threat'. Fekete argues that such racial profiling not only institutionalises discrimination, it actually 'gives terror networks a formula for greater success' (p.43), since by default it provides the criteria which security services do not consider 'suspicious'. David Miller's chapter also discusses the current preoccupation of the security state with 'terror', concentrating on the propaganda apparatuses of the UK and, to a lesser extent, US governments. Miller demonstrates a quite frightening degree of complicity between governmental propagandists and

3

the news media in whipping up waves of panic regarding the presence of Muslim terrorists in the UK. Dubious intelligence is fed to journalists; which, because it appears credible to most mainstream journalists, is reported as the authoritative views of experts; and, in an 'almost absurdly circular' fashion, these same reports have been used as evidence in the deportation of Muslims. Miller shows that it is this circularity, in which the actions of journalists and security services appear to substantiate each other, that has contributed to the success of the 'terror threat' propaganda campaign.

The book then moves to examine certain institutional and occupational issues of news production in more detail. Julian Petley's chapter on the Press Complaints Commission (PCC) suggests that the application of journalism's own professional codes of practice does not encourage fair and accurate representations of Muslims either. The PCC Code of Practice requires newspapers to 'avoid prejudicial or pejorative reference to a person's race, colour, religion, sex or sexual orientation', but Petley shows that they are failing in their role to censure newspapers who violate this code. Despite receiving 586 complaints about discrimination (19.8 percent of complaints received, a rise from 1.7 percent in 1993) not a single one concerning racism or religious discrimination has ever been upheld by the PCC. In response, Petley provocatively concludes that the PCC is part of the problem of press racism, not part of the solution, and should be replaced by a statutory right of reply.

The final two chapters of this section discuss the employment of Muslim journalists. In the first, Peter Cole examines the continuing disparity between white and minority ethnic journalists in mainstream newsrooms, particularly those of local and regional newspapers. Despite finding dreadfully low numbers of black and minority ethnic journalists, Cole does detect 'a new recognition at a senior level in these major publishers that recruitment of journalists from the ethnic minorities was an issue that had to be addressed'. (p.71) The work that remains to be done to bring about significant improvement, Cole concludes, can only occur through the use of champions in the industry, cross-industry commitment to change and a concerted effort of journalism educators – both inside and outside the industry – to attract and retain black journalists. Of course, the mainstream news media are not the only journalists on the block, and in the second chapter discussing employment, Isabelle Rigoni looks at the Muslim minority press in France and Britain. Her discussion demonstrates the significance of Muslim minority media – not only to the Muslim journalists who work for such publications, but also to the wider Muslim communities who view (and use) the Muslim news media as forums to represent their views and identities. Less positively, the chapter demonstrates the role that Islamophobia plays in constructing the identities of Muslims in 'the West'. Many of Rigoni's interviewees suggest that it was in reaction to Islamophobia that they (re)identified themselves as Muslims and that it was Islamophobia that provoked them to re-engage with social concerns of Muslim minorities, such as discrimination. The media she studies function as a palliative to such social exclusion, making their users feel that they can be Muslims in the West; and that 'British and Muslim' and 'French and Muslim' are complementary rather than contradictory identities.

The second section of the book examines the impact of context on media output. It is output that tends to be the most focused on and controversial area in discussions of Muslims and the news media. Examined here is the reporting of the mainstream media (mainly printed) in four 'Western' countries, those countries where one might expect (due to context) the most distorted representations: the UK (press, Poole and Richardson), the US (media in general, Karim), Australia (press, Manning) and Israel (press, Korn).

Using a combination of quantitative and qualitative methods of content analysis, the findings of the research that follows illustrates the negativity of the mainstream media towards Muslims. Muslims are most likely to be represented as terrorists (Poole, Korn and Manning) or cited as terrorist sources, whilst ordinary Muslims are marginalised (Richardson). A conflictual framework dominates (Korn, Karim and Manning). Other common themes found by these authors include the illegitimacy, criminality, violence, extremity, fanaticism, sexual aggression and disloyalty of Muslims. Religion is often given as an explanatory factor for behaviour, and overall an official hegemonic viewpoint dominates.

Furthermore, several chapters show the impact of recent events on reporting in the authors respective countries. How, for example, September 11th (Poole, Karim and Manning), the war in Iraq (Poole and Manning) and the Palestinian intifida (Korn) have narrowed the framework of reporting whereby US led ideas/understandings of these events, or in the case of Korn, an Israeli official consensus, dominates even local news. This homogenisation is more likely to take effect during crisis points, in times of war, for example.

Despite the force of dominant discourse, however, counter spaces exist within national contexts. As content is politically (and commercially) driven, local circumstances allow for some variety in representation as demonstrated by the reporting of the liberal press in Israel and the UK. However, Manning's chapter on reporting in Australia shows how US definitions of the war on terror have been concretised on an international scale, despite its different historical and political context. Although coverage of Muslims in the mainstream press has increased in the context of recent events (Poole, Richardson and Manning), it seems that this has been at the expense of alternative reporting, which remains marginal.

Through a combination of quantitative (Poole, Richardson and Manning) and qualitative approaches (Richardson, Karim, Manning and Korn) the *what* and *how* of Muslims' representation is established. Quantitative techniques allow us to establish what is newsworthy about Muslims whilst qualitative techniques analyse meaning. Karim in his chapter, for example, outlines the 'core stereotypes that characterise dominant Western representations of Islam' (p.119) as well as the selection, construction and emphasis that takes place through the representation of high profile cases (such as the kidnapping of Private Jessica Lynch) which contribute to a particular public knowledge about Muslims.

What is more, having established a news framework, these findings illustrate the strength and consistency of this framework over time. Karim demonstrates how even the unusual becomes routinised as new events are forced into existing frames of reference. Hence, Muslims are 'Othered' in a mediated world where simplistic notions of good and evil peoples find currency.

As these chapters focus on mainstream images in the mainstream media we feel it important to question whether new media forms are offering a space for alternative voices to be represented, heard and strengthened. Does the Internet offer us a really revolutionary tool for a more democratic future? Gary Bunt explores this question by examining how Muslims across the world are utilising the Net as an outlet for a range of political, religious and cultural activities. The chapter demonstrates how a technology that is decentralised and allows for connectivity and interactivity can be harnessed for countering dominant representations, enhancing dialogue and encouraging participation. However, the Islamic nature of Muslims' surfing activities should not be over emphasised. It should not be assumed that Muslim uses of the Internet are greatly different from general surfing habits. There is also the problem of access: the low levels of take up in Arab countries, for example, demonstrate how offline inequalities are reinforced in the online world. Whilst the Internet does allow for a diversity of voices and a place where Muslims can overcome their marginalisation, many of their activities remain at the periphery of Net consumption. As with other media forms, the capabilities of technology do not mean they will be used in a particular way. The struggle for control of new technologies is clearly demonstrated here.

Content illustrates the norms and values of particular media and the wider society in which it is located. It provides a cultural indicator of conceptualisations of a nation, the 'in' and 'out' groups. A central interest in content, however, is its links to 'effects'. We can only say something further about this relationship with reference to audience research. In the final section we consider the impact of the media on Muslims themselves, both community media on minorities within the UK (Ahmed) and transnational media forms on wider Muslim societies (Zayani and Pintak) before returning to understandings of media events by Western audiences (Philo and Berry).

As we have seen from Gary Bunt's chapter in the previous section, alternative media offer audiences both another source of information and a voice to the marginalised, indicating a greater democratic potential. The first three chapters in this section show how there is a greater need for this following events such as September 11. Such key events reinforce the need for communities to make connections, unify, voice opinions and counteract negative representations, hence there was a clear need for this gap to be filled socially, culturally and politically. For Ahmed, this role has been performed for British Muslims by new forms of community media whilst Zayani and Pintak argue that Middle Eastern satellite television, especially al-Jazeera, has been of particular importance.

The findings of their research show the importance of these particularistic media for providing the marginalised or disenfranchised with a sense of identity and therefore a wider sense of community. For example, in Britain, Ahmed argues, dissatisfaction with the mainstream and minority press (focusing on national/racial groups and often printed in second languages) and a growing sense of religious identity saw the development of Muslim media forms that specifically recognised this British Muslimness. For Ahmed this identity is 'active' resulting in consciously driven media consumption, which then results in the strengthening of these identities. The emergence of this Muslim media in the UK has given Muslim voices more access to the mainstream media as the journalists working for them become recognised as credible professionals.

The importance of identity is also emphasised by Zayani who illustrates the role of satellite news channel al-Jazeera in unifying and mobilising opinion in the Arab world. He argues that the fledgling channel has given what traditionally has been known as 'the Arab street' a voice. This and the loss of control (by the authorities) of people's media consumption has introduced an element of popular pressure not only in the Arab Middle East but also at an international level. However, Zayani also stresses the complexities of this process. It is not simply a straightforward case of al-Jazeera influencing public opinion. The channel allows people to relate to each other, interact even, outside their own private worlds and for the circulation of ideas. Public opinion, which already had a presence, is given publicity, and hence becomes visible.

These complexities are reiterated by Pintak who shows that, despite the polarised rhetoric of US and Arab leaders reproduced in the news media, there is little difference in the attitudes to the US of Muslim viewers of CNN, the BBC or al-Jazeera. On the one hand then the 'perception gap' between the US administration and Muslims around the world appears to be caused by the framing of events in a simplistic way on opposing sides, creating 'rhetorical borders' which are reproduced by the media, yet this again is too simplistic. Pintak shows how people interpret events through their own worldview, however it has been framed. In fact they will select items from the news that support their own perspective even if the thrust of the content is in opposition to this. This confirms audience theory that suggests audiences are discriminating and selective in their interpretation of media events. However, the role of the media in reinforcing dominant viewpoints through framing is also illustrated by Philo and Berry. Their extensive research into public understandings of the Israeli–Palestinian conflict is a useful end piece as it studies the different stages of the communication process, as we have done in this book in its entirety. They demonstrate the relationship between production processes, content and audiences, showing how news about this event is constructed. Content is decontextualised, ahistorical, sensationalist, relies on official sources and uses specific language to frame events in a particular way. Their findings show that Western audiences express an understanding of the conflict that relates to the way it has been framed. The last two chapters together demonstrate that resisting news frameworks about 'the Other' requires important situational knowledge and experience.

What is clearly evident from this work is the role of the media in processes of democracy. The media, particularly these alternative sources, offer Muslims a revitalised public sphere. Processes of identification and unification are enhanced as an 'imagined community' becomes apparent. This has been more necessary in times where Muslim identities have become a target for criticism. However, this raises a further issue for democracy. These media forms might give people a voice but if this is then ignored within wider politics it may have serious consequences leading to Muslim dissociation. The reliance on television for news demonstrated by Philo and Berry's research shows the responsibility of the news media for informing people. Yet if it leads to the confusion also found in their audiences, how is an informed debate possible? Philo and Berry's success in filtering their research through to the public sphere and, in particular, the professional sector which is under analysis, demonstrates one way in which we might start to have an effect on representations. The responses of journalists, however, illustrate the constraints that they are under, as we have tried to demonstrate in the first section of this book. Philo and Berry suggest that only a reconsideration of the structure and development of news will make some impact on creating the democratic public sphere needed here.

We have tried to incorporate the whole 'cycle of communication' here to illustrate the workings of journalism when it comes to the representation of Muslims. However, these sections are manufactured for easy analysis. The chapters themselves demonstrate the lack of clear, discrete boundaries: Karim shows how an analysis of context and production is necessary for understanding content; Ahmed, Philo and Berry illustrate how an analysis of production is vital for understanding audiences. What this demonstrates is the workings of social power: audience understanding of events can be severely limited by news frameworks; public perceptions then feed back into policy; and for Muslims, the negative representations in circulation produce a climate where they are further repressed by heavy-handed legislation and military power. This book shows how the cycle of communication comes full circle, how journalism contributes to social reality.

Part 1
Context, Politics and Production

1. New Labour, Multiculturalism and the Media in Britain

Siobhan Holohan

In recent years the term multiculturalism has been embraced in Western societies who want to build cultures of tolerance and equality for all citizens. Contemporary British politicians, regardless of their party affiliation, would be foolish to ignore the needs and desires of any group able to cast a vote. For this reason politicians now regard the rhetoric of multiculturalism as an essential component of their everyday speech. What is more, this trend towards outward expressions of inclusiveness has not gone unnoticed by the media, who increasingly report on the wonderful diversity of multicultural Britain. Indeed the picture that is often painted about contemporary Britain is one that suggests that, despite its problems, our society is heading in the right direction. In response to this position there have been several attempts to locate the idealistic concept of multiculturalism in public policy, most notably in the 2000 Race Relations (Amendment) Act, which came about after criticisms of institutional racism outlined in the Macpherson Report (1999) and the Parekh Report (2000), which attempted to point a way forward towards a truly multi-ethnic society. But what is actually revealed when we take a closer look at the discourse of difference? What does multiculturalism mean to the various groups competing for recognition in today's chaotic public sphere?

World events such as the terrorist attacks on New York and Washington and the war in Iraq have highlighted just how fragile cross-cultural relations continue to be in our global society. Instead of the harmonious existence portrayed in a good deal of contemporary political and media rhetoric, we are witnessing a far more antagonistic relationship between British 'insiders' and those who still exist on the fringes of white British society by virtue of visible religious, cultural, or ethnic difference. Attempts by the press to deny the hostile relationship between white and minority ethnic Britons simply underscores the reality that tensions really do exist. Therefore, in an effort to unravel the myths from the realities, this chapter seeks to trace the discourse of self/other relations within the context of New

Labour's politics and the push by media agencies to present an image of harmony in contemporary Britain.

The Roots of Race Relations in Great Britain

It is a common myth that the population of Britain has ever been united in terms of ethnicity, religion or culture. Historically people have migrated either to escape trouble or in search of work. In Britain ethnic populations have always contributed to the building of the nation state. For instance the historical period immediately after the Second World War saw migrant labour welcomed into Britain in order to help boost the post-war economy. Yet until quite recently it was considered acceptable to divide people in terms of perceived racial difference. In the post-war years the British Empire was still fresh in public consciousness. White Britain could 'open its doors' precisely because it believed that the new entrants were second-class citizens brought in to fill the jobs that no one else wanted. As a result of this popular imaginary the nation could be safe in the knowledge that generosity to its colonial cousins could not possibly backfire on its own citizens. The idea that white people were somehow naturally more intelligent and better suited to superior jobs discounted the idea that the new immigrant workforce would ever achieve more than their colour allowed (Anthias and Yuval-Davies 1992).

But race relations took a turn for the worse as various ethnic populations began to form separate communities in order to avoid harassment. Although driven to this strategy of group formation by overt discrimination in housing and work opportunities, the white working-class population, buoyed by political flag waving and press scaremongering, saw large communities of blacks and Asians as a threat to their British way of life. In 1968 Conservative MP Enoch Powell notoriously sought to exploit this fear of the other. His inflammatory 'Rivers of Blood' speech, which was critical of the perceived privileges afforded to the 'Commonwealth immigrant' under proposed amendments to the 1965 Race Relations Act, further aggravated the antagonism between cultures:

> For these dangerous and divisive elements the legislation proposed in the Race Relations Bill is the very pabulum they need to flourish. Here is the means of showing that the immigrant communities can organise to consolidate their members, to agitate and campaign against their fellow citizens, and to overawe and dominate the rest with the legal weapons which the ignorant and the ill-informed have provided. As I look ahead, I am filled with foreboding; like the Roman, I seem to see the River Tiber foaming with much blood.

While Powell was widely condemned by political leaders and sacked from his position in the shadow cabinet, his views were symptomatic of a wider discontent that followed the decline of secure white identity. It was against this turbulent backdrop that the first Race Relations Acts in 1965 and 1968 gave ethnic minorities the legal authority to protest against overt discrimination in the workplace, education and housing. In this regard the Acts gave some definition to the debate about how migrants to Britain should integrate into majority society. Nevertheless, following the experience of socio-political racism throughout the 1960s and 1970s, black activists in Britain wanted to maintain race as a privileged site of political struggle. Within this framework the category of race worked as a discursive reminder of power relations and inequality in Britain in order to provide a platform for social and political criticism.

According to this idea writers such as Stuart Hall and Paul Gilroy sought to apply a New Left model of critical theory to reveal how discourse worked to maintain social inequality. After Hall et al.'s (1978) earlier attempts to theorise ethnic conflict using the example of mugging, Hall and Jacques (1983) expanded the idea of antagonism in *The Politics of Thatcherism*. In this work they explained how the political ideology of market forces promoted by Margaret Thatcher's administration allowed racism to flourish under the discourse of equality. The paradox of this situation was that it was precisely the politics that sought to universalise difference that sustained ethnic conflict. That is to say that ethnic difference became the most basic form of identification for groups of people who felt that they had no identity under market capitalism.

The urban street protests that flared up in the 1980s took place in response to Thatcher's increased emphasis on a law and order state. The common identification of the protests as 'riots' followed the logic of the Conservative's zero tolerance policy on domestic insurgence. According to writers such as Benyon and Solomos (1987) black protesters, aggrieved by increased police 'stop and search' powers that targeted their communities, were portrayed as criminals bent on violence and destruction. Supported by widespread press coverage of the protests as evidence of mass deviance, the legal and cultural criminalisation of urban blacks was able to pass off without too much opposition. For a time racism continued to exist beneath the surface of British society. Apart from occasional eruptions of violence, which came to highlight racial antagonism, ethnic conflict became dispersed into ordinary everyday life where it was normalised as an accepted part of social relations. For this reason anti-racists thought it important to continue to draw attention to the racism beneath the surface of popular representation

v the myth of a multicultural harmony with occasional
ıal violence to persist unchecked.

The Multicultural Dilemma

Since the demise of what Kundnani (2000) has called 'Thatcher's
monocultural society' and the rise of Blair's multicultural imaginary,
critical anti-racism seems to have been discarded in favour of theories of
difference adequate to the reality of the global market. Whereas the idea of
anti-racism is to attack racism through its opposite (anti-racism), the
postmodern theory of multiculturalism seeks to move beyond the idea of
self/other opposition to embrace the politics of cultural difference. For this
reason the postmodern understanding of identity, put forward by authors
such as Charles Taylor (1994), can be seen to refer to policy adopted by
countries such as Canada and Australia in the 1970s. In these countries
multicultural policies were introduced to back the attempt to promote
polyethnicity (Kymlicka 1995). In this sense multiculturalism meant that
(white) migrant settlers could, indeed should, maintain their specific
cultural identity, rather than adopt the cultural signifiers of the host nation.
This new socio-political agenda insisted upon an ethic that was inclusive of
all, and privileged none. No one religious, cultural or ethnic group could be
seen to benefit over another, but rather everyone would gain by merit.
Embracing this ideology of mass democracy, multiculturalism suggests that
all cultures are different but equal.

Thus, theoretical multiculturalism evolved from the recognition that we
are all different. This recognition became a criticism of the essentialism of
the racist/anti-racist binary, which, according to theorists who advocate
difference, merely replicated constructions of race. Outwardly this position
grounds Hall's (1992) identification of the mythologies that show the idea of
race to be the naturalisation of cultural difference. Hall's argument is that in
order successfully to create the subject of the nation state, national identities
must be formed around what Benedict Anderson (1983) previously called
'imagined communities'. Here, identity is constructed around a set of
shared, or collective, myths about how the nation was formed in order to
illicit patriotism and allegiance to that nation. However, Canadian political
theorist Will Kymlicka (1995) explains that such shared myths, which are
adopted by state institutions as discursive tools for interpolating subjects,
also work to separate those that do not adhere to the current rules of
nationality. In other words, the idea of the insider always creates an outsider.

Against the construction of identity around national myths, which work
to exclude those who pursue different cultural practices, multiculturalism

puts forward an ideology that embraces difference. For Hall this can be observed in the formation of new identities where the 'oscillation between Tradition and Translation' (Hall 1992: 310) produces hybrid identities peculiar to the time and place in which they occur. In these communities people may remain close to their cultural roots, but also take on characteristics of the place in which they now reside. Hall imagines that this hybrid identity might take on the history and character of several different national and religious cultures that have been thrust together by post-colonial migrations. Multiculturalism therefore promotes difference above national identity and its exclusionary structures. In this respect it is also, like postmodernism, against the idea of a unified nation state.

However, it is clear that in many ways the idea of multiculturalism reflects the central tension of contemporary politics. How is it possible to reconcile the demands of multiculturalism and a globalised economy *and* uphold the demands of the nation state that confers authority on the political representatives who must try to negotiate the tension that is constitutive of this global/nation bind? Their very positions as elected representatives of nation states mean that contemporary politicians are faced with the conundrum that multiculturalism can never really embrace the idea of the cosmopolitan individual, because this would mean the collapse of their own national territories.

New Labour and Postmodern Politics

When New Labour was elected to government after eighteen years of Conservative rule it appeared to signal a change in momentum for British society. After Thatcher, John Major's Conservative government had made attempts at modernisation by introducing an ideology that centred on moderate conservatism. According to this ideology Major sought to water down the old style antagonism characteristic of the class politics that had previously been the focus of Tory rule. While in speeches to the Tory faithful he maintained the national myth of 'warm beer and cricket on the village green', by affirming his own Brixton roots Major also sought to emphasise the meritocratic nature of British society. His implication was that in 1990s Britain anybody could make it, regardless of their class, gender or ethnic background. The political purpose of this affirmation of the American ideology of a meritocratic society was to expand the Thatcherite strategy that sought to fragment mass political opposition.

However, Major's extension of Thatcher's strategy was a failure. Whereas the working classes could understand Thatcher's idealisation of hard work, achievement and lawfulness in terms of her shopkeeper roots,

Major's attempt to broaden this strategy to Britain's ethnic population was unbelievable. While Thatcher could pass for the austere working-class matron bent on self-betterment, Major could never pass for a young black man from Brixton. Instead his attempt to connect to Britain's non-white population came to emphasise the gulf between conservatism and the minority ethnic population.

At the same time as conservatism started to lose its credibility, Labour made a more successful pitch to the newly fragmented British electorate. Following their third straight electoral defeat, socialism was consigned to the dustbin of history. Neil Kinnock, the figure who seemed to epitomise traditional working-class identity through his Welsh roots, was also cast aside. In order to replace socialism and Kinnock, Labour became New Labour; socialism became third-way politics; Kinnock became Blair. Where Major and the Conservatives had failed to replace the haves/have nots political terrain with a universal middle-class model, Tony Blair and New Labour were successful.

In terms of Britain's minority ethnic population, the end of strict state control and the embrace of a neo-liberal market philosophy meant that certain pillars of British migration law had to be taken down in order to afford greater freedom of movement. New Labour started to dismantle clauses in British migrant settlement law upon their arrival in office (Back et al. 2002). For example, the 'primary purpose' law, which stopped foreigners from marrying British citizens to settle in the UK, was repealed. The purpose of this reform was to slacken border controls. Whereas such reform would have been problematic for the Conservatives, who remained the party of landed wealth, the gradual lowering of border controls was seen to be essential by New Labour. According to their economic policy such measures were necessary to improve Britain's relation to the global economy. Such moves could increase economic efficiency at home, but also enable what Bauman (2000) has called the liquid class to be more successful in their international transactions. From this point of view it is possible to see why the late 1990s became New Labour's multicultural years. Multiculturalism was a signifier of Britain's embrace of the political ideas of social inclusion, individualism, meritocracy and the globalisation of economic forces. Each of these innovations took place under the watchful eye of the caring, hands-off state.

The fly in the ointment for New Labour's utopic vision stemmed from incidences of racial violence left over from Tory rule. However, turning a problem into an advantage was simple for New Labour's professional spin doctors, who were able to turn an event that should have been an indicator of the existence of racism into an episode that could illustrate the

multicultural idealism of New Britain. Consequently the r
black teenager Stephen Lawrence was repackaged as a lefto'
divided by class and race. In contrast to the racism of old
Britannia' became an image of a nation united by a common multi-culture.
The icons of Cool Britannia, such as pop groups Oasis and the Spice Girls,
were mass cultural figures that could transcend boundaries of race, class
and gender and therefore show how Britain was a truly inclusive society at
the turn of the new millennium. Arguably the case of Stephen Lawrence
exemplified this movement towards multiculturalism due to the
'acceptable' characteristics of the Lawrence family (Holohan 2005). The
case had stagnated under the Conservatives. However, under New Labour
Lawrence became a sign of multicultural Britain, whereas his accused
killers became symbolic of the racial violence we needed to leave behind.

The turning point for race relations came when, four years after the
murder of Stephen Lawrence, the new Home Secretary, Jack Straw,
instigated an inquiry into the investigation by the Metropolitan Police under
the direction of Sir William Macpherson. After the failure to convict anyone
for the crime, Lawrence's parents were vocal in their condemnation of the
investigation. In this regard the case had been problematic for the press who
were faced with the family of a murdered black man accusing Britain of
being racist. However, unlike previous conflictual relations between the
press and black Britons, the Lawrences were able to effect a campaign that
centred on their inclusive identity traits, which in turn enabled them to
criticise the racism inherent in certain quarters of British society. The *Daily
Mail* in particular embraced this contemporary version of a normal and
pathological England. While the accused killers embodied white thugs,
akin to football hooligans (another pet topic for the *Daily Mail*), the
Lawrences were portrayed as a hard working, church going family unit. It
was these qualities that epitomised the multicultural ethos of New Britain.

However, this idealist vision of social inclusion was shattered after the
publication of the Macpherson Report in 1999. In the report, Macpherson
concluded that there was real evidence of institutionalised racism in the
Metropolitan Police. Although race relations had legislated against
discrimination on the basis of racial difference in work, education and
public services, until Macpherson's findings and recommendations the
police force had been exempt from this rule. Initially it had been omitted
upon the thought that anti-discrimination legislation would hamper police
in their inquiries if suspects were from ethnic minorities. To newspapers
such as the *Daily Mail*, which were famous for standing by the values of the
law and order society, institutional racism was a problematic accusation.
Indeed, in the midst of the flood of criticisms of the report, *Daily Mail*

columnist Stephen Glover summed up the oppositions argument when he stated that the report had effectively said that 'white Britons are a nation of racists' (24 February 1999).

At the same time that Macpherson was investigating claims into racism in the police force, an independent think tank, The Runnymede Trust, set up the Commission on *The Future of Multi-Ethnic Britain* (2000). Under the direction of Bhikhu Parekh, the Commission's aim was to 'analyse the current state of multi-ethnic Britain and to propose ways of making Britain a confident and vibrant multicultural society at ease with its rich diversity' (viii). Arguing that the multicultural vision is far from achieved, the report notes a need to change old ideas of what it means to be British at every level of daily life. Suggesting that former models of multiculturalism may have come to the end of their useful life, Parekh argues that we need to move towards a more tangible dialogue between cultures. Importantly for Parekh, this dialogue must be embedded in social, legal and political institutions.

Echoing conclusions from the Macpherson report – that policies need to be developed that rest on the recognition of individual identity – Parekh continues by advancing the idea of a 'common culture'. In this vision for a multi-ethnic future, citizens would be encouraged to forge new wide-ranging identities rather than focus on their differences, and institutions would be asked to provide services that respond to the diverse needs of every community. In order to achieve these goals the Commission also suggested that the idea of what it means to be British needs to be rethought, to include the many cultural and historical experiences of the UK's diverse population. The response to the report from the right-wing press was much the same as that which greeted Macpherson's effort to open dialogue between state institutions and ethnic citizens. Interpreting the report's findings within its own ideological framework, the *Daily Telegraph* dismissed it as 'drivel' (11 October 2000) and at the same time seized the opportunity to promote a new wave of nationalism and parochial conservatism:

> Still, we should be grateful to the Commission members for one thing: they have overreached themselves in their excitement, and have unintentionally put their governmental sponsors on the spot. The Conservatives now have an excellent chance to make good their past silence on Macpherson. They must expose the Government's collusion in this attempt to destroy a thousand years of British history. (12 October 2000)

Resistant to the idea that the cultural heritage of 'Britishness' could be construed as being racist, sections of the media began a campaign that privileged the notion of the UK as an inclusive nation. Anne-Marie Fortier (2005) chronicles this move in her analysis of the media's reaction to the Parekh Report, where she argues that articulations of pride and shame left multiculturalism open to a revised construction. For the right-wing press, multiculturalism under New Labour was no longer about inclusiveness but about marginalising the majority of 'British' (meaning white) subjects. However, this renewal of the 'us and them' binary included a new dimension. Instead of funding a return to antagonistic race relations, the press sought to exploit the ideology of multiculturalism to advocate the erasure of ethnic difference. Against what it regarded as a discourse of shame about British history coming from the Parekh Report, the press presented a succession of articles that expressed national pride from black and Asian Britons. Pop stars, sports men and women, business people and politicians came forward to endorse a universal ideal of Britishness. In just one example musician Craig David was quoted in the *Daily Mail* saying 'I'm proud to be British and call myself British. If you're not proud to be British then you're living in the wrong place' (12 October 2000). In yet another extract from the *Mail*, Raj Chandran declares his subject status when he states 'the truth is that nobody forced me or any other immigrant to become British. I did so by choice' (10 October 2000). This idea of choice proved crucial to the debate. The logic ran that if you are here, you must have chosen to be here, therefore abide by 'our' rules and accept 'our' history (Fortier 2005). At once the ethnic citizen was both hailed as a British subject and refused subjectivity. Running parallel to media-led concerns about immigration and asylum, it was clear that a return to the nation state was paramount. This move indicated a move toward what Back et al. (2002) have called the new assimilationism.

New Divisions

The government was eager to respond to such criticisms in order to prove its commitment to presiding over a liberal multi-ethnic society in the run up to the 2001 general election. In the April of that year Robin Cook, then Foreign Secretary, made attempts to respond to what he saw as increased pressure from the opposition to push the immigration and asylum questions. Stating that 'Chicken Tikka Masala is now Britain's true national dish, not only because it is the most popular, but because it is a perfect illustration of the way Britain absorbs and adapts external influences', he wanted to invoke the idea that Britain had moved on from petty squabbles over identity. After making such definitive moves towards establishing a multicultural state, the 2001 election proved a more difficult time for Blair. New Labour's policies of inclusiveness were in stark contrast to the real-world conditions experienced by many still living in ghettoised communities. This was none more evident than when disturbances broke out in South Asian Muslim communities across the north of England. Sparked by British National Party election successes and far-right activities in Oldham, Bradford and Burnley, the riots provoked a media response that paralleled representations from twenty years earlier (Holohan and Poole 2002).

The operation of an anti-Islamic discourse was clear from reports that suggested that any legitimate protest had been hijacked by rogue elements inciting violence on the streets. Again newspapers such as the *Daily Mail* presented images of damage to property and speculated on the financial cost of the disturbances, which ran into millions of pounds. For his part, Blair condemned the actions, stating that protest should be enacted via the acceptable political channels. In response to the disturbances, the government commissioned reports that sought to find a solution to the renewed antagonistic race relations. In these reports self-segregation was seen to be problematic (Kundnani 2001). Self-imposed divisions in schooling, housing and work were thought to be behind the failures of multicultural integration. In this respect ethnic antagonism was seen to be indicative of a wider cultural mis-recognition between communities that was only accentuated by their self-imposed physical separateness. In response to this process of self-segregation, which seemed to be creating ethnic ghettos in Britain's towns and cities, the Community Cohesion Report called for migrant settlers to pledge 'primary loyalty' to Britain. Mirroring the use of allegiance ceremonies in Canada and the United States, and in particular the passage of the Patriot Act, this recommendation saw an attempt by government to interpolate subjects into the constructs of identification of the nation state.

Recent events in the United States and Iraq have made the ethos of inclusion even more problematic. The terrorist attack on the World Trade Center in New York saw the idea of Islam as an enemy of the West take on new significance. What is more, domestic matters such as immigration and asylum have been discursively tied to a perceived security threat. In response to the 'terror threat' Home Secretary David Blunkett's *Secure Borders, Safe Haven* (2002) White Paper called for the implementation of citizenship ceremonies and the necessity for all migrants to Britain to obtain English language skills. In this way New Labour's multiculturalism could be seen to regress towards a strong idea of national identity evocative of Powell and the theory of ethnic assimilationism. Thus Blunkett has seemed to turn his back on the early days of New Labour, which sought to dismantle borders in hope of inclusive society, through his emphasis on patriotism and monocultural identity. New Labour's conflicting politics and rhetoric mirrors the problem of upholding the reality of an equal and inclusive multicultural society. The changing agenda of Blair and Blunkett reflect the challenges that face anyone attempting to unite the seemingly irreconcilable philosophies of multiculturalism and nation statism. In this sense multiculturalism is necessarily bound up with struggles over the meaning of belonging (i.e. what it means to be British) rather than with any tangible realisation of inclusion or recognition.

2. Anti-Arab Prejudice in the UK: the 'Kilroy-Silk Affair' and the BBC Response

Fred Halliday

This article features an edited letter from Professor Halliday to the BBC, dated 11 January 2004, responding to and commending the BBC's decision to suspend the daytime talk show of the presenter Robert Kilroy-Silk. This followed a controversial public debate provoked by an article written for the *Sunday Express* (a middle-market conservative tabloid) by Kilroy-Silk in which he made sweeping generalisations about Arabs including:

> We're told that the Arabs loathe us. Really?... What do they think we feel about them? That we adore them for the way they murdered more than 3,000 civilians on September 11 ... That we admire them for the cold-blooded killings in Mombasa, Yemen and elsewhere? That we admire them for being suicide bombers, limb-amputators, women-repressors? ('We Owe Arabs Nothing', *Sunday Express*, 4 January 2004)

In this article, the arguments of which are amplified in his book *100 Myths about the Middle East* (Saqi, 2005), Halliday draws on his own experience teaching about, researching on, writing about and visiting the Middle East. Halliday advocates the promotion of 'critical debate and judgement on sensitive matters' such as the Middle East, for example by explaining that there is no 'one' Middle East problem, but a set of interlocking separate ones. Here we focus on four 'observations' as contributions to the debate.]

The Contribution of 'Arabs' to the UK

First, if we argue about the historical contributions of one culture to another, we would have to recognise that, in the past century, Europe, including the UK, for all the positive it has given to the Middle East has also set a bad example – anti-Semitism as a modern ideology (e.g. the Protocols of the Elders of Zion), genocide on an unparalleled scale in Europe and colonial countries such as the Congo, brutality in general during war, racist and ethnically purist nationalism, and so on. Middle Eastern peoples have certainly picked up on some of these imports, but we should remember – as should Kilroy-Silk, Berlusconi, Huntington and their ilk – where they came from. Secondly, if we look at historic obligations, one of the Arab peoples to whom the UK does owe a special debt are the Yemenis who coming through Aden, in their thousands, and in common with other colonial seamen from Malaya, China and the West Indies, volunteered in such large numbers for the merchant navy in the Second World War and who suffered considerable and under-recognised losses in the Battle of the Atlantic. On the memorial on the Liverpool docks to these men there are many Yemeni names, an index of what was contributed in a battle which, as we now know, brought Britain to within weeks of surrender. Thirdly, in talking of what has been contributed and by whom, it is mistaken, as some replies have done, to try and answer this taunt in its own terms, by pointing out what some supposedly unitary Muslim or Arab civilisation has contributed. A case can certainly be made on this, and leaving out philosophy, mathematics, art, trade: to take the least significant point, it is striking that the main square in our capital city has an Arab name *Taraf al-Ghar*, that one of the two main cultural centres in London has the name of a Persian fortified gatehouse, *Babkhane* or 'Barbican', and that one of our main football teams is named after the Arabic for a military engineering works, *Dar al-Sina'a*, or Arsenal.

More serious points can and will be added, but the real point is that the whole premise of the argument is wrong: Arab culture, like all others, is a hybrid, based on interaction with other civilisations, religions and languages; it borrowed, fused, invented, and passed on its riches to others.

Arab Political Discussion

One impression given by the Kilroy-Silk argument may be that his remarks about dictatorship in the Arab world need to be said here because they are not being said in the Middle East. This is a ridiculous and ignorant claim. We do not need Kilroy-Silk's flat-footed generalisations about Arabs to make this point, and he should not be allowed to get away, as he tries to do in the press, with proclaiming himself as a champion of human rights in that region.

Anyone who has worked over recent years, as I have, and have many BBC journalists, with Amnesty International and Human Rights Watch will know that they have published many, detailed, iterative and denunciatory reports on Middle East states, the violations of human rights, gender conventions and the rules of war. These are all in the public realm. So are many measured and precise studies by Middle Eastern writers themselves, published often outside their own countries, on repression by their own states: just for the record, I would mention, as examples of two countries, Kanan Makiya and Falah Abd al-Jabbar on Iraq, and Ervand Ebrahamian and Reza Afshari on Iran. There is a large literature, some of it in translation, be it by feminists (including the excellent NGO (non-governmental organisation) 'Women Living Under Muslim Laws' and women short story writers from the Arabian Peninsula), intellectuals, and members of ethnic minorities like the Kurds, on their experiences.

Most Middle East states are authoritarian, despite cosmetic tolerance of NGOs and 'civil society', their media are often of a formality that outdoes Brezhnev on a bad day, and there is in particular far too much collusion by Western journalists, especially those working for English-language papers in the region, all of which are a disgrace from one side of the Middle East to the other, with the fancies of power. I too have been photographed in my time 'exchanging views' on a Louis XV sofa with some minister or dean. On one occasion, I read in the paper a report of the deep discussions I had had with the chairman of the local university, and the historic cooperation agreement I had signed between our two higher education systems: the only thing was that, the previous day, my visit had been cancelled and never took place.

There is also a dreadful practice of quoting selectively from what other people say, removing all criticisms of 'the Arab world' or of Muslims. Recently I gave an interview to a Gulf paper on Muslim–Western relations, and made my conventional point that there are idiots in the West who try to exploit this, but also idiots in the Middle East who do the same thing the other way around. Next day the headline ran: 'British Professor Says West Still Prejudiced Against Islam'. Until recently books were relatively freely circulated in the Arab Gulf states and shown at annual book fairs, but this has changed recently, under the influence of conservative Muslim groups operating from below. Books by non-Muslims like myself, but also by liberal Muslims, like the Algerian Mohammad Arkoun or the Egyptian Ziad Abu Nasr, are now banned as well. I think local states have too easily run for cover on this, but the pressure to silence is not coming just from above. The BBC has, of course, no need to be reminded of this, with the two notorious examples of the Arab reaction to the film 'Death of a Princess' in, I think, 1981, and the sudden pulling of the plug on the BBC Arabic TV service, after it rebroadcast a Panorama programme on Saudi Arabia, in 1995 – the latter episode being one in which, if I may say so, the BBC did not acquit itself in what one might call the Falklands Spirit.

However, the idea that people in the Middle East do not know this, do not express it and that there is not a lively critical, and sardonic, culture about those in power is the opposite of the truth. Indeed Arabs often complain that the British do not have a culture of political humour (when did one last hear a joke about Blair, or the Royal Family), but at any party or private gathering you go to, in the Arab world, Iran or Turkey you will find people retailing these jokes, many of which are of an unbroadcastable kind, involving mollahs, donkeys, lecherous tigers, the more outrageous orthodox views on personal conduct (Jews and Muslims, whose clerics are obsessed about these things, always understand each other's jokes on this matter), the sons of incumbent presidents, and the private practices of their rulers. I do not want to romanticise these things, and I have sat through my fair share of official speeches in the region, but I have had over the years far more lively conversations, and hilarious and indiscrete discussions, with Middle Eastern friends and colleagues than I have had in the often uneasy, *bien-pensant*, salons of the Western world.

An example of this popular scepticism: a few months after the revolution in Iran, in the summer of 1979, I was in Tehran. On the roads out of town in the evening rush hour little boys would try to sell food or string or whatever, but also something known as *Kitab-i Shukhi-yi Ayatollah Khomeini*, 'The Ayatollah Khomeini Joke Book', which turned out to be a selection of the most preposterous sections of his writings on personal hygiene, married life, and, with the imagination of a failed novelist, quite a lot else.

Arabs and Iranians are also very aware, and in private very voluble, about the conduct of their rulers. One Arab army officer, who I had known for about twenty minutes, once cheerfully told me: 'All our rulers are thieves.' Most people in Iran detest the ruling mollahs, something which accounts for the fact, one that few in the UK realise, that Salman Rushdie is very popular there, even when they do not know what he said; one Professor of Literature at a noted Arab university told me a while back that *The Satanic Verses* was the greatest Muslim novel of the twentieth century, a judgement with which I do not actually agree.

These things are not measurable, but my sense of travelling in different places, including Latin America and East Asia, is that Middle Eastern people are less thin skinned, much more able to laugh about themselves, their neighbours and their rulers, than elsewhere in the world. The gold medallists in this regard are for my money the Egyptians, whose jokes about their leaders, from Nasser onwards, are outstanding. The Iranians come second, though their conspiracy theories are by a long chalk world champions, beating even the Serbs and the Chinese (75 per cent of whom, so a recent poll tells, believe SARS was invented by the CIA to undermine their economic success).

Getting Prejudice in Proportion: Between Complacency and Alarmism

We cannot aim to prevent, or eliminate, all racist stereotyping in the media, and public life, and it is self-defeating to try to do so. In talking to Muslim and Jewish colleagues about their respective concerns, I do argue that, while we must remain firm on these questions, they have to accept that some degree of this rubbish will last for decades. 'The West' as a whole, whatever this catchall phrase means (in my view not much) is not embarked on some global 'anti'-campaign. Dr Conor Cruise O'Brien, one of my heroes, has said that 'Anti-semitism is a light sleeper', to which some might reply that it never went to sleep in the first place. But there is change, up and down, in this regard, and not every derogatory aside, many of which are given double use against Jews and Irish alike (e.g. not 'fitting in', not 'being on side', not being 'entirely rooted in this country' etc.), is the last stop before genocide. Given that, it is important to identify whether and how far the trends are getting worse, or better. As a number of members of the UK British community have recently argued, there are certainly more cases of anti-Jewish racism by Muslim immigrants in Europe. We saw this in the 2001 British general election where people like Mike Gapes MP were targeted, in a way that went beyond legitimate criticism, by pro-Palestinian groups in Essex; yet the overall trend may be much more mixed, and certainly does not give support to the idea of some underlying European anti-Semitic regression, a point talked up to excess in the USA.

Beneath public and polemical debate, there is also what I sense is a false claim of historical continuity. This is of more than academic interest. In theoretical terms, I am what is termed a 'modernist' in the sense that I set ideas, practices and institutions in the context of the modern world, and question, while I do not always deny, their link to earlier times. I am opposed, unless these can be proven, to claims that somehow these things go back centuries, and are products of deep civilisational structures: this is what I have termed 'Fault-line Babble'. It sounds wise and great to talk about these things as ancient trends, but this is often inaccurate. Prejudice of any kind has to be reproduced across the generations, and if there is such contemporary racism it is for contemporary, not atavistic, reasons. Prejudices also change: in Auschwitz, as Primo Levi wrote, the term 'Muslim' was used to denote those who had lost the will to live and become completely passive, the complete opposite of today's *jihadi* youth; ditto, changing stereotypes of Jews as being passive being replaced by ones of Israelis as ferocious soldiers. Everyone now goes on about how important the Crusades are in modern resentment among Muslims against the West, but my impression is that until a few years ago, and until Saddam and Osama began going on about them, no-one and no-one away from the Mediterranean area, such as Iranians or Pakistanis, cared about the issue at all.

This change in political culture is also pertinent to the question that is central to the Kilroy-Silk argument, namely the attitudes of the British public as a whole to Arabs and Muslims. Far from this being some deep colonial residue, my research (on the oldest Muslim community in the UK, the Yemenis) and general sense suggest that the very categories of 'Arab' and 'Muslim' were never until the last ten years particularly common in the UK political culture, in contrast to, say, France where, because of the North African connection, they held the place which for us is held by South Asians. A simple historical test on this concerns two events in Indian history, the Black Hole of Calcutta of 1756, and the 1857 'Mutiny' or 'Uprising'. Everyone who knows British history knows about these, but I wonder whether one in a hundred, or a thousand, could tell you (a) whether the perpetrator of the Black Hole was Hindu, Muslim or Sikh and (b) what the religion of the 1857 rebels was. In post-1945 British colonial history, there have been many enemies, objects of stereotypical hostility (the pro-Zionist Stern and Lehi Gangs, Mau Mau, EOKA, Malayan communists, the IRA to name but some) but few of these were Muslim or Arab, or categorised as such. One cannot be sure of this but I have no recollection of any work of British colonial history, or its aftermath, that propagates negative stereotypes of Arabs. This is not true elsewhere, as a quick look at the Tintin comic books, published in Belgium, and full of now dated images of Arabs with camels and clad in burnous and Berbers among others, will show: in parentheses, on the occasion in early 2004 of the 75th anniversary of the first episode, Tintin in Russia, these were re-issued on DVD but with the volumes on the USSR and the Congo removed, one can only assume for different reasons, and that the portrayal of Arabs was still deemed acceptable.

The entry into UK political discourse of categories of Arab and Muslim may owe something to the presence of British forces in Egypt in the Second World War, but it is mainly a result of the Rushdie affair of 1989, an own goal by self-apppointed spokesmen of the Muslim community in this country which some, at least, have come to reconsider. When Muslim representatives say to me that Rushdie's novel should be banned because it offends them, I refer them to the verses of the Qur'an concerning Jesus Christ, a prophet for Muslims, but who, according to the holy text, was not the Son of God, was not Crucified, and did not rise from the dead, all claims that are, by normal Christian standards, blasphemous. My suggestion is to leave the issue of blasphemy alone.

In this vein, and against the natural tendency to see such attitudes as endemic in non-Muslim/Gentile culture, and talking with Jews and Arabs, and others, I find that this issue, of unstated historical premise, is vital. I try to notice historical discontinuity as much as continuity, to persuade them not to think in terms of some timeless 'Anti-whatever' prejudice lodged in the subconscious of the Western, or Christian or modern psyche, and to focus on the most egregious examples, of which the Kilroy-Silk case or the promotion of the 'Protocols of the Elders of Zion' are certainly examples. This means that racist prejudice, of all colours and beliefs, is a fact of today's multi-ethnic, and transnationally globalised, world: like the rain, or earthquakes, it is a fact we have to live with, but can, and should, take reasonable precautions to contain.

Another premise concerns singularity, the belief of those who protest that the prejudices against them are, somehow, unique. Certainly, they are felt as such, but, as with say unemployment or crime, these evils may, without denying some uniqueness, be set in an aggregated context. One of my first, academic but also political, instincts is to take any one instance of prejudice and challenge its singularity, to put it in comparative perspective – in other words complaints about anti-Semitism and Islamophobia (a term I do not like and think is inaccurate, preferring anti-Muslimism) should be matched by what we know about other prejudicial views. Everyone tries to claim that they, and implicitly they alone, or especially, are victims of some external, global, conspiracy against them. All view any attempt people like me, or the BBC, make to say things are not so bad, or are changing for the better, as blindness and collusion, yet this too needs to be said: one has only to look at the changing coverage by the *Sun* of black and gay issues over the past three decades to see how things do get better. I liked very much what I heard a Catholic bishop on the BBC saying, in response to a question about what realistically we could do about anti-Semitism. His reply was 'Vigilance and Solidarity', to which I would only add, to cover both education and the media, including the BBC, 'Information and Education', an ongoing, never completed, task.

Robust Secularism: Against 'Islam-Lite'

My last thought may appear contrary, but is one that I have come to on the basis of quite a number of years teaching, researching and broadcasting on, and in, Middle Eastern countries, and that is that, in an attempt not to offend 'communities' and 'faiths', in some ways the BBC and media can be *too soft on 'Islam'*. I do not mean this in regard to religion as belief in the supernatural, and the rituals attached to this, but in regard to accepting without comeback or criticism claims, many of them claims which any Muslim would know to be preposterous, which supposed 'representatives' of the Muslim world and Muslim community in the UK make. It is evident that representatives of such groups are not subjected to the kind of civil, but informed and insistent, questioning which is given to politicians or people from mainstream public life.

I have been live on the World Service, and in the immediate aftermath of September 11, and to my considerable embarrassment, with representatives of violent and bigoted Muslim groups whose identity has not been vouchsafed to the listeners, and who have propounded a wholly inaccurate and sectarian view of what 'Islam' is supposed to be. Here the presenter made no attempt to cross-question or challenge what this particular fanatic, all dressed up in reasonable-sounding phrases, had to say. As I wrote to the World Service at the time, if I had been asked if I agreed to appear with this man, or had been warned he would be brought in during a one-hour studio discussion, I would have refused. Another striking example of this indulgence of bigots was to be heard on the *Today* programme, 12 January 1999, in connection with Muslim attitudes to the kidnapping of British tourists in Yemen, four of whom were, if I recall correctly, shot later that morning. The person being interviewed told John Humphreys that the BBC audience should know that military training was a duty for all Muslims, and that in every mosque in Britain, young Muslim men were receiving military training. Now both these claims are false, in dogma and empirical fact respectively: but the interviewer did not come back at him, because he was not briefed on how to come back, or/and because he/his editor/the BBC were worried about appearing to contradict a self-proclaimed, if utterly mendacious, 'representative' of something we have come to call 'the Muslim community'.

I have often heard interviewers asking Muslim representatives about the 'Islamic' view on this or that, assuming, which is quite false, that there is one, single, reading of the issue in question – the status of women, the environment, globalisation or whatever. As an observer of politics, sociology *and money*, I would have to say that there is no such thing as a single 'Muslim' community in the UK, any more than there is a single 'Jewish' or 'Christian' one. We are already well down a slippery slope of communitarian and relativist indulgence when we allow supposedly 'holy' or 'devout' men to represent all those who come from their own countries. They are free to say what their personal view is, or what one particular interpretation of the holy text is, but not to claim that their opinion is representative or indicative of a unitary sacred message (which on all questions, other than the unity of God, does not exist).

Some courageous voices within the UK, such as independent and open-minded Muslim foundations and intellectuals, and the resolute and much abused Yasmin Alibhai-Brown, have sought to represent the variations of Muslim society, not least those of nation, class and gender, but they are very much the minority in the media. Such diversity among Muslims in the UK was present, but largely unseen and unreported, during the Rushdie affair, 1989–91. We recall that The Satanic Verses only became an issue months after the book was published and when political groups in India and Pakistan began to make a fuss about it.

The attitude of the Yemeni community on Rushdie was to say, and do, absolutely nothing. Their argument was very simple: if the man has committed blasphemy (which, incidentally, he did not, because in English this means insulting God and Muhammad is not, like Christ, supposed to be divine, and to claim divinity for the Prophet in Islam is itself blasphemous), then Allah will punish him. The main problems facing the Yemenis in Sheffield and Rotherham were unemployment, integration of newly arrived Yemenis, racist attacks on pensioners on the upper deck of buses and funding for community projects. The Yemenis were not alone (but had more reason than most to suspect) in thinking that the hullabaloo about Rushdie had involved some transfer of funds from fundamentalist donors, keen to appear more militant than their Shiite rivals in Iran, to South Asian 'community' groups here.

In this context, I would make a plea for what many of my colleagues and most politicians seem to regard as a lost cause, a starting point of secularism in the analysis of public and political life. This means not atheism, the denial of religion and belief in the divine, but a separation, in public life and in analysis, between the claims of religion and the realities of political and social life. Some effort has been made in recent years to broadcast more programmes about 'understanding' Islam and the Muslim world but most of this, be it on the BBC or the independent channels, is usually 'Islam-Lite', apologetic and inaccurate public relations which leaves the viewer no sense of the power structures, oppression of women and ethnic minorities, the manipulation of texts and the very variety of opinion within these countries. No one watching such programmes would be prepared for the variety of inter-ethnic tensions within the Muslim world, the possibilities for various interpretations of the Qur'an (a process known as *naskh*), or the very lively debate about the implications of Islam for economic and social life that have taken place in Iran, Pakistan and Egypt over many decades. To take an obvious example of such simplification: our pious clergymen here all tell us that Islam is against alcohol, whereas the Qur'an itself, in its earlier chapters, enjoins the believer to take wine (*khamr*) for good health and, among other sensual delights (for men only, I hasten to add), promises 'rivers' of it in paradise;

moreover the culture, cuisine and social life of most Muslim societies has given a central role to alcohol and its delights over many centuries as is evident, in the Arabic, in the poetry of Abu Nawwas, and in Persian in that of Hafiz and Omar Khayyam.

These sympathetic TV documentaries about Islam often do a disservice, not a service, to the peoples and cultures of these countries. They can, therefore, tell us a bit about architecture and culture in these countries but are wholly misleading about people's lives and attitudes. This contrast is immediately evident if, instead of bland commentaries on the greatness of some single Islamic civilisation, one reads novels by contemporary Turkish, Iranian and Arab writers, such as the Egyptian Neguib Mahfouz, or the cinema of Muslim countries – such as the recent flowering of Iranian cinema, the films of the Egyptian Yusuf Shahin, or the very moving, but not widely distributed in the Middle East, Lebanese film *West Beirut*, which describes the breakdown of social cohesion and the rise of violence at the beginning of the Lebanese civil war in 1975. Similarly I tell students that if they want to get behind the official views of Israel they should read Israeli novels by David Grossman or Amos Oz. The stick has been bent rather too far in favour of the supposedly 'devout' and 'sage' in recent years. It is, more generally, misleading in broadcasting to run to holy writ or supposed 'tradition', the latter too often treated in indulgent fashion, that is to analyse modern inter-ethnic and political issues in terms of religion and the interpretation of holy texts. I also doubt if holy writing itself has much relevance when people choose to trade with, or murder, their neighbours. People do not consult holy texts when they buy a car, go to work, brush their teeth or go to a football match. This is quite apart from the fact that the texts, depending on which bit you chose, give a variety of answers.

To sum up, I think that the action you (BBC) have taken with regard to this gentleman (Kilroy-Silk) will be widely welcomed and commented on here and in the Middle East. Firmness in the face of such prejudice and ignorance will be a test of the BBC's credibility here and abroad. It will both reflect and encourage the work that many people have been engaged in over recent years to sustain balanced, if ever sniped at, coverage of the Middle East, to raise awareness of anti-Arab and anti-Muslim prejudice up to the levels of prejudice against others, to reduce unchallenged stereotyping to more common levels, even if such attitudes do not, for the reasons I give here, ever completely disappear. I know a number of Arab intellectuals, trades unionists and diplomats in this country, all of whom are very fond of it, as are the Turks, Iranians, Kurds and Israelis that I come across: they are the first to recognise that there is also a problem in the

Middle East and that the goal should be reasonable containment of debate within civil limits, and education, not a total suppression.

[This letter was sent to the Director General of the BBC in January 2004. At the time of going to press no letter of acknowledgement or substantive reply from the BBC had been received by the author.]

3. Racial Profiling and the War on Terror

Liz Fekete

In the US, human rights groups and anti-racist campaigners have fought long and hard for legislation to outlaw racial profiling in law enforcement. But is a similar racial profiling being institutionalised in counter-terrorism measures in Europe?

According to Professor David Harris of the University of Toledo College of Law – a leading expert on racial profiling – criminal profiles are sets of personal and behavioural characteristics associated with particular offences that police use to predict who may commit crimes in the future, or identify what type of person may have committed a particular crime for which no credible suspect has been identified or eye-witness description provided. Criminal profiling becomes racial profiling when these characteristics include race, ethnicity, nationality or religion.[1]

Campaigns against racial profiling in Western democracies largely arose because of racially biased policing towards minority communities – whether it was of Afro-Americans in the US, Aborigines in Australia or of the African-Caribbean community in the UK. Racial profiling involves the singling out of groups based on race for a different form of policing. This may take the form of surveillance and intelligence gathering on whole communities and raids on meeting places and places of worship, based on suspicion alone, coupled with the constant use of identity checks on the streets. Landmark campaigns against racial profiling, such as the campaign to scrap the SUS laws in the UK,[2] were historically part of wider campaigns against institutionalised racism.

Profiling Threats

There is another form of racial profiling connected to immigration and anti-terrorism policies that has been developing, largely unnoticed. One reason for this is that the primary instigators of systems of data collection that lead to racial profiling are heads of states and civil servants. In the EU (European Union), the collection of extensive personal data on asylum seekers for general surveillance purposes started in the 1970s, with the activities of the Trevi group of ministers and police chiefs, and its associated working groups. Their forums perceived migrants and refugees as a threat to European security, with the very act of crossing international borders to seek asylum effectively criminalised.[3]

Subsequently, the security issue was used to justify the use of measures, such as compulsory fingerprinting, usually associated with serious criminal investigation against all asylum seekers. The threat to security also legitimised the storage of information on all asylum seekers on the Schengen Information System (SIS) – the EU's largest computer database and at the heart of the EU's internal security system. SIS is the first supranational investigation system for law enforcement agencies and can be accessed from local terminals in all participating states. The database is comprised of records put in by each of its EU member states, which are then accessed by other state agencies. The SIS database, which contains basic information, is backed up by the SIRENE Bureaux in each state, which provides on request more detailed information and intelligence. A further computerised database on asylum seekers is provided by EURODAC, established in December 2000, which stores fingerprints of asylum applicants and allows for electronic data transmission between member states and the database.

In time, data registered on SIS was extended to include not just personal data on asylum seekers but also on foreigners defined as 'Third Country Nationals', who were likewise viewed as a security threat. What this collection of data on foreigners signifies is a new form of administrative racism, best described as xeno-racism, that targets foreigners irrespective of colour.

The Institute of Race Relations (IRR) has described in other contexts how frequently racist structures applied to one group in society are soon extended to others. And this is precisely what is happening post-September 11. Today, European security services have used the 'War on Terror' to extend the surveillance structures already operational against asylum seekers and foreigners to profile other groups perceived to constitute a 'threat'. Since Islam represents 'threat' within Europe, the EU and member states are building up 'risk profiles' of Muslim residents, even though they may be citizens. The Muslim community is thus being caught up in the ever-expanding loop of xeno-racism documented below.

Creating Databases on Muslims

The EU heads of state, senior police officials and civil servants, through forums such as Trevi, have sent out a strong signal to security services that foreigners, and particularly foreigners from 'the Islamic world', constitute a threat to Europe. This determines the security services' priorities in terms of intelligence gathering.

Germany's Office for the Protection of the Constitution (BFV) is one of three national intelligence services gathering information on domestic and foreign terror groups. The BFV, it would seem, interprets its remit in such a way as to build up profiles on foreigners and the Muslim community per se, as witnessed by the release of statistics on the foreigner and Muslim community in its 2003 annual report.[4] The BFV's profiling of foreigners will be greatly strengthened by federal interior minister Otto Schily's decision to establish a federal database for 'Islamist' terror suspects. This is a move that has alarmed the Central Council of Muslims in Germany. Chair, Nadeem Elyas, points out that unless the term 'Islamist' is properly defined, innocent Muslims risk falling under suspicion.[5]

The danger now is that the German government might pressure the EU to establish a similar database. Already, Schily has called on the EU to follow the German model and establish an EU-wide database on 'Islamist terrorism'.[6] In fact, the BFV statistics have been compiled through the most extensive system of religious profiling in Europe. Following the events of September 11, the federal government introduced a system of computer scanning for 'Islamic terrorists'. But instead of compiling records on individual suspects with a proven connection to terrorism, the security services literally trawl for information on Muslims. Public and private institutions have been placed under a duty to hand over to the police authorities information from databases on individuals whose personal profiles corresponds to specific criteria on the police's search grid for potential terrorist sleepers. By April 2002, the federal state's criminal investigation department had assembled six million personal records and singled out well over twenty-thousand potential suspects, even though there was no concrete evidence against them. To qualify for inclusion on this list a suspect had to be, amongst other things, of (presumed) Islamic religious affiliation, 'from an Islamic state', and not previously come to the notice of the criminal investigation department.[7]

According to the BFV's 2003 annual report, 57,300 foreign individuals are 'radical' with 31,000 Muslim radicals active in twenty-four Islamist organisations, which have a total membership of 30,950. But, again, the BFV's assertion seems to be based on suspicion rather than concrete evidence. It is enough, it seems, to be suspected of 'Islamic religious affiliation' to warrant intrusive surveillance and be included in intelligence gathering. A German Muslim citizen can be monitored if he or she belongs to a Muslim organisation that the German state perceives to be influenced by 'radical Islam' even if that organisation does not advocate violence and even if the individual has no criminal record or links with terrorism.

The subjectivity of the intelligence services' approach to defining Muslim organisations as a security threat is demonstrated by the BFV's collation of information on the membership of Milli Görus. Milli Görus is an organisation that does not advocate violence. Indeed, it is generally perceived, in terms of its ideology, to be close to the moderate Islam practised by the Justice and Development party (AK) – the ruling party in Turkey that seeks to govern in cooperation with Turkey's secular establishment. Despite the fact that no criminal proceedings have ever been taken against Milli Görus for involvement in terrorist activities, interior minister Otto Schily describes this legal organisation's view on integration as 'dangerous' and implies that it represents one of the greatest threats to Germany's security. Schily's view is, at best, based on the ignorance of the German security services on the situation in Turkey. Or could it be that the German security services' close relationship with its Turkish counterparts has coloured the view of Germany's interior minister who, in his pronouncements, inadvertly reflects the Turkish military's fear for its own future under an Islamist government?

There are similar concerns about the impartiality of the Dutch intelligence services. Again, the concern is that the Dutch intelligence services may be politically motivated in their classification of specific organisations within the Muslim community as comprising 'threat'. The General Intelligence and Security Service (AIVD), which is working closely with the Immigration and Naturalisation Department (IND), warned in its 2002 annual report that networks of radical Islamic terrorists posed a threat to the country.[8] From here however, the AIVD went on to single out groups within the Muslim community that it claimed to be working against integration and for separatism, and somehow connected these groups to the security threat posed by 'radical Islam'. The principle organisation named by the security services as a potential security risk is the Arab European League (AEL), with the AIVD citing its attitudes to integration as alarming. The AEL is a movement, mainly of young Muslims, that rose to prominence in Belgium after the racist murder of a young Muslim in Antwerp (an area where the extreme-Right Vlaams Blok is the largest political force in the municipality). It has since established a branch in the Netherlands. In Antwerp, the AEL had attempted to monitor the activities of the police – whom it accuses of institutionalised racism – including the failure to protect the Muslim community from racial violence. It has also mounted a sustained critique of Belgian integration policies, which, it argues, are based on assimilation. Though its methods may be controversial, and though its critique of the police and government may prove uncomfortable for the establishment, the tendency to view its membership as a security threat demonstrates a subjective assessment rather than one based on concrete evidence of terrorist activity.

Impact on Policing

The security services' preoccupation with Islam as 'threat' is leading the police to target Muslim meeting places and religious places of worship for raids, which are more often than not carried out on the basis of suspicion rather than concrete evidence of terrorist activity. At the same time there is an increase in identity checks on people of Muslim appearance. And it is at this point, on the streets, that the political decision to target the Muslim community as a national security threat spills over into racial profiling, as it is most often 'racial characteristics' that signify to the police religious identity.

The German system of building-up religious profiles in the Muslim community has had a direct effect on the policing of the community and is leading to widespread alienation. Nadeem Elyas, chair of the Central Council of Muslims, has said that police searches on more than eighty German mosques and over one thousand apartments and offices belonging to Muslims had 'achieved nothing', adding that the community felt that they were not being treated as 'partners' in the war against terror.[9] On 10 December 2003, the police carried out the largest raid in post-war history, searching 1,170 Muslim homes, businesses and other premises. The raids were on individuals who had subscribed to the newspaper of the banned organisation, the Caliphate State. Information as to who subscribes to a religious magazine could only have been gleaned from security service databases. But as human rights organisations have pointed out, subscription to a religious magazine is not reason enough to justify an indiscriminate raid, targeting a whole community, including families and children. In fact, it amounts to the arbitrary targeting of Muslims. In the event, the raids led to just four people facing further investigation.[10]

It is, however, in the UK where the direct link between anti-terror laws and increased racial profiling is at its clearest. In the UK, in 2003 the IRR reported a 28 percent increase in the number of Asians stopped and searched, with a massive 40 percent increase in Asians stopped and searched in London – the largest increase ever recorded in a single year for any group.[11] Nationally, Asians are now two-and-a-half times more likely to be stopped and searched than whites. This racial profiling is all the more disappointing given that the disproportionate use of stop and search by the police of the black community was acknowledged as discriminatory by Sir William Macpherson in his landmark investigation into the murder of Stephen Lawrence, which for the first time recognised institutionalised racism in policing.[12] As a result of this, the Race Relations (Amendment) Act 2000 was passed which made it unlawful for police officers to discriminate on the grounds of race, colour, ethnic origin, nationality or national origins when using their powers. Subsequently, in April 2003, new guidance on the use of stop and search came into effect that clarified that searches were only meant to be based on 'reasonable grounds for suspicion'. That was defined as 'suspicion based on facts, information, and/or intelligence' and specifically excluded suspicion on the basis of a person's race or on generalisations about ethnic groups. However, new stop-and-search powers under the Terrorism Act 2000 allow police officers to take a suspect's ethnic origin into account when deciding whether to search someone under suspicion of terrorism. In fact, the number of people from Asian backgrounds stopped and searched by police under anti-terrorist legislation has increased by 300 percent. Lord Carlisle, in his 2003 annual review of the Terrorism Act, disclosed that the stop and search powers available under the act had been subject of twenty-eight-day rolling authorisations for the area covered by by the Metropolitan and City of London police forces and that they had been used in almost every police authority in the country.

Databases on Foreigners

Through the Schengen Information System (SIS) the EU has been building-up vast amounts of information on Third Country Nationals in a process linked to the EU's tough stance on immigration and asylum that started long before the events of September 11. However, following the events of September 11, the German government proposed the creation of a centralised population register and centralised registers storing data on Third Country Nationals present in the territory of the Union. This was then incorporated into the Council's Anti-Terrorism Roadmap and led to the introduction of a new system of 'alerts' on SIS and the introduction of a European central register of Third Country Nationals present within the territory of the EU. Most recently, the Visa Information System (VIS) has been set up to store personal data (including biometric identification data) on an estimated twenty million visa applicants to the EU each year.[13] This is with the view to tracking those who overstayed their visa period (for work or visiting) or their residence permit period. Crucially, information is not stored on people because they have been involved in any criminal offence, but simply by dint of the fact that they are foreigners and as such had the potential to commit an immigration offence in respect of overstaying visas or residence permits. This, under Dr David Harris' definition cited earlier, clearly amounts to racial profiling, as the data relates not to any offence already committed but to the potential immigration offence of overstaying a visa.

At the member state level, it is, once again, Germany which is at the forefront of pioneering a system whereby the security services have comprehensive on-line access to all information on foreigners stored on the Central Register of Aliens. In the past, security services had to provide specific justification for data requests. Now they are able to carry out searches whether or not there is a concrete threat to justify them. Foreigners applying to visit Germany also fall under the scope of the new legislation, with fingerprints and digital photographs taken and stored by German consulates abroad. Immigration authorities and security services have also been mandated to scrutinise all those who issue invitations to visa applicants (and even people with close connections to applicants).

Recently, the German government announced that, in future, all foreigners visiting Germany for more than three months would be monitored more closely, by cross-referencing with biometric data when issuing visas. In June 2002, the government introduced a system whereby citizens from twenty-two countries would be subject to special checks before getting visas to enter Germany. These could include inquiries from German secret services or the requirement that visa applicants be fingerprinted at German embassies.

The system of computer scanning pioneered by Germany could easily spread across Europe. In the UK, under powers introduced under the 2002 Nationality, Asylum and Immigration Act, iris scans and fingerprints can now be collected and stored on computer when visas are applied for. Applicants from Djibouti, Eritrea, Ethiopia, Sri Lanka, Tanzania and Uganda now have to have their fingerprints computer scanned when they apply for a visa and these scans are stored on a database that a number of UK state agencies, including the police, have access to. Greek human rights groups were concerned that additional scrutiny of immigrant groups in the run-up to the Olympics could fall over into religious profiling.

Profiling and Internal Controls

The establishment of computerised databases on foreigners also legitimises increased identity checks on the streets, as the police trawl for suspected 'illegal immigrants' amongst settled minority communities. That police use racial characteristics to single out people for checks has long since been an issue on the Continent, particularly in France and Belgium, where police harassment arising from such internal controls has been a source of resentment in minority communities, especially amongst young people of North African origin. But EU-wide databases are ensuring that such checks become systemic. And a further stimulus for the profiling of foreigners has been provided by an EU-wide deportation programme for rejected asylum seekers, coordinated by the EU Expulsions Agency. With most EU countries now setting targets for expulsions of asylum seekers, more identity checks on public transport will become commonplace. In August 2004, in the UK, the mayor of London spoke out against the profiling of foreigners on the London Underground by immigration officials who, in cooperation with the British Transport police, are stopping those suspected of illegal entry and asking them to produce papers proving their right to British residence. Although Home Office guidelines explicitly prevent police from stopping people because of their accent or appearance, immigration officials, it appears, are targeting people on the basis that they speak non-European languages.[14]

Such checks, by their very nature, are based on suspicion and led to abuse of rights, as evidenced by the case of Bicha Monkokole Kasembele, who was stopped at Brussels South Station during identity controls. Despite being in possession of a perfectly valid identity card, Kasembele was detained by police because they suspected her identity card was not her own and that she had entered Belgium illegally. She was taken to a detention centre and served with a deportation order. Kasembele's lawyer, who managed to secure her release, pointed out that 'foreigners – and those who may look like foreigners – are not given the same rights as Belgians to be brought before a court on arrest'.[15]

Databases on Foreign Students

In Germany, Denmark and Norway the intelligence services have specifically targeted foreign students as a high-risk group and embarked on a process of religious profiling of non-EU students. The German government first placed a duty upon universities to hand over personal data on overseas students, suspected not of any criminal offence but of 'Islamic religious affiliation'. The sleeper/perpetrator profile drawn up by the Federal Criminal Investigation Department includes the following criteria: male students and former students; aged between eighteen and forty of presumed Islamic religious affiliation; coming from Islamic states; with legal residence status; are or have been, studying technical/scientific subjects between 1996 and 2001; are financially independent; travel a lot (sometimes training in flying); and have not so far come to the notice of the criminal investigation department.[16]

Under new anti-terrorist laws, the Danish Intelligence Service (PET) has been given a broader mandate to exchange information on immigrants, and PET now has the authority to investigate all individuals applying for Danish citizenship. PET's attempt to gain access to information on foreign students comes under the label of 'preventing the spread of weapons of mass destruction' and raising 'awareness that terrorists could register as students to access information or equipment that may be used to produce weapons of mass destruction'.[17]

The Norwegian Police Security Service (PST) is also attempting to inaugurate a scheme to register non-Western students on the grounds that students could gain knowledge that could be used to develop weapons of mass destruction. The PST has started to register non-Western students at the universities of Bergen and Oslo. And it is now seeking to extend the system of registering foreign students to private companies. This accords with provisions in the new anti-terrorism law that make it mandatory for an employer to inform about the suspicious behaviour of employees and allows for greater use of camera surveillance in the workplace.[18]

Dissent against Racial Profiling

Amnesty International (US) has produced an excellent briefing paper on racial profiling in which it points out that racial profiling not only institutionalises discrimination and undermines basic human rights, but also undermines national security and gives terror networks a formula for greater success. This was confirmed in October 2002, when a group of senior international anti-terrorism law enforcement officials released a memo entitled 'Assessing Behaviours'. The experts assert that the only effective method of identifying potential terrorists is to focus on suspicious behaviour, not race.

Dissent in Europe, too, is growing, with critics arguing that the suspicions and stereotypes that these policies engender is creating a climate of xenophobia, which also undermines national security. Arild Humlen, head of the Norwegian Bar Association's commission for asylum and immigration law, believes that the security services should not be allowed to ask for information on foreign students per se, and that PST is contributing to a 'collective suspicion' being rendered against a group.[19] The Director of Education at Bergen University, which has apparently registered 500 foreign students with the PST, says that the system is 'unwelcome' and the University takes care not to submit more than the minimum information necessary.[20]

Many of the examples above come from Germany, where racial profiling is more systematised than in European member states. But where the system is at its most intense, so too is the opposition. A lawyer and parliamentary consultant Rolf Gössner has been involved in an evaluation of computer scanning. He concludes that far from enhancing national security it is undermining the police and the law. The police and security forces can barely cope with the enormous mass of accumulated data, the evaluation of which ties down hundreds of police detectives and is highly costly.[21] Thilo Weichart, who is the chair of the German Association for Data Protection as well as deputy data protection officer in Schleswig-Holstein, argues that 'The greater ease of conducting computer scans for suspects and of telecommunications surveillance, and the extended control of migrants has so far failed to contribute demonstrably to clearing up terrorist crimes.' Police successes are based on 'classical criminological work' and computer scanning for 'sleepers' has been an expensive failure.[22]

4. Propaganda and the 'Terror Threat' in the UK

David Miller

Since 11 September 2001 both the US and UK governments have comprehensively overhauled their internal and external propaganda apparatus. These have been globally coordinated as never before to justify the 'War on Terror' including the attacks on Afghanistan and Iraq and the assault on civil liberties at home.

There is very little public debate on the propaganda apparatus and very few people know of the extensive machinery that has been built up in the past two years. The machinery has a number of parallel elements in the US and UK and the efforts are also coordinated globally between the US and UK. In the US the White House has the Office of Global Communications that sits at the top of the global pyramid. The Office was set up by the Bush White House based on the experience of the Coalition Information Centers (CIC) that operated during the Kosovo and Afghanistan conflicts. These drew on the propaganda expertise of the British government and are reported to have been the idea of Alastair Campbell the No. 10 Press Secretary (Foreign Affairs Select Committee 2003). The CIC was set up in October 2001 for the Afghanistan campaign with offices in Washington, London and Islamabad to coordinate across time zones. According to reports it was this initiative that sparked information sharing to ensure that the US and UK (and other governments) 'sang from the same hymn sheet' (Day 2002). The CIC was made permanent under the auspices of the White House with the creation of the Office of Global Communications (OGC) in July 2002. It was the OGC that fed out the lies about the threat posed by the Hussein regime including the faked and spun intelligence information supplied by the UK and by the secret Pentagon intelligence operation, the Office of Special Plans. This was set up by Rumsfeld to bypass the CIA, which was reluctant to go along with some of the lies.

From the White House the message is cascaded down to the rest of the propaganda apparatus. In the US, the State Department Office of Public Diplomacy is responsible for overseas propaganda; in the UK there is a parallel apparatus. The Ministry of Defence (MoD) and the Foreign Office

45

have the biggest propaganda operations of any UK government departments and their efforts are coordinated with Downing Street. The co-ordination is accomplished by means of a cross-departmental committee known as the Communication and Information Centre, later changed back to the Coalition Information Centre as it had been in the Afghanistan campaign. It is based administratively in the Foreign Office Information Directorate, yet directed by Alastair Campbell and run from Downing Street.[1] Campbell also chaired a further cross-departmental committee at No. 10 – the Iraq Communication Group. It was from here that the campaign to mislead the media about the existence of weapons of mass destruction (WMD) was directed. In particular it oversaw the September dossier on WMD and the second 'dodgy' dossier of February 2003, which was quickly exposed as plagiarised and spun.

The propaganda apparatus below this has four main elements. First is the external system of propaganda run by the Foreign Office. Second is internal propaganda focused on the alleged 'terrorist threat', coordinated out of the Cabinet Office by the newly established Civil Contingencies Secretariat (CCS). Third was the operation 'in theatre' in Iraq. Lastly, the US and UK military psychological operations teams undertaking overt and covert operations inside Iraq. All of these operations have their own contribution to make in the 'War on Terror' although most public debate (in the US and the UK) has focused on the system of embedding journalists and latterly (in the UK) on the Downing Street operation overseen by Campbell. This article focuses on the internal propaganda apparatus that has overseen the dissemination of information about the alleged 'terror threat' in the UK.

UK Resilience and the Civil Contingencies Secretariat

Without attracting front-page attention the Blair government has quietly presided over a revolution in internal propaganda systems for dealing with national emergencies. The overhaul was set in motion in July 2001 as a result of the foot-and-mouth crisis and drawing on the experience of the floods of winter 2000 and the cost of fuel protests. Based in the Cabinet Office and overseen initially by the most senior propaganda official in the civil service, the Head of the Government Information and Communication Service Mike Granatt, is the Civil Contingencies Secretariat. It works closely with another new body, the Health Protection Agency which encompasses parts of the Department of Health disease surveillance operation and the MoD's chemical and biological labs at Porton Down. Under the rather chilling website title 'UK Resilience', this network of organisations also works closely with the Special Branch and MI5. They tap straight into the CIC, chaired – until his departure from government – by Alastair Campbell. The aim of the CCS is said to be to improve the UK's 'resilience' to 'disruptive challenge'.[2] It has already seen action in the fire-fighters dispute – an indication of the orientation of the CCS towards state rather than public service agendas. Post September 11 it has been centrally involved in circulating information on the alleged 'threat' from Islamic 'terrorism'.

The CCS houses a 24-hour monitoring spin operation called the News Co-ordination Centre (NCC), which stands ready for use in the event of the next emergency. It has also (in the wake of September 11) established a wide ranging review of information handling in an emergency situation, undertaken by a working party involving government press officers and senior media executives together with police and local authority crisis planners. The Media Emergency Forum has produced a long report that the CCS claims 'reflects a more productive relationship' with the media.[3] The approach taken by the CCS is more sophisticated than previous emergency planning responses that allow the government simply to take over the broadcast media. However, that system is still in place – according to Mike Granatt, forced out as Director General of the GICS in early 2004, 'we've got a system that was put in place for nuclear war. We could press the button and pre-empt every transmitter in this country'. But this would be counter-productive. 'Voluntary' agreements with the media are seen as more effective. Granatt (2003) says: 'We need a credible active, sceptical – rather than cynical – system of news reporting...Anything we do to subvert the process of giving trust in that is wrong...If the BBC or ITN... said we think you should do this because the government says so, we would be lost.' So productive has this been that it has occasioned little attention in the media.

It was the new propaganda apparatus that oversaw the release of the information on the alleged discovery of ricin in January 2003 and that ordered the tanks to Heathrow in late 2002, following an intelligence tip-off, reported as a suspected surface to air missile attack on the airport. In the case of Heathrow, Granatt (2003) has noted:

> I will now confess to you. I sat at all the meetings that decided to do that, and I have seen agony cross their face before...Ministers actually considering putting tanks at our biggest economic asset...After what I sat and heard, doing it was absolutely necessary and I can't tell you more – I'm very sorry about it but that's the fact. But I can tell you first hand there was no lack of sincerity and nobody does that because it's going to make some

propaganda point for a war that at that point, wasn't entirely certain anyway.

What Granatt and others sat and heard was the intelligence assessment of the threat. Whether or not the threat was genuine or just more dodgy 'intelligence', no one was arrested and no surface to air missiles were found. Militarily, the effectiveness of light armoured vehicles, with a top speed of thirty-eight miles an hour, against a SAM attack launched at some distance from the airport remains opaque. But according to senior sources involved in the decision: 'You don't catch rockets in an armoured vehicle. That is not the point. Part of the point of these things may be deterrence. So visibility is another part of the game.' Visibility – otherwise known as propaganda.

In the case of ricin, the information was released, after deliberation in the Civil Contingencies Secretariat, under the name of the then Deputy Chief Medical Officer Dr Pat Troop.[4] She conducted a joint media briefing at Scotland Yard with the police. Troop (2003) has maintained that the information that ricin had been found was released because 'what we didn't know when we started was whether or not we were then going to find lots more Ricin somewhere else and therefore it was felt the public had the legitimate right to know'. According to a senior source involved 'the broadcasters' response was very positive. They told us afterwards it enabled them to go straight to air...because they were talking to people they believed were trustworthy and experts in their fields'.[5] The CCS released the information in the knowledge that it would potentially prejudice the trial of the people arrested in connection with the find. As Mike Granatt (2003) noted, prejudicing a trial comes way down the list of priorities after 'public safety'.

The claim that the information was released for public health reasons ushers in a new era of threat warning and assessment where the threat of terrorist attack is whipped up on shaky evidence for our own good – a very New Labour propaganda solution. The 'threat' from ricin in the 'environment' was clearly very small. The poison has to be ingested, inhaled or injected. Even if we suppose that the warning genuinely was given by civil servants operating in good faith, the information on which the warnings are based depended on the 'intelligence' services. Their collective lack of understanding of Islamic activists together with their own overhauled spin apparatus makes it difficult to discern whether the information in such cases is based on genuine, if misinterpreted, intelligence or deliberate fabrication, as was the case of the MI5 leak that a planned gas attack on the London Tube had been foiled (Miller 2003).

The case of the London Underground is instructive in that the arrests occurred on 9 November 2002 with little fanfare. Two days later Tony Blair made his Lord Mayor's speech in which he stated that there was a 'real' threat. The following weekend *The Sunday Times*, following briefings from MI5 linked the arrests to a 'suspected Al Qaeda terrorists' gas attack plot (17 November 2002).

> Fleet Street scrambled to follow up the sensational tale... the Independent on Sunday said the Algerians may have been planning to place a dirty nuclear bomb 'on a ferry using a British port'. [The Observer] said they had been charged with plotting to 'release cyanide on the London Underground', as did pretty much everyone else. Broadcasters repeated the story. (Cohen 2003)

The story was boosted by the 'green light' from No. 10 to follow it up, leading *The Sunday Times* to defend its story as being based on 'reputable security sources' (Cohen 2003). Reputable maybe, but how accurate are they? This link surprised the lawyer for one of the suspects since as he put it, 'none of the allegations which had entered the public domain over the past few days had been put to his client' (*Guardian* 19 November 2002). The Algerians eventually were charged with having false passports, and no evidence whatsoever of gas or dirty bombs was produced. Some commentators, such as Simon Jenkins, the former editor of *The Times* complained:

> I was outraged by the smallpox scare story [of 3 December 2002]. It was a clear repeat of the previous weekend's lobby story of 'gas horror on London Tube', itself an echo of the Home Office 'dirty bomb' story two weeks earlier. These Whitehall officials are panic happy; careless of the cost and worry they cause others... This is the third weekend in a month that a terrorism threat has emanated from Whitehall. Terror stories are always the easiest for government to sell. Headlines write themselves and the pictures always 'burn or bleed'. (*The Times* 4 December 2002)

For some commentators the combination of repression and media frenzy stirs uncomfortable memories of Ireland. Faisal Bodi argued: 'For all the hysterical headlines warning of a Bin Laden in our backyard, the reality is a picture of political repression of Muslims that is starting to resemble the experience of Northern Ireland's Catholics throughout the Troubles' (*Guardian* 21 January 2003). Like Ireland, the arrests are high profile and the outcomes usually much less dramatic. Also like Ireland, the media coverage ensures the possibility of a fair trial will be prejudiced, potentially leading to a series of unsafe convictions. According to Home Office figures, covering 11 September 2001 to June 2004, 609 people have been arrested and 99 of them have been charged with offences under the Terrorism Act 2000. As of 30 June 2004, there had been fifteen convictions. Of the fifteen convictions at least eight were of white people, six of whom were convicted for displaying Ulster loyalist symbols. It is important to stress that the number of convictions for planning or carrying out specific acts of terrorism is zero (Athwal 2004).

It seems that the wave of arrests signals – at best – the confusion and panic in the police and intelligence services. Under the cloak of the Terrorism Act the police are simply sweeping the Muslim community in the hope that they strike it lucky against an unknown threat. According to press reports, 'From the beginning, senior officers privately recognised there would be "collateral damage" – petty criminals or even innocent individuals temporarily detained in the police trawls. But they decided it was a price worth paying' (Burke and Bright 2003).

Where there is 'intelligence' the quality of it reportedly has been suspect. The strongest connection between the people arrested in the past year has been that many have been from Algeria. It is well known that two key Algerian opposition groups have been active in the UK since the 1992 election was cancelled for fear that it would be won by Islamists. The 'intelligence' on some of the Algerian suspects arrested in the UK reportedly has emanated from Paris, and some experts say the information comes from 'tainted official sources in Algiers'. In addition, neither opposition group 'has ever been directly connected to bin Laden' (Burke and Bright 2003).

Spook Spin?

In a 2001 deportation case against nine men detained without trial for over 7 months, the defence asked Martin Bright, Home Affairs editor of the *Observer*, to analyse the prosecution evidence linking the defendants to terrorism. In a piece submitted to the court and available only on the *Observer* website he notes that 'by far the largest proportion' of evidence was simply press cuttings reporting such links. In 'almost absurdly circular' fashion these were based largely on unattributable briefings from intelligence sources.

Information from intelligence briefings from foreign or the domestic services becomes common currency and is then repeated by journalists who are starved of any real information. Reputable journalists report the denials of the Islamists themselves, but the fact that someone denies being a terrorist is never considered to be much of a story. As increasing numbers of dissidents have been rounded up in Britain and elsewhere it has become increasingly difficult for journalists to check their stories properly... We have therefore been thrown back on an increasingly narrow set of sources: essentially the police and the intelligence services. (Bright 2001)

In recent years MI5 and MI6 have overhauled their information operations and now have named press officers who deal with designated reporters in each media outlet. Bright notes that, 'In the case of the *Observer*, I deal with MI5.' As he notes: 'Most journalists feel that, on balance, it is better to report what the intelligence services are saying, but whenever the readers see the words "Whitehall sources" they should have no illusions about where the information comes from' (Bright 2001).

Of course it would be wrong to see this as a wide-ranging conspiracy in which the government, the police the secret state are all engaged. Key elements of the state clearly genuinely believe the briefings they get, and in fact much of the state apparatus has to act as if the briefings are true regardless of what they actually believe. A useful way of looking at it is proposed by Martin Bright of the *Observer*:

I believe that the police and intelligence services are genuinely concerned and that the threats are largely real (in their minds at least they really believe an attack is imminent and inevitable)... But I do not know for sure and I don't believe the police have any understanding of Islamist politics and so what they perceive as a threat may be nothing of the sort.[6] (Bright 2001)

As Bright notes in his court submission, the same goes for MI5's press officer. He has 'no expertise in Islamic or Arab affairs and simply acts as a conduit' (Bright 2001). Furthermore, it may well be that Tony Blair genuinely is convinced that there is a threat. As he put it in an interview with *Newsnight*: 'I mean, this is what our intelligence services are telling us and it's difficult because, you know, either they're simply making the whole thing up or this is what they are telling me' (6 February 2003). And it doesn't seem likely that they are making *all* of it up. Nevertheless, there are reasons to doubt the 'genuine mistake' line of argument at least some of the time. One good reason for scepticism is the past record of the intelligence and defence establishment. As Bright himself notes, in the past information was slipped out informally and, 'Sometimes the stories that resulted were true and sometimes not' (Bright 2001). Others have revealed the deceptive information operations of intelligence agencies (Leigh 2000; Dorril 2000). But the best reason to doubt the Prime Minister is that there is abundant evidence that Downing Street and MI5 have engaged in both spin and deliberate mendacity. If the Hutton inquiry shows anything it is that almost the entire apparatus of government is mired in deception. Moreover, as the case of the London underground showed, MI5 have themselves been engaged in deception on the terror 'threat'.

The propaganda apparatus, run under the auspices of the Civil Contingencies Secretariat, appears credible to most mainstream journalists and ensures effective wall-to-wall coverage for stories based on dubious sources, which played very nicely into the propaganda campaign to legitimise the attack on Iraq. Its key function – apart from indulging the paranoic fantasies of the intelligence services – is to provide cover for the ever-expanding power of the state to subvert civil liberties and to undermine dissent. While the propaganda campaign to launch the attack on Iraq has to some extent unravelled, propaganda on the terror threat seems much more successful.

5. Still no Redress from the PCC

Julian Petley

This book contains numerous quotations from British newspaper articles that, in one way or another, constitute highly negative representations of Muslims. Many readers will no doubt be tempted to ask whether complaints about any of these articles have been received by the UK newspaper industry's own watchdog, the Press Complaints Commission (PCC), and, if so, what has happened as a result. The short answer is that complaints have indeed been received, but absolutely nothing of any significance has resulted from them. The longer answer constitutes this chapter.

The Press Complaints Commission's *Annual Review 2002* reveals that a total of 2,630 complaints of one kind or another were received that year. This was down on the record of 3,033 in 2001 but significantly higher than the average of the previous three years. One third of complaints the PCC found to be outside its self-imposed remit. In the case of 26 percent of the remaining 1,799 complaints, the PCC announced that: 'No breach of the Code was established, or no further action was required by the PCC after the editor of the publication concerned made an appropriate offer to remedy any possible breach' (PCC 2003: 6). The PCC actually adjudicated a mere thirty-six cases, upholding seventeen and rejecting nineteen. This means that it adjudicated only 2 percent of the complaints which it investigated, and upheld only 1 percent.

The *Annual Review 2003* (which, interestingly, is strikingly lighter on statistics than its predecessors, and thus much more difficult to analyse) reveals that the Commission received a record 3,649 complaints – 39 percent higher than the previous year. Of these, only twenty-three (0.6 percent) were adjudicated. However, according to the PCC's own inimitable *Alice in Wonderland* logic, the fewer complaints it adjudicates the more successful it considers the process of 'self-regulation' to be. On this basis, the PCC's most successful year would be that in which it adjudicated not a single complaint, at which point, presumably, it would regard its peculiar modus operandi as having reached the peak of perfection.

Inaction on Press Racism

Just how peculiar this actually is can be judged by the way in which it deals with complaints concerning race or ethnicity, most of which fall under Clause 13 of its Code of Practice. This clause states that: 'The press must avoid prejudicial or pejorative reference to a person's race, colour, religion, sex or sexual orientation, or to any physical or mental illness or disability.' It also states that: 'It must avoid publishing details of a person's race, colour, religion, sexual orientation, physical or mental illness or disability unless these are directly relevant to the story.' In 2002, 17.9 percent of complaints to the PCC concerned discrimination – up from 13.5 percent the previous year. The *Annual Review 2002* rather coyly notes that the increase might have something to do with the 'continuing reporting of debate about issues relating to asylum seekers and refugees' (PCC 2003: 6). None of these complaints were upheld, and yet this was the beginning of the period in which, as former *Mirror* editor, Roy Greenslade, claimed in the *Guardian*, 3 February 2003, many papers have conducted an anti-refugee campaign 'misinformed by hatred, lies and exaggeration which have played on people's fears and prejudices'. In his view, 'Underlying all that has been written is a vile racist agenda,' with papers 'appealing to the basest of human instincts: suspicion of the alien. That is racist in principle and in practice.' By 2003 the figure had climbed to 586 (19.8 percent) and 17.2 percent of rulings concerned this clause. Only inaccuracy accounted for a larger number of rulings and complaints relating to the representation of ethnic or racial groups, which can also sometimes be considered under Clause 1 of the code, which relates to accuracy. This states that: 'Newspapers and periodicals must take care not to publish inaccurate, misleading or distorted material,' adding that: 'Newspapers, whilst free to be partisan, must distinguish clearly between comment, conjecture and fact.'

However, PCC inaction on press racism is hardly confined to the early years of the new millennium. According to an analysis of ten years (1991–2000) of PCC adjudications, undertaken by Chris Frost (Chair of the National Union of Journalists (NUJ) ethics council), the period was marked by a steady rise in discrimination complaints: from 1.7 percent of all complaints received in 1993 to 10.6 percent in 2000. In 1993, 1.1 percent of complaints adjudicated concerned discrimination, and in 2000, 5.4 percent. During this period the PCC adjudicated only thirty-eight complaints concerning discrimination (5.6 percent of the total number of complaints adjudicated) and only six were upheld. The upheld complaints concerned discrimination against gay people and the mentally ill, and none concerned race, although sixteen (42 percent) of the original thirty-eight did so. Frost (2004: 112) concludes that:

> The significant and rather dramatic finding here is that not a single complaint of discrimination on the grounds of race or ethnicity has been upheld by the PCC. Since 42 percent of the adjudicated complaints concerned race, it is reasonable to assume that at least this many of the complaints made also concerned race ... This would suggest that approximately 600 complaints have been made in ten years on the grounds of race discrimination.

In order to understand PCC inaction on press racism, it needs to be realised that the PCC believes that the purpose of the discrimination clause is 'to protect *individuals* from prejudice – not to restrain partisan comment about other nations' (*PCC Report* No. 42). The position of the Commission was further clarified in a speech at Green College, Oxford by its then Acting Chairman, Professor Robert Pinker. As he explained, the code 'draws a clear distinction between the personal and the collective aspects of discrimination' and the Commission 'does not accept complaints on matters relating to issues of taste and decency', issues which, in its view, are frequently the basis of complaints about discrimination. The crucial point here, however, is that these are entirely self-imposed and self-denying ordinances: no-one other than the PCC has drawn up the discrimination clause in the code, and no-one other than the PCC has decided how it will be interpreted. There is thus not the slightest point in Pinker bleating about examples of 'the worst type of journalism which all too easily can bring the whole of the press into disrepute' and 'lapses in editorial judgement' in articles pertaining to race and ethnicity, or in the PCC collectively wringing its hands over xenophobic tabloid coverage of Euro '96 as 'shrill and poorly judged' (*PCC Report* No. 35), when the plain, simple and unavoidable fact is that the PCC *chooses* to avoid confronting such journalism.

'Robust Opinions'

Let us now examine how the PCC has dealt with complaints about the representation of Muslims and Islam under these clauses. This is not at all an easy task, given the remarkably few complaints about these subjects which the PCC has actually adjudicated, and the absence from its reports of significant details of the numerous complaints which it has decided fall outside its all-too-narrow remit.

On 16 January 1995, Robert Kilroy-Silk – whose vitriolic attacks in the *Express* on Muslims long predate his infamous 'We owe Arabs nothing' piece of 4 January 2004 – wrote:

> The Iraqis are publicly cutting off the ears and hands of and branding the foreheads of thieves and army deserters. They claim this ferocity is sanctioned by the Koran. Moslems everywhere behave with equal savagery. They behead criminals, stone to death female – only female – adulterers, throw acid in the faces of women who refuse to wear the chard, mutilate the genitals of young girls and ritually abuse animals. Nor are non-Moslems immune to their depravity. They conspired to kill the Pope, placed a death sentence on Salman Rushdie for writing things they did not like, murdered several of his supporters, threatened the life of a Moslem author who said, rightly, Islam treats women as second-class citizens, and indiscriminately murdered Western holiday-makers in Algeria, Egypt and elsewhere – just because they were Westerners.

When a reader complained to the PCC, the paper's editor told the Commission: 'The point about columnists in newspapers is that they express their own opinions . . . What he's done is taken various things that irritate him and put them all together but they are his opinions. He's not actually attacking all Muslims. He's just attacking the ones he doesn't like.' The PCC duly rejected the complaint on the grounds that: 'The column clearly represented a named columnist's personal view and would be seen as no more than his own robust opinions' (quoted in Runnymede Trust 1997: 26–7).

Nor is the kind of sentiment solely the preserve of right-wing newspapers. Thus on 18 August 2001, Julie Burchill used her regular Saturday *Guardian* column to lambaste the positive view of Islam recently presented by the BBC's Islamic Week. She concluded:

> That's Islam, then – fun, fun, fun! Not a mention of the women tortured, the Christian converts executed, the apostates hounded, the slaves in Sudan being sold into torment right now. Call me a filthy racist – go on, you know you want to – but we have reason to be suspicious of Islam and to treat it differently from other major religions. I don't think that either Judaism or Christianity, for a start, have in recent times held that apostasy – rejecting the religion one was born into – should be punishable by death . . . While the history of the other religions is one of moving forward out of oppressive darkness and into tolerance, Islam is doing it the other way round.

A few weeks later, on 29 September, it became clear from the regular column by Ian Mayes, the Readers' Editor of the *Guardian*, that more than half a dozen complaints had been received by the Press Complaints Commission, but Mayes also revealed that most of these had been rejected, and one can only assume that the rest received the same treatment, as there is no mention of any of them in any edition of the *PCC Report*.

Attention focused again on the *Express* when, on 15 November 2001, its columnist, Carol Sarler, wrote a piece headed 'Why do I have to tolerate the rantings of bigots just because they are Moslems?'. Describing herself as a 'conscientious, secular liberal' she stated that although 'we are constantly told that "the vast majority" of Moslems in this country are "moderates"', when it comes to unqualified condemnation by British Muslims of the events of September 11, 'with the barest handful of notable except-ions...the silence is deafening'. She also complained that proponents of multiculturalism

> ...seek allowance for cultures other than the indigenous to be accepted in their entirety – and the bottom line is that when it comes to Islam, that acceptance is something a liberal cannot properly offer. We are not allowed to pick and choose: love the food and pinch the kohl but reject the beaten wives, hate the suppression of women and find repugnant the Halal butchery.

She also stated that: 'Every Moslem state today is a cauldron of violence, corruption, oppression and dodgy democracy' and the Qur'an is described as 'no more than a bloodthirsty little book that is firmly rooted where it should have stayed – in the times and values of the early seventh century when it was written'. Also to her distaste was the 'tolerance that allows an indigenous population to host another that hates us and says so, in loud, haranguing, roving gangs that terrorise our inner cities in the name of Allah'. Admittedly, Inayat Bunglawala, Secretary of the Muslim Council of Britain's media committee was given a reasonable amount of space to reply on 20 November, but what is of greater significance in the present context is the PCC's response (in *Report* No. 56) to a reader's complaint that Sarler's article infringed the accuracy and discrimination clauses of its Code. According to the PCC, the gist of the complaint was that the remarks quoted above were 'incorrect in their generalization'; however, the *Express* defended itself by arguing that, as the article was headed as comment and clearly distinguished as the opinion of the columnist, it could not be in breach of the accuracy clause; furthermore, as in the article no specific persons were subject to prejudiced or pejorative attack based upon their race or religion, it could not be in breach of the discrimination clause. The PCC happily agreed with this defence, adding for good measure that:

> Regarding the alleged inaccuracies, the Commission noted the reporter made no factual claims regarding every Moslem, but rather drew attention to certain situations that she believed happened within certain Islamic societies. The entire article was presented, in accordance with the Code, as the opinion of one reporter, and did not purport to be a purely factual account of this complicated issue.

Standard Responses

What these examples demonstrate is that the PCC has certain standard responses to complaints about newspaper representations of race and ethnicity. The first is to argue that newspaper columnists are as free, within certain broad limits, to express their own opinions on these matters as they are on others. Thus, for example, the *Annual Review 2003* notes that many complaints under Clause 13 concern 'general issues to do with a newspaper's editorial stance on controversial subjects such as immigration. Such subjects may arouse strongly divergent views, but, providing they are presented in accordance with the Code's provisions on accuracy, do not normally involve a breach of the Code' (PCC 2004: 4). However, the problem with this formulation, and other similar ones routinely trotted out by the PCC, is that many of the views on race and ethnicity aired in British newspapers are based almost entirely on inaccuracies of one kind or another. For example, the Kilroy-Silk piece quoted above does not, whatever the *Express* editor may claim, single out *certain* Iraqis or *some* Muslims for their 'savagery': Kilroy-Silk is clearly stating that this is how Muslims *as a whole* behave, which, demonstrably, is factually inaccurate. Similarly, Julie Burchill's dislike of Islam appears to be based at least in part on her belief that it is a tenet of that faith that apostasy is punishable by death – but this is a view held only by certain minority sects within Islam, and thus, again, Burchill's position rests on at least one serious factual error. Likewise Carol Sarler's indignation about the 'deafening silence' from most British Muslims in the wake of September 11 is also grounded in her apparent ignorance of the actual facts of the case. Thus on September 11 itself the Muslim Council issued a press release which stated that: 'Whoever is responsible for these dreadful, wanton attacks, we condemn them utterly. No cause can justify this carnage. We hope those responsible will swiftly be brought to justice for their unconscionable deeds.' On 13 September a meeting of Muslim organisations convened by the Council issued a statement which made it clear that: 'We utterly condemn these indiscriminate terror attacks against innocent lives. The perpetrators of these atrocities, regardless of their religious, ideological or political beliefs, stand outside the pale of civilised values.' And on 29 September the Council convened a meeting of leading Islamic scholars and mosque leaders that condemned the attack in the strongest possible terms on the grounds that Islam holds that it is a criminal act to take the life of a human being without the due process of law. The meeting's conclusions were then circulated within the UK for wider endorsement by the Muslim community. However, these responses were either ignored or heavily downplayed by significant sections of the press – which puts Sarler's 'deafening silence' in a completely different light. (For further details of these responses see Muslim Council of Britain 2002: 18–19, 29–37). Nor, of course, is it true to say that *every* Muslim state is a 'cauldron' of violence, nor that the indigenous population of the UK is hosting another that hates it. These are simply wild accusations that fly in the face of the known, and easily verifiable, facts.

However, like certain kinds of postmodernist, the PCC appears not to believe in the distinction between fact and opinion.[1] It is, of course, perfectly possible to distinguish between the two, and indeed one would have thought that this would be one of the prime responsibilities of any media regulator. As Roy Greenslade pointed out in the *Guardian*, 10 March 1997, after the PCC had rejected, on grounds similar to the above, a complaint from Victim Support against a Barbara Amiel *Telegraph* column: 'If there is pressure on the reporter to write a factually accurate story, then the commentator faces just as much responsibility to write factually accurate comment. His or her opinions may be controversial, but they have to rest on truth.' Or as the late lamented Paul Foot (2000: 80) trenchantly put it:

> It is no good denying political bias – everyone is naturally and properly affected by it. The question is not how to disguise political bias but how to justify it. And the answer is by finding out and presenting the facts. Facts are the crucial standard by which opinion can be judged.

The problem, however, is that across most of the British press the distinction between news and editorial has entirely collapsed, and the Code's requirement that newspapers must distinguish clearly between comment, conjecture and fact is routinely breached on a daily basis: for example, many *Mail* and *Express* front page stories, and especially those about immigration, read just like editorials – and particularly strident ones at that. Clearly, opinion (especially when robust) sells, as does appealing to insularity, prejudice and bigotry. Were the PCC a genuinely independent body, it might be expected to take a stand against this kind of partisan pollution of the news, but as it is paid for by the papers that it is supposed to be regulating it is hardly likely to hit them where it hurts – in their pockets. So, having neither the resources nor the will to decide whether the facts on which an article is based are true or false, the PCC routinely falls back on evasive and hopelessly inadequate formulations such as: 'It is not the Commission's job to establish the facts of the matter when two parties dispute the accuracy of an article but to consider, under the Code, whether sufficient care has been taken by a newspaper not to publish inaccurate material' (*PCC Report* No. 52). Thus the way in which the PCC interprets the first clause of its Code means that it is a wholly ineffective measure against what most people would understand by inaccuracy, and that newspapers whose very trademarks are the conflation of news and views have absolutely nothing to fear from the PCC.

The second standard reason for the PCC's rejection of complaints about press representations of race and ethnicity is that the articles in question do not attack specific individuals. This is also frequently given as a reason for rejecting third-party complaints about such articles. However, after its hearings into privacy and media intrusion, the Culture, Media and Sport Select Committee noted that Friends, Families and Travellers, a national voluntary organisation serving the travelling community, had reported that it had submitted over six hundred complaints to the PCC regarding discriminatory references to gypsies and travellers in the press. The majority of these had not been accepted and none had been upheld. 'Perhaps the PCC would concede,' the Committee suggested, 'that this is evidence, despite its efforts, of a problem that just will not produce a technically valid complainant, i.e. one related to a named individual – with regard to discrimination and racism this is often the whole point' (House of Commons Culture, Media and Sport Committee 2003: 32). The Committee concluded that, 'A new and more explicit approach to the acceptance of third party complaints' would be a beneficial reform as 'this is as important in issues of prejudicial and pejorative references to minority groups as it is on privacy matters' (ibid.: 31).

The issue of third-party complaints has also been taken up, in a rather wider context, by the campaigning body MediaWise:

> Any refugee, black person or homosexual might reasonably object if a newspaper published inaccurate or prejudicial material about

refugees, black people or homosexuals, even if they themselves are not mentioned by name. After all, they are the ones most likely to bear the brunt of any public displeasure that ensues. To argue that this is unlikely to happen flies in the face of reason, since there have been innumerable instances of outbursts of public rage against paedophiles (during the *News of the World*'s 'name and shame' campaign), travellers and asylum seekers. Nor is it unreasonable for readers who are not members of the group under attack to complain if they feel that inaccurate or prejudicial material is likely to distort perceptions, cause harm to others, or skew the responses of policy-makers. We are all equal members of an open democracy, so public misperceptions generated by inaccurate or sensational stories matter to us all. (Jempson 2004: 33)

Furthermore, they argue, third-party complaints should be permissible on the grounds that: 'We are all diminished when community relations break down as a result of inaccurate or sensational coverage' (ibid.: 39).

Name and Shame

For all the reasons outlined above, I would argue that the PCC is quite hopeless as a bulwark against negative representations of Muslims and Islam in the press. Since it is paid for by newspapers, and its Code Committee is stuffed with editors, some of whose papers are front runners in the Islamophobia stakes, I find it extremely difficult not to regard it as part of the problem rather than part of the solution. Indeed, since many people who are daily affronted by press racism are only too well aware of the nature of the PCC and of the narrow restrictions which it has conveniently imposed upon itself, the only real surprise is that the PCC receives as many complaints about racial discrimination as it actually does.

Is it worth complaining at all, then? The Runnymede Trust thinks that it is. In their view: 'A critical mass of complaints will affect the general climate of opinion, such that columnists and editors think twice before printing the more "robust" of their opinions...A critical mass of complaints will also, it is reasonable to assume, affect how the Press Complaints Commission interprets its own code of practice' (Runnymede Trust 1997: 27). This, personally, I very much doubt. Much more likely, in my view, to affect the press, the PCC and the 'general climate of opinion' will be various forms of what the press loves to call 'naming and shaming': critical articles in papers such as the *Guardian* and *Independent*, as well as in the trade magazine *Press Gazette*, and items on radio and television programmes about the media, exposing and examining specific instances of Islamophobia in the press: there's nothing that journalists like less than being criticised by other journalists. Similarly, complaints to the PCC can serve as useful ammunition for its many critics if complainants can manage to publicise their unsatisfactory dealings with it (see, for example, Petley 1997, 2004), either through the various media or via bodies such as the Campaign for Press and Broadcasting Freedom, MediaWise or the National Union of Journalists. It would also be extremely useful if such bodies, and indeed any organisation concerned with how the media represent certain issues or social groups, could include on its website a section devoted to exposing and analysing media misrepresentations of these issues or groups – a kind of do-it-yourself right of reply, in fact. And finally, books such as this also perform a useful 'naming and shaming' function in that they write press racism, and PCC complicity with it, into the historical record. Newspaper articles themselves are notoriously ephemeral, but critical writing about them far less so, and papers which would like to be able to present themselves as bold, courageous members of the 'fourth estate' increasingly find themselves having to compete with far less flattering representations – after all, all that most people know about the *Mail* (apart from the fact that it's extremely right-wing) is that in the 1930s it was an ardent admirer of Nazi Germany and Mosley's Blackshirts.

Finally, though, the only remedy against the kind of journalism encountered in this and other chapters of this book is, in my view, a statutory right of reply. However, this is hotly opposed by the Department of Culture, Media and Sport (DCMS), which at the time of writing is having a fit of the vapours over a perfectly sensible recommendation of the European Parliament and the Council of the European Union for 'considering the introduction of measures into [member states'] domestic law or practice to ensure the right of reply across all media'. Following a consultation with press and broadcasting interests (and, note, no-one else) on this matter, the DCMS sent a briefing note to all UK MEPs that condemned the proposal as 'unwieldy, bureaucratic and impractical', adding that: 'The UK has a voluntary system arbitrated by the Press Complaints Commission to ensure a right of reply in the printed press, and in online versions of print newspapers. This works well and we do not believe that it is necessary... to enshrine the procedures in law.' Since the PCC has not insisted on a right of reply to any of the articles quoted in this chapter, and elsewhere in this book, it is extraordinarily hard to see how the present system can be said to be working at all, let alone working well.

6. Mixed Communities: Mixed Newsrooms

Peter Cole

Introduction

The recruitment of ethnic minority journalists to newspapers is now on the agenda of the publishers. But it has taken a long time to get there and too little has been achieved so far. Broadcast journalism recognised the problem and did something about it nearly ten years ago, and those who led the way would be the first to admit that much more needs to be achieved. Yes, there are black and Asian faces on our television news programmes, but there are few in senior positions in editorial management.

Newspaper journalism has lagged behind, first in recognising the problem and second in doing anything about it. National newspapers, with their large editorial staffs and ability to recruit from the regional and local press, have made some ethnic minority recruitment progress. But regional and local newspapers, even in areas of high non-white population, have achieved so little that those with a single black or Asian reporter in the newsroom tend to be proud of the fact.

This chapter examines the available data about ethnic minority employment in journalism, particularly newspaper journalism. It looks at the reasons given for the low level of recruitment, at the lack of attraction of journalism to young people from ethnic minority backgrounds, at measures being taken to improve the situation and at the comparatively superior performance of broadcast journalism.

Ethnic Minority Reporters in British Newsrooms

Remarkably little research attention has been given to this issue. Many publishers have been reluctant to provide, or in some cases even gather, ethnic minority recruitment data. Some take the view that it is sufficient simply to say that they recruit the best person for the job, and ethnicity is not a factor they consider. Others maintain that they do not receive applications from the ethnic minorities, or that they recruit from colleges and universities who do not take significant numbers of ethnic minority students on to their courses. Others say that journalism is not an attractive career option for ethnic minorities, particularly those from Asian communities. Reasons or excuses, the result is poor ethnic minority representation in the press, particularly the regional and local press. And it begs the question, why has broadcast journalism done so much better?

One comprehensive and thorough survey of employment in journalism has been undertaken. *Journalists at Work*, claimed as the most detailed survey of journalists in the UK ever undertaken, was produced in 2002 by the Journalism Training Forum, a body set up under the government sponsored Publishing National Training Organisation. Through a detailed questionnaire it sought journalists' information and views on training, recruitment and conditions. In the section on the personal characteristics of journalists the questionnaire identified journalists as white, Asian/Asian British, black/black British, Chinese and other. The survey found 96 percent of journalists in the UK were white and highlighted 'concerns about the level of diversity in the industry'. It said:

> The occupation is not ethnically representative – more than nine out of ten are white, with small proportions from ethnic minority groups. Given the predominance of the industry in London and the South East and in other urban areas, it might be expected that the occupation would have a greater proportion of people from ethnic minority backgrounds. (*Journalists at Work* 2002: 26)

Ian Hargreaves, chair of the Journalism Forum, said in his introduction to the report: 'The case for a programme of action to address the issues of social and ethnic diversity raised in the survey is compelling.' At the press conference in London to launch the report senior representatives of print and broadcast journalism – Bob Phillis, chief executive of the Guardian Media Group, and Clive Jones, the then chief executive of Carlton Television – both spoke forcefully on this aspect of the report. The lack of ethnic minority representation in the media, particularly the print media, was disgraceful and had to be addressed. Both called on publishers, editors and media managers to prioritise the issue and bring about change. Two and half years later there is more discussion of the issue, more awareness at a senior level in the media that present levels of ethnic minority representation are indefensible, some small steps to improving the situation, but little significant change.

Writing in *British Journalism Review*, Joy Francis (2003: 68) of the Creative Collective remarked that 'it is like pulling teeth to establish how many ethnic minority journalists are earning their crust in national and regional newsrooms'. Francis paints a very negative picture of progress made in the employment of ethnic minority journalists in mainstream media in Britain. She had received funding from the American Freedom Forum's internship programme for young ethnic minority journalists to encourage a similar scheme in the UK. The American programme, run by John C. Quinn, former editor of *USA Today*, had placed 500 students on three-month placements, and 71 percent of these interns subsequently had gained a foothold in the industry.

Francis had been told that British newspapers would be 'hard nuts to crack', and while the Creative Collective has managed to organise some internships at papers, such as the *Manchester Evening News*, *Bradford Telegraph and Argus*, *Nottingham Evening Post* and *Scunthorpe Telegraph*, as well as *The Times* and *Financial Times*, Francis still finds that 'the wider print landscape isn't all that pretty to look at'. She writes:

> Mutterings that ethnic minority journalists can't quite cut the mustard are still audible. Jobs continue to be sealed in pubs and bars on the back of a recommendation from a friend of a distant friend. Figures on the numbers of asylum seekers depriving Brits of their birthright or black men who are terrorising middle class white families aren't in short supply in the tabloids or broadsheets. (Francis 2003: 68)

It was in the light of the Journalism Forum's sparse but gloomy data on ethnic minority employment in the media, conversations with Clive Jones (now managing director of ITV News) about his experiences with ethnic minority recruitment in television, and national and regional newspaper editors and editorial directors, that led me to think further work on the subject was needed. Joy Francis's comment that simply gathering data was like pulling teeth was true in my experience too. Publishers might declare (usually off the record) regret or embarrassment at the lack of ethnic diversity in their newsrooms, but corrective action was never high on their executive agendas. It seemed to me that we needed specific data, qualitative and quantitative, and we needed answers to a number of questions. As chair of the Society of Editors (SoE) Training Committee, I was in a strong position to initiate such a project.

The Society of Editors is the representative body of national and regional newspaper editors and senior broadcasters. It campaigns on issues of press freedom and other legislative matters affecting the reporting of information to the public. It is consulted by government and public and private bodies. It takes a strong interest in training and recruitment. Its annual conference, held in different parts of the country each year, is a prestigious occasion attended by the most influential figures in the media and other areas of public life. In short, the Society of Editors was a significant body to draw attention to the diversity issue and to influence change.

Rather than take the macro view produced by the Journalism Forum's industry-wide survey, we decided our work should be more focused. While '96 percent white' confirms observation of the print media in towns and cities across the country it does not fill in the detail. It might be the case that in areas of high black and Asian population ethnic minority media employment is high, and the 96 percent figure is accounted for by the absence of minority ethnic journalists in a wide range of places with little or no ethnic minority population.

The SoE survey, it was decided, would focus on a series of case studies of regional newspapers publishing in areas of high minority ethnic population. These were: Birmingham, Bradford, Burnley, Harrow, Leeds, Leicester, Manchester, Oldham, Stoke and Uxbridge. We needed to know the extent to which national and regional publishers regarded ethnic minority employment as an issue, what were the causes of the problem, what were the effects of lack of diversity in the newsroom, what measures were being taken and could be taken to correct the situation. The result was a report, *Diversity in the Newsroom*, published by the Society of Editors in 2004, and presented to the SoE's annual conference (Society of Editors Training Committee 2004).[1] The figures for the ten newspapers we considered were stark (see Table 6.1).

Table 6.1. *Regional Press Employment Data*

City	Paper	Circulation	Ethnic minority population (percentage)	Editorial staff	Ethnic minority staff
Birmingham	*Evening Mail*	104,000	30	93	7 (7.5%)
Bradford	*Telegraph and Argus*	47,000	22	65	2 (3.1%)
Burnley	*Express*	20,000	11	38	1 (2.6%)
Harrow	*Observer*	13,000	43	12	1 (8.3%)
Leeds	*Yorkshire Evening Post*	75,000	9	68	0 (0%)
Leicester	*Mercury*	90,000	38	120	4 (3.3%)
Manchester	*Evening News*	148,000	10	112	6 (5.4%)
Oldham	*Evening Chronicle*	27,000	14	34	1 (2.9%)
Stoke	*Sentinel*	75,000	7	92	5 (5.4%)
Uxbridge	*Gazette*	20,000	14	10	1 (10%)

Source: *Diversity in the Newsroom*, Society of Editors Report, 2004.

Editors' Views

In each case the editor of the newspaper featured in the case study was interviewed, and comments helped to paint a picture of industry attitudes to and experiences of ethnic minority recruitment. Here are some examples of their comments. Roger Borrell, editor of the *Birmingham Evening Mail*, has strong opinions on the employment of ethnic minority journalists, and as the Table 6.1 above shows has made progress in recruitment. He says:

> When I arrived in the office as editor three years ago it was like walking into the Johannesburg Star in 1952. There were plenty of black people around, but they were cleaning the toilets. It seemed appalling to me, having walked through the streets and seen the mix there. There was one minority ethnic journalist on the staff then. I had to do something about it. You can't reflect the community unless you reflect its mix. We still have no minority ethnic staff in senior positions on the paper.

According to a National Opinion Polls survey in 2002, the *Birmingham Evening Mail* is read by 23,000 Asians in the Birmingham and Coventry area, almost 14 percent of the Asian population and 5 percent of the total readership. No national newspaper is read by more than 12 percent of Asians in the area.[2]

While Borrell, in common with most of the editors interviewed, stresses that ethnic minority reporters are used as true generalists, rather than being encouraged to concentrate on ethnic and race relations issues, he accepts that the paper gains valuable knowledge of the communities it should be serving by employing journalists from those communities. He cites one journalist who used to be an advertisement rep on the *Daily Telegraph*. 'He has been a bridge to the Muslim community,' says Borrell, developing a huge number of contacts the paper did not previously have. The paper gave him a sabbatical to learn Arabic. 'I think having a more representative newsroom, employing more minority ethnic staff, is the right thing to do,' says Borrell, 'not the right business decision.'

Perry Austin-Clarke, editor of the *Bradford Telegraph and Argus*, had to deal with the Bradford riots of 2001 and, by common consent, the paper covered the trouble and its aftermath and inquiry reports very well. He says that employing minority ethnic journalists is extremely important to him. 'We ought to be better able to reflect the make-up of that community on our staff.' However, in 2004 there were two ethnic minority reporters on the staff, two fewer than two years earlier. The editor says it is 'almost impossible' to find minority ethnic recruits. Austin-Clarke says his paper has made extensive efforts to attract minority ethnic applicants to journalism. They have gone into mono-cultural schools, targeted careers events, even staged their own recruitment events in Asian areas, 'with little interest or success'. For the past three years the paper has joined *Big Issue*, *The Times* and a handful of other regional papers in pioneering an ethnic minority placement scheme with the Creative Collective, where the paper paid for three-month internships for minority ethnic candidates. None of them converted into a full-time trainee.

Chris Daggett, editor of the *Burnley Express*, stresses that his ethnic minority population is concentrated in one area of considerable social deprivation. Burnley gained national prominence with disturbances in 2001 – which Daggett says were not race riots – and a rising profile, including election of councillors, for the British National Party (BNP). Daggett is now chairing an East Lancashire project team that is seeking to build a relationship between the ethnic minority communities and his paper. 'I have more faith in this project than in simply hiring more minority ethnic reporters,' he says. He further states:

> We cannot change things overnight, but we are working in the right direction. The riots in 2001 had a big effect on me. They made me realise how powerful a paper is. We didn't realise what impact we could have. We still have to build links into the ethnic community. There is no flow of stories coming in. We don't know who to contact. It takes a long time to build up the contacts.

Nick Carter edits the *Leicester Mercury*, and has over the years been one of the regional editors most preoccupied with the employment of ethnic minority journalists. Leicester has one of the highest Asian populations in the country and it will not be long before this community becomes a majority. Carter sees the need to recruit journalists from the minority ethnic community as very important because the paper serves a diverse community. If the paper is not seen to be working hard to write about this community, then ethnic minorities will not recognise commitment. Carter says: 'As an industry we need to get better at understanding the communities we want to serve. Lots of areas are changing drastically and editors ignore this at their peril. The real need is to get better at bringing in a mix of people.' But the *Mercury* finds problems with minority ethnic recruitment, a 'huge issue' according to Carter. 'The Asian community doesn't see journalism jobs as sexy compared with traditional favourites like accountants, doctors and dentists, and other potentially high-earning jobs.'

Paul Horrocks, editor of the *Manchester Evening News*, has to serve a range of communities spread throughout the ten towns of Greater Manchester. He says there was a deliberate policy to increase the number of minority ethnic editorial staff.

We talked, across the company, about the fact that our staff was almost all white, and not reflective of our circulation area. It was hard to tackle some stories if we didn't have people who understood the culture. It was important to increase our knowledge base. We now have a good, or better, base for understanding the background and culture of a significant proportion of our potential readership.

Philip Hirst is managing director of the *Oldham Evening Chronicle*, having previously been its editor. There was racial violence in Oldham in 2001, and there has been an increased BNP presence in Oldham. Hirst admits that sales of his paper to the Asian community, which makes up 14 percent of the potential audience, are 'too small to be quantifiable'. Nevertheless:

A positive effort was made to court the Asian communities. There were meetings with Pakistani and Bangladeshi representatives. They said we were racist. They said we only reported bad news about their communities. We agreed upon a pact: they tell me their good news; I would use it if it was worth it and would tell them why I wasn't using it if it wasn't suitable. The meetings were fierce, stormy but a good exchange of views. They took me at my word and we have not looked back. The newspaper now reflects the Asian communities here far better than at any time in the past.

Trinity Mirror Southern's Editorial Director, Marc Reeves, is responsible for both the *Uxbridge Gazette* and *Harrow Observer*, two papers serving communities with large Asian populations. Each paper has one ethnic minority reporter. 'While in Uxbridge,' says Reeves, 'it could be argued that the proportion is very broadly in line with that of the general population, Harrow's numbers are considerably out of step.' Reeves warns of the dangers of lack of understanding of the minority communities the newspapers are serving.

The *Harrow Observer* recently ran a story that caused ructions within the Hindu community and the local authority. We were approached by a local Hindu group that wanted to draw attention to the fact that one local authority was giving minimal support to Divali events. We ran the story only to find that the council was in fact linking up with many groups to help the celebrations and we had in fact been duped by a very small Hindu splinter group. Our lack of detailed knowledge of the finer points of Hindu community issues had come back to bite us. Furthermore, and more seriously, the story had been written by the one Asian reporter in the newsroom. Our editing process had fallen completely into the trap of tokenism. We had assumed that our responsibility to reflect ethnic community issues was taken care of by the fact we had an Asian reporter. What it showed was that the responsibility goes a lot further: every news editor, sub and photographer needs a much deeper level of understanding of different communities.

It was the lack of understanding of the ethnic communities, brought about by a failure to employ their representatives, who like any community contained a variety of views and political attitudes, that caused this confusion. The paper fell into the trap of thinking all Hindus thought the same!

Applications

Most of the editors interviewed said they received very few applications for reporting vacancies or traineeships from the ethnic minorities. Roger Borrell (editor of the *Birmingham Evening Mail*) said that out of two or three letters a week, some ten or twelve a year are from minority ethnic applicants. There is a noticeable reluctance among some Asian groups to go into journalism, and Borrell says parental pressure is a factor, 'I often hear that "Dad wants me to be a solicitor".'

Perry Austin-Clarke (editor of the *Bradford Telegraph and Argus*) said he received hardly any applications, and the supply from recognised pre-entry college courses was 'non-existent'. Even in the most aspirational communities in cities like Leicester, journalism was not seen as a worthwhile career by many families who encouraged their children to aim for jobs as doctors, lawyers, accountants and entrepreneurs. Journalists were regarded as badly paid and pretty low on the social scale.

Combine that with the extremely poor levels of educational attainment in an area like Bradford, where the Asians come from the poorest parts of Bangladesh and Pakistan, and it leaves very few people with the aptitude or interest to join newspapers. Those who do look for media jobs are keen to go straight into radio or TV.

Major Regional Publishers

All the individual newspapers referred to in this chapter are owned by large publishers: Trinity Mirror, the biggest, owns 230 regional newspapers; Newsquest, part of the American publisher Gannett, owns 216 titles; Northcliffe, the regional arm of Associated Newspapers, owners of the *Daily Mail*, publishes 110 titles; and Johnston Press 241. The Society of Editors survey detected a new recognition at a senior level in these major publishers that recruitment of journalists from the ethnic minorities was an issue that had to be addressed. Johnston Press, for example, had conducted a survey of employment patterns across all its newspapers and found that 'less than one percent' of its editorial staff came from ethnic minority backgrounds. Trinity Mirror's editorial director, Neil Benson, said that 'Newsrooms are traditionally a bastion of the white middle classes, and making them representative is proving a difficult nut to crack.'

Both these publishers have introduced bursary schemes to encourage young blacks and Asian trainees to join pre-entry journalism courses at colleges and universities. Trinity Mirror has its own training school and Johnston Press is starting a scheme to fund young people from the ethnic minorities through college and university journalism courses. At present these bursaries are few in number.

National Press

The national newspapers have a slightly better record in this area, but those who have achieved most in the area of ethnic minority recruitment will be the first to say that too little has been done so far. Take the *Guardian* that since 1991 has run the Scott Trust bursary scheme which funds places on postgraduate journalism courses at three nominated universities (City, Sheffield and Goldsmith's). There are at present six of these a year, and priority is given to ethnic minority applicants. The beneficiaries of these bursaries are not guaranteed employment on the *Guardian* or other titles in the Guardian Media Group, but some have been taken on. In 2004 the *Guardian*'s editorial staff of 411 included 20 from ethnic minority backgrounds.

The *Financial Times*, owned by the Pearson Group, is one example of a newspaper that is making significant progress in the diversity issue. It has a diversity manager and an explicit strategy aimed at increasing ethnic minority representation in its newsrooms. There is careful monitoring and collection of data, an intern scheme, and open days to attract potential applicants to its training scheme. The *Financial Times* London editorial staff of 400 has 7 percent from an ethnic minority background. The newspaper's commitment to change is evidenced by the commitment of its chairman Sir David Bell to tackling the issue. He has brought together senior editorial management from other national newspapers to discuss ways of improving the situation.

Broadcast Experience

The initiative by Sir David Bell at the *Financial Times* mirrors the actions taken some years ago in broadcasting. There the starting point was commercial – an awareness by a few leading figures in the television industry that, in multi-cultural Britain, large sections of the ethnic minority communities were not watching the programmes the broadcasters were putting out. Clive Jones, then managing director of Carlton TV, was one of these, and he has championed the issue since 1996.

> Our sales department and the advertising agencies were telling us that there was a significant group that was simply not watching our programmes. We commissioned research. We found that Asian audiences preferred satellite and cable television. They like quizzes, not game shows. They liked natural history programmes. They hated *This Morning* [an early morning programme], dirty things like sex. They hated *EastEnders* because they never saw a father with a child. They switched off. The first black character seen on *Corrie* was breaking into a house.[3]

ITV newsrooms were targeted with a view to improving minority ethnic representation. In 1996 Carlton newsrooms contained 5 percent minority ethnic staff; in 2003 the figure was 13.6 percent.

In October 2000 Britain's leading broadcasters agreed to set up the Cultural Diversity Network (CDN). For the BBC and the commercial stations there was a compelling business case as well as an ethical imperative to take action. Black and Asian audiences are an important and growing segment of the audience and attracting and retaining them was a priority. CDN members support cross-industry initiatives and share expertise, resources and models of good practice, including setting targets for ethnic minority employment, including senior executive levels. The key to its success has been the involvement of all the main television companies and the fact that they were represented at chief executive level.

A number of CDN members have set themselves firm targets for minority ethnic employment. The BBC announced in January 2004 that it had hit its initial target of 10 percent of staff and 4 percent of senior management from minority ethnic communities. Its new target for 2007 is 12.5 percent of all staff and 7 percent of senior management. ITN is near to its stated target of 10 percent of staff; Channel Four is at 10.4 percent of all staff (target 11 percent) and 5.1 percent of management (target 8 percent).

The broadcasters have invested in training schemes aimed at ethnic minority candidates. Both ITV and the BBC offer bursaries for postgraduate vocational courses at journalism schools, which are targeted at the ethnic minorities. In attracting young black and Asian graduates into broadcasting, particularly broadcast journalism, the CDN has placed great emphasis on the value of portrayal and role models. The BBC and ITN have a number of black and Asian newscasters and correspondents who have undoubtedly encouraged young people from ethnic minority communities to believe that talent is the key to success.

The Future

The broadcast experience demonstrates that the issue of ethnic minority employment requires champions and cross-industry commitment if change is to occur. The Cultural Diversity Network provides a model of how change can be achieved. The recent involvement of senior figures in the newspaper industry, regional and national, suggests that the mood for change may be coming about. There is a growing realisation that newspapers cannot properly report the communities they serve if those communities are not represented on editorial staffs. Changing demographics and multiculturalism cannot be served by a journalism that represents a different world, one that no longer exists in Britain. Ethnic minorities will not connect with newspapers that neither understand them nor bother to employ them. Successful newspapers reflect the communities they serve and if potential audiences are significantly multicultural and multi-ethnic, then those who report them and seek to understand them need to be the same.

Clearly a great deal remains to be done. Several publishers are now pursuing the bursary route, targeted funding of pre-entry journalism courses for aspiring journalists from the ethnic minorities. Journalism education has changed greatly over the past twenty years. What was once a craft apprenticeship, particularly in the regional press, is now predominantly a graduate career. That means the universities and colleges providing journalism education also have a key role to play in promoting diversity in newsrooms. Like the employers of journalists, universities and colleges must take their share of responsibility for the current situation. Like the employers of journalists they need to play their part in changing that situation.

7. Islamic Features in British and French Muslim Media

Isabelle Rigoni

In Western Europe, the identity constructions and religious engagement of Muslim communities are based on a variety of individual and collective strategies, upon which the specifics of national setting have a decisive influence. In the vast panorama of the British community media (Cottle 2000; Husband, Beattie and Markelin 2002), the Muslim news media – created by and for Muslims and asserting itself as such – and the Muslim associative media committees became skilful and demanding interlocutors, functioning like agents of pressure on the authorities. In France, the specifically Muslim news media constitute a new generation, different from the media based on a national or cultural, rather than a religious, membership community.[1] In this context, young people who foreground a Muslim identity occupy an increasingly important place on the European public scene.

This chapter draws upon interviews with young Muslim people involved in community news media that I conducted between 2001 and 2003 in Great Britain and in 2003 and 2004 in France. I wish to present some particularly illustrative cases of the Muslim news media production in Great Britain and France – specifically, how they are the fruits of a foregrounded religious identity expressed by Muslim actors of the younger generation. First, through portraits provided by the actors themselves, I will underline the various stages of individual routes to such a foregrounded religious identity and explore these young Muslims' motivation for social action in the public sphere. Second, through discussing various initiatives by these various news organisations and media associations I will show how the group is reconsidered and how public space is reappropriated.

Individual Routes to Faith

The various stages of engagement in Islam and the Muslim media vary intensely according to individual routes. Despite this variation, all of those interviewed share a renewed reflection and engagement towards Islam. My qualitative research demonstrates that young Muslims can be grouped into three types that reflect their origin and path to Islam.

Discovering Islam and faith

Converts occupy a relatively important place – quantitatively and qualitatively – within the Muslim media in Great Britain, especially among the younger generation. According to its ex-editor Shagufta Yaqub, about half of the contributors to *Q-News* magazine are converts. The majority are British, but with some exceptions such as Hamza Yusuf – an American of Greek Orthodox origin who converted to Islam – who is one of the most popular and the most emblematic converts of the Anglo-Saxon world. Today, Yusuf is Professor of Arabic and director of Zaytouna Institute in San Francisco, organises and coordinates conferences in Great Britain and contributes to Muslim magazines like *Q-News* as well as mainstream newspapers like the *Guardian*.

Other examples are not rare within the British Muslim organisations and news media. Consider Sarah Joseph, for example, the first woman to become editor of a Muslim magazine – *Trends* – in Great Britain. Joseph converted to Islam when she was sixteen years old and studied Religious Studies at higher education. After her stint as the head of *Trends* magazine in the second half of the 1990s, she transferred to a consultancy in Islamic business and now provides training courses. Nevertheless, she still appears on the media scene, for example on television programmes like *Panorama*.[2] In France, until recently, the community press was almost exclusively produced by young French Muslims with family origins in the Maghreb. For a few years, several converted intellectuals have collaborated with *Hawwa* or *Oumma.com*.

The routes of the converts contrast dramatically with the commonly widespread image of the convert disseminated by some mass-circulation mainstream media – simultaneously representing a 'victim' and a 'threat to society'. This type of alarmist interpretation has the particular effect, if not the *aim*, of causing or encouraging the primary fears of an expansionist Islamic force, and to give credence to the assumptions of a 'clash of civilisations' (Halliday 1996; Ferguson 1998; Gabriel 1998; Jacobs 2000; Poole 2002). The British Muslim press opposes this partial vision, preferring to highlight the (far more common) examples of adult converts who maturely made their choice at the end of an intellectual process. Some covers of magazines illustrate this choice, such as the cover of *Q-News* below (January–February 2002). Here, Yvonne Ridley, the ex-war correspondent for the *Daily Express*, is pictured wearing an Islamic veil, her azure-blue gaze directed towards the sky as if infused with the faith.

Figure 7.1 *Q-News*
Lifting the Veil

In France, the media representation of Islam, particularly on television, is often an ideological construction that confuses proselytism and religion, Islamism and Islam (Yavari-D'Hellencourt 2000; Geisser 2003). The aim seems to be to show the intrinsic incompatibility of this religion with one of the central values of French modernity: laic secularity. In this context, the journalists of the mainstream media seem particularly uncomfortable with the phenomenon of conversions, which they quasi systematically locate in the context of imprisonment. The Muslim media try to counterbalance the absence of positive or attractive portrayals in the mainstream media in order to relativise the negative images given in many reports and thus provide political support and personal identification for Muslims.

Rediscovering Islam

Within the British news media, a significant number of young Muslims, whose families emigrated from 1960 to 1970, rediscovered their faith when they were teenagers or while growing up. In contrast to converts, this rediscovery stands as a second reading of Islam compared to that practised by their immigrant families. Their religious engagement is maturely intellectualised and Islamic practice is reinterpreted, giving a new direction to their faith.

The route of Shagufta Yaqub is interesting in more than one way. When we meet in a London café in June 2002, Shagufta is veiled, wears green clothes of several tones, her arms laden down with the newly printed latest issue of *Q-News*. *Q-News* is a well respected, independent Muslim monthly magazine that combines national and international coverage across sections covering politics, social issues, fashion and sport. She described the target audience as 'The young British Muslims, probably between 18 and 45, Muslims whose first language is English, and who have university degrees in the UK.' With a circulation of 15,000, it is distributed mainly in Great Britain but also, since September 2001, in some areas of the United States, Canada, South Africa and some Middle-Eastern countries. She was only twenty-four years old when she became editor of *Q-News* in 2000, and her meteoric rise and prestigious position merited mention in several articles in national British newspapers (the *Independent*, the *Observer* and the *Guardian*).

Her religious engagement came only at the end of an intellectual process. Born in Pakistan, Shagufta was one year old when she arrived in

Britain (South London). The search for roots in her teenage years led her to turn to 'Asian culture', but her interest in Islam awoke whilst at university, where she studied 'Islamophobia' as part of her diploma in Sociology and Communications. This strictly academic interest in Islam evolved into a religious conviction at the end of a trip to Egypt. She adopted the Islamic veil in 1999, at the age of twenty-three, at which point she had already worked as a journalist at *Q-News* for two years. The evolution of her faith has had a double price: within her family, who accept her adopting of the veil with difficulty, but especially within wider British society, which sometimes views her with suspicion:

> People treat you differently. Since September 11, it has been very difficult. People think you're responsible. It has been quite hard. In a way it has been getting worse [than after Salman Rushdie affair]. But I think more people are curious about Islam, they ask questions. They said that the best selling book was the Qur'an, for many months after September 11. I think that's a good sign because people are learning more, so there will be more understanding about Muslims.

The personal investment related to faith, and to Islamic practice more specifically, implies a particular choice of life, which was translated in this young woman's case by a professional reorientation. Shagufta Yaqub

> [...] always wanted to be a journalist. I studied media and wanted to work for the mainstream, the *Guardian* or something. But I became more religious and I just thought I would not be comfortable working in a media setting. Because a lot of the media is, I think, quite unethical. I had new and different values and I didn't think that they would be compatible with working in the [mainstream] media. So, one day I discovered *Q-News*, I just went: that's it.

While Shagufta suggests the difficulty of working within the mainstream media, her strong investment in the Muslim press concerns a personal choice in close connection with its recent religious engagement. But this choice does not prevent her from occasionally contributing to national daily newspapers, such as the *Guardian* and the *Independent*, or with broadcasts of the BBC and even of European television channels, as was the case after September 11. Shagufta perceives these activities as a 'complement' to her engagement with the Muslim news media: simultaneously they play a role in educating a readership ('people who want to know make the effort to learn') and a role advertising the magazine. For example, *Q-News* has been described as a 'must-read' magazine (*Independent* 31 October 2000) and the 'greater Muslim voice in Europe' (*Observer* 23 September 2001). As Shagufta affirms: 'That was a good publicity. The *Guardian* article [after September 11] brought us a few hundred subscriptions, and it wasn't Muslims subscribing but other people interested in Islam.'

Inayat Bunglawala is another example of this younger generation engaged in the revival of the British Muslim media. We met in June 2002 in a halal snack bar in the district of Whitechapel, the only one near to his place of work, a complex of high-rise office buildings, where he works in data processing. His parents, of Gujarati origin, were never involved in religious organisations. However, during his adolescence in the mid 1980s, Inayat developed an awareness of what he calls a growing Islamophobia within the British media and wider society. Indeed, Islamophobia (Runnymede Trust 1997) played as important a part in the rediscovery of Islam by Inayat as by Shagufta Yaqub. Inayat became a practising Muslim in 1987, at the age of eighteen. His religious engagement was motivated by mysticism (a renewed faith) and pragmatism (to act here and now):

> when I was growing up in the 1980s and the early 1990s, we felt powerless, we didn't have a body that could respond to this [Islamophobia]...I wanted to do something practical. I don't believe Islam is just reading the Qur'an...We wanted also a body who represents us and also who would go and meet journalists to put our point of view across. Because they had their views and we had no way of articulating ourselves.

Inayat was very active in the 1990s: he created an Islamic association, later part of The Young Muslims UK (YMUK); became the editor of *Trends* in 1996; and joined the Islamic Society of Britain (ISB). Nevertheless, he estimates that these actions were not enough to introduce knowledge of Islam into British society. From its inception in 1997, Inayat was responsible for the media committee of the Muslim Council of Britain (MCB) – one of the fifteen committees of the organisation. His roles are to monitor all articles published in the dominant press concerning Islam or Muslims; to write occasional articles in the mainstream national dailies; and to lobby the mainstream British media (press, radio and television) with a view to influencing their reporting.

Having been educated in English schools and socialised in British society, the rediscovery of Muslim faith and practice by Inayat has, without question, influenced his way of life. While the most visible change of Shagufta Yaqub is her veil, for Inayat it is social relations as a whole and in particular relations between men and women that have changed. Like Shagufta, he perceives his work explaining Islam to have a double function: educational and promotional. The same applies to the representatives of the mainstream media and some politicians, whom he regularly meets in order to push the point of view of the MCB.

Faith as a heritage

The last type of actors are characterised by continuity in the transmission of the faith. Coming from believing families – although not always practising – they profit from their religious heritage, or more simply from the values and the moral rules, transmitted from parents to children. Even if the practices are renewed and adapted by this younger generation, this does not constitute a rediscovery of the faith as in the preceding example.

Briefly let us consider Rehana Sadiq, who played a key part in the creation of the female branch of The Young Muslims UK at the end of the 1980s, before becoming an active member of The Islamic Society of Britain. Rehana was three years old when she left Pakistan for Great Britain and settled in the city of Sheffield. The mother of four children, she currently works as Muslim chaplain in the hospitals of Birmingham while following postgraduate courses in psychosocial assistance and psychotherapy. From the same generation, Munir Ahmed is a father of four children and a doctor. President of the ISB and former president of the YMUK between 1989 and 1991, he has devoted himself to the teaching and the propagation of Islam since the beginning of the 1980s. These two people are far from being isolated examples.

In France there are many similar cases. Dora Mabrouk, editor of the women's magazine *Hawwa*, is, like other contributors to the magazine, a Muslim woman born in France. She chose to wear the veil before engaging in the media sphere. Within the web-magazine *Aslim Taslam*, the religious heritage of the voluntary journalists is even more obvious.

Being Muslim in the Public Sphere

Positioning in the public sphere is essential for these young associative and media actors. The various ways of engagement in the public sphere, related to a renewed understanding of religious identities and memberships, also affect relations with the Other and with the wider society. Two phenomena appear to be of primary importance.

On being 'British Muslim' or 'Muslim and republican'

One of the pillars of the British as well as French Muslim media is that of the individual membership of a community. However, this affiliation is generally not expressed as a purely religious community – as the *ummah* – but as a community that combines religious and national membership. Being 'British Muslim' or 'Muslim and republican' are at the heart of identity claims of these young people.

For Shagufta Yaqub (*Q-News*), living her Islamic faith is perfectly compatible with her British Muslim identity – in a way that would not be the case, according to her, if she had chosen to foreground a Pakistani identity. Shagufta, like many other young British Muslims, asserts a double allegiance – perceived as a complementary commitment to a nation and a religion, rather than as an unrealisable allegiance to two nation states. For Zahid Amin (Radio Ummah), a 'sense of belonging' is central to this commitment:

> When you feel someone is pushing you away you don't feel you belong. When you feel you are alienated, then you don't feel you belong. I think if the radio can help to make people feel more comfortable, to feel that you can be Muslim in the West, you can practice your religion in the West, then I think people will feel more the sense of citizenship. In the same way that people feel they can be Jewish and be in the West, or they can be Buddhist and be in the West.

Figure 7.2 *Q-News* British, Muslim and White

From time to time, the media iconography illustrates this complementary commitment, as this cover of *Q-News* (May–June 2002) shows. The cover combines the British Union flag and an Eastern mosaic above the title 'British, Muslim and White' – white being understood in opposition to Asian, stressing that all young British Muslims do not want to be placed in an unspecific Indo–Pakistani categorisation.

The same discussion takes place among the Muslim media elite in France, where the collective commitment is reframed as a simultaneous allegiance to the Republic and to Islam. Dora Mabrouk, editor of *Hawwa*, summarises it well: 'Ourselves, young Muslim women born in France, we grew with the republican values.' Jocelyne Césari (1998) shows that the transplantation of Islam to a French democratic space led to a cultural revolution related to an experiment of the minority condition in a pluralist context, inserting this religion in postmodern transformations.

80

Femininity, feminism and Islam

The recent increase of young Muslim women finding gainful employment and social responsibilities in the public sphere constitutes another important phenomenon to British as well as French Islam. A self-described 'Islamist feminism' was developed from 1980 to 1990, on the initiative of urban and cultivated women, who sometimes went as far as to dispute the male monopoly of the defence and the practice of Islam (Khosrokhavar 1997). These young women militate for a new and theorised practice of Islam, a phenomenon that is also observable internationally (Göle 1993; Abdelkhah 1998). Their adherence to Islam is often worked out in reaction to a sexist reading of Islam and often in direct contrast to that of their parents who, according to these women, are sometimes connected with antiquated forms of religion (Amiraux 2001; Rigoni 2001; Weibel 2000).

This tendency, which mixes Muslim femininity and feminism, is strongly felt in some titles of the British and French Muslim press. When Fuad Nahdi, creator of *Q-News*, gave editorial control to Shagufta Yaqub, the magazine changed, becoming more aesthetic:

> The magazine became younger, more positive and more feminine! [laughs] I've put nice colours in there; you know I think women are more concerned about appearance. I worried about the magazine; I put pictures on the cover and good photographs...Fuad was very 'get the news out there', he had a very different approach.

Yaqub also developed new sections: a page devoted to the books for children, another intended for 'lonely hearts', a third on relationship problems. Female problems and medical aspects of sexuality are no longer viewed as taboo subjects: since the end of the 1990s, and for the first time, *Q-News* in Britain and *Hawwa* in France – both edited by young women – tackle questions relating to beauty and well-being, contraception, sterility and so on. However, editors and journalists are generally opposed to sections strictly reserved for women. When I raised the question, Shagufta Yaqub was emphatic:

> We don't believe in that, that women need to have a separate section. We're interested in everything you know! If we have something that would be classified as women, we would put it in the family or domestic issues. I think everything can be read by everyone. Women should be concerned by the whole magazine, in politics, in everything.

81

Fareena Alam, then twenty-six years old and editor of *Q-News* since 2004, adds: 'Our readership is probably female to 65 percent. I think that it is just a coincidence. We target the men as much as the women.' Dora Mabrouk, editor of *Hawwa*, explains: 'We want to offer to the Muslim woman a foundation in which she can recognise herself and find subjects of reflection. But we also address to the non-Muslims [including men], to help them to carry a new take on Islam.'

The Islamic veil brings to some young women additional resources in terms of moral legitimacy, with respect to the family and/or the Muslim population. Veiled by conviction, they intend to promote the redefinition of the 'Muslim female identity'. Those who are not veiled also find their place: for Dora Mabrouk, 'what we want is to replace the woman at the heart of social activity. Veil or not, we do not make any difference' (*Le Monde* 11 May 2000). For these young women, change is enacted by individuals and not by the group or the system. It is a question of getting rid of the image of traditional femininity and to acquire a social identity. These practising and urbanised young women seek in Islam, not the promise of a collectively egalitarian way of life, but a means of personal and individual emancipation.

Islam in Action

'Faith in action' is not a phrase reserved for Islam; the expression has for a long time been employed by British Catholic organisations that, like their Muslim and Jewish counterparts, regard collective action as a religious duty. In Islam however, the duty of propagation of the faith – *dawah* – adds an additional dimension to 'Islam in action', which is no longer reticent about acting in and on the political arena.

Towards social legitimation

Fuad Nahdi, creator and former editor of *Q-News* and former correspondent of the agency Associated Press, highlights the importance of social action. In handing over control of the magazine to a young team whose average age was twenty-five years, one of his declared goals was to indicate a new direction to the young British Muslims who had 'lost their reference marks'. The way he chose was the 'centre path': on the one hand to prevent the proliferation of a too rigorous Islam; on the other hand to try to reach and reclaim the young people who took part in the riots of Bradford, Burnley and Oldham, in the north of England, during spring and summer 2001. He states: 'We must invest ourselves in the creation of a positive identity for them, therefore we create the right kind of Muslim.'

An individual using themself and others as a model for personal conduct is a leitmotiv that is found in the majority of the community media, whether ethnic or religious. Several testimonies make a point of mentioning individual, religious and/or social successes. Mezan Ahmed, a listener of Radio Ummah, writes in the Web guest book: 'Hello brothers in Islam. I really enjoy listening to your radio station because I as a muslim have lost my ways a little bit and after listening to your radio station it has really woken me up' (29 November 2002). Irfan Patel expresses the same sentiment: 'Sallam ALL at Radio Ummah. First let me say great shows and everything. You have inspired me a lot... and I want to give up my life that i use to live and I want to become Islamic and pray... Thank u from the bottom of my heart' (15 November 2002).

Radio Ummah cultivates the image of a young and dynamic radio station, which is simultaneously anchored in the Muslim faith and the Western world. The iconography of its website (Figure 7.3), representing young Muslims close to others listening to hip-hop, is intended to unify two identities considered to be complementary rather than contradictory. In the same way, the logo of The Young Muslims UK – a stylised letter 'M', for Muslim, in the shape of a green diamond, the colour also referring to Islam – recalls the iconography used by rap groups and in fashion films.

Figure 7.3 Logos of The Young Muslims UK and Radio Ummah

Hence, the Muslim media, like Muslim associations, attempt to confer a social legitimacy to both the group and to the individual. Beyond their role of an ideal model, they provide a broad range of services that the authorities are not able, or are less able, to provide.

A renewed political engagement

Religious communities consider themselves within their rights to want to invest in the political sphere. Young Muslim media actors often militate for a renewed political engagement motivated by two principal concerns: the fight against discrimination and to improve modes of representation.

My interviewees all mentioned the question of discrimination, often related to Islamophobia. For a long time associated with a discourse of victimisation, such discrimination is not viewed by all as an entirely negative phenomenon. Indeed, as suggested earlier, prejudice and discrimination were often the catalyst for them (re)discovering their faith. The position of Shagufta Yaqub (*Q-News*) illustrates this change well:

> Islamophobia is good because it forces you to change who you are and see yourselves as Muslims. A person I know did a study on converts and he found that a vast majority of converts to Islam... were converting because initially they had [heard] something bad about Islam and they wanted to find out what is this awful religion. They read the Qur'an and then they transformed. So I don't worry too much when there is that bad publicity about Islam because the people who want to know take the trouble to learn.

Politico-legal claims are never very far from this idealistic vision. The claim for their recognition as a religious minority, carried by the first generation of associative and media campaigners, has been taken up again by the new generation. Inayat Bunglawala (Media Committee of the MCB) summarises:

> In the UK, British Muslims are not protected under the Race Relation Law. In 1976, they passed a Race Relations Act which protects Jews and Sikhs because they are a race, but Muslims are not classified as a race. The Runnymede Trust report and the Home Office's double report [in 2001] recommended the introduction of legislation on religious discrimination. This is something we campaigned for for many years...I think the ministers recognise this but there is lots of opposition from liberal groups who fear that the legislation would be used to silence any criticism of Islam – and that's not the intention.

In Republican and centralising France, the question of the representation of Muslims is largely taboo. However, anti-discrimination campaigns have increased since the end of the 1990s – within the authorities as well as in the Muslim media. Oumma.com is one website that publishes more on this topic than some other media outlets.

The Muslim community media are used as a sounding board and a source of information for the Muslim citizens who believe that they are discriminated against, while in other contexts associations and even institutions occupy this role. Zahid Amin refers to the online programmes of Radio Ummah as a forum where

People phone in and they tell their stories, and also ask for advice as well. They say: 'what can I do? What is the law that I can call upon this case?' There's a lot of live discussions, phone-ins, which were very interesting, very shocking in some cases.

Second, we need to consider the major issue of political representation. While the question of discrimination entails exclusion, political representation evokes inclusion. The majority of the Muslim media work for social and political inclusion in their country of residence. They are used in particular to pass on the actions of lobbying – actions that constitute a good example of this strong will of the Muslim communities to be, and to play, an active part in society.

In Britain, figures like Ahmed Versi, editor of *The Muslim News*, and Iqbal Sacranie, Secretary-General of the MCB, are well known by politicians and representatives of the mainstream news media, with whom they occasionally collaborate. Inayat Bunglawala explains: 'If we note something unfair or bad, we take down our telephone immediately and call ministers, MPs and media to ask them for clarifications.' Organisations such as the Media Committee of the MCB, the Islamic Society of Britain Open Group or The Muslim Public Affairs Committee (MPAC) are all very active on the Internet via their websites and their mailing lists.

In France, on the other hand, the Muslim media are not that adept at lobbying. Granted, Oumma.com disseminated information about the List Euro-Palestine[3] at the time of the European elections of June 2004. However, this website predominantly constitutes a forum of expression for intellectuals challenging the political world on current affairs that affect Muslims in France or the Islamic religion as a whole, and is markedly less enthusiastic about lobbying than the British Muslim media. Admittedly, the Averroes Club – created in 1997 and joining together more than 150 professionals working in the media and artistic spheres – has adopted the mission 'of sensitising the decision makers with a greater visibility and a better representation of the minorities in the media'. However, its action does not relate specifically to Muslims. If, according to Jocelyne Césari (1998), 'French Islam entered the age of citizenship', claims for religion still emanate significantly more from the associative rather than the media sector.

Conclusion

The ways of engaging with Islam are diverse for young intellectual Muslims working in the media and associative sectors. Notwithstanding the case of converts, young Muslims are not a homogenous group: while some *received* their faith as a family heritage at their earliest age, others *rediscovered* their faith as adults. The reinterpretation of oneself and the group acts through identities and strategies mobilised in order to buttress or support individual or collective claims. Very often questions of discrimination associated with 'Islamophobia' and of socio-political representation are at the root of individual routes to faith, engagement in community media and in the fight for group recognition. On the whole, the Muslim media in Britain and France testify to the search for socio-political legitimation of Muslims' multiple affiliations/allegiances: to a nation state and to a religion. The main stake in this search can thus be summarised as: how are we to be Muslims in the West? The modes of action and the claims of young Muslim journalists are in the main fundamentally linked to citizenry. At another historical, social or political time, these young people would have perhaps turned to other identity logics and vectors.

Part 2
Media Output

8. The Effects of September 11 and the War in Iraq on British Newspaper Coverage

Elizabeth Poole

Introduction

This chapter examines coverage of British Muslims in two British broadsheet newspapers from 2003. The aim is to compare these outputs to previous coverage (from 1994 onwards) to determine whether the 'framework of reporting' has altered in any considerable way since the two major world events in the chapter title. I am using the definition of 'news framework' employed by Hartmann et al. (1974: 145) in their study *Race as News*: 'the set of inferences about what it is related to, that define an area of subject-matter, and provide the terms in which it is discussed'. I will be drawing on my own previous research (Poole 2002), using the same methodologies and categories of analysis to allow for a direct comparison.

I have used a quantitative method of content analysis. Quantitative content analysis is interested in measuring frequencies. A measure of frequency is useful for analysing the attention and thus importance given to particular stories in relation to a certain subject, in this case British Muslims. It can therefore reveal when and how British Muslims are newsworthy, thus providing a useful cultural indicator at a particular historical moment.

The newspapers examined were the *Guardian, The Times* and their sister Sunday papers, the *Observer* and *The Sunday Times*, chosen for their differing political/ideological stances, the *Guardian* being left of centre and *The Times* conservative. *The Times* is owned by Rupert Murdoch's News International and has a current daily circulation of 616,706, whilst the *Guardian* is controlled by the Scott Trust, a non-profit making organisation, and sells 358,625 copies daily (Alden 2004).

In order to ensure the sample was representative, *all* articles including the terms Muslim(s) or Islam, from 2003, were selected for analysis. This ensured that only content that explicitly referred to Muslims or Islam was selected. It is my argument that many people would not recognise articles to be about Muslims unless this is specified (i.e. they may not recognise Muslim names) and, importantly, the aim is to identify the type of stories in which Muslims are categorised, revealing assumptions made in relation to these groups of people.[1] Previous research, examining the representation of Muslims internationally in the British press (Richardson 2004), has found a framework of reporting that centres on conflict and violence. The focus on British Muslims allows us to examine whether the local context allows for more variety in representation whilst the inclusion of (non-British) Muslims in Britain offers an opportunity for examining nuances based on 'foreign' signifiers.

The aim then is to identify the sort of material and patterns of coverage that have been made publicly available in different papers over a period of time, from 1994 to 2003. Crucially the recent inclusion of 2003 allows us to determine the impact of September 11 and the war in Iraq on approaches to the reporting of Muslims in Britain.

Global Coverage

An examination of the number of articles covered about Islam in its international entirety allows us to contextualise the British situation. The data illustrates that the main significance and focus on Islam continues to be global. This extensive coverage of global events will be significant in the public's awareness of Muslims. What is significant from Figure 8.1 is the huge

Figure 8.1. *Comparative Frequencies of the* Guardian *and* The Times: *Global Coverage*[2]

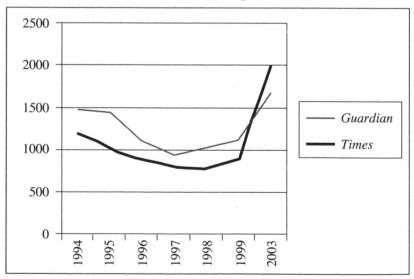

increase in coverage of both global and British coverage in 2003. Coverage of international events has almost doubled, and of home events more than doubled. The war in Iraq, of salience to the British press, clearly has had an impact here but more significantly this has also had an effect on the percentage of articles about British Muslims. This has risen from 12 percent in 1994–6 to 20 percent of overall coverage in 1999 to 25 percent in 2003, a quarter of total coverage. Whilst this is a continuation of a pattern that has been developing in the last ten years, there now seems to be a clear correlation between the reporting of world events involving Muslims and British Muslim communities. This is further demonstrated by the increase in coverage in March (when war broke out in Iraq) of both global and home events. This month records the highest number of articles on Muslims in 2003, both at home and abroad, in both papers.

Equally significant and a further continuing trend is that *The Times* has now overtaken the *Guardian* in terms of the amount of coverage (see Figure 8.2). I have previously argued that the *Guardian*'s more extensive coverage of Islam has been based on a more accommodating and tolerant approach to the Other that allows space for alternative voices and interests whilst the more traditional, establishment news values of *The Times* means it is less likely to take an interest in items with less cultural proximity (Islam) unless they have extreme news value. I would now

Figure 8.2. *Comparative Frequencies of the* Guardian *and* The Times: *British Coverage*

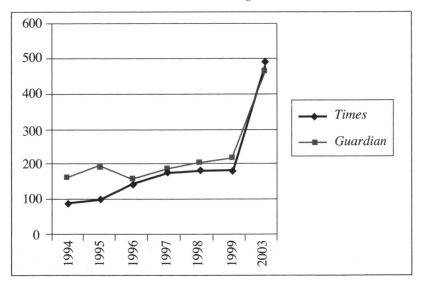

argue that the events of September 11 and the war in Iraq have given Islam that kudos to the conservative press. As we shall see, these events have allowed for the construction of Muslims within a more limited and negative framework which is more likely to be reinforced in the conservative press.

Domestic News

This section explores press coverage of British Islam. Table 8.1 reiterates the figures previously presented within the global context. It also shows the continuing parity between the Sunday papers, perhaps reflecting their greater focus on softer news, features etc.

Table 8.1. *Coverage of British Islam, 2003*

Newspaper	No. of Articles	Percentage of total articles
Guardian	314	35.9
The Times	388	44.3
The Sunday Times	90	10.3
Observer	83	9.5
Total	**875**	**100**

In this section, I will be mainly focusing on the prominent topics of news items about British Muslims. By 'topic' I mean the overall subject category of an article (Hartmann et al. 1974). This focus allows for an identification of the type of material presented to the public on Islam and, therefore, the likely concerns and agenda of the prevailing majority (ethnic) groups. Topics are selected on the basis of their news value and carried for a given time depending on considered importance. The pressures of the market and limited space mean some issues are marginalised or excluded from debate whilst others are always approached in the same way. Increased coverage then, implies that an issue has some salience or importance to the interests of powerful groups in a particular social context. Islam's ability to be newsworthy relies on established notions of who Muslims are and what they represent to (interpretations of) British culture.

The data presented here reveals a continuation of the narrow framework of reporting and the close correspondence in the types of issues covered between papers, indicating the assumptions (cultural consensus) being made about what constitutes news in relation to Islam. This restrictive representation is demonstrated by the fact that differentiated groups of people can now be defined in terms of thirty-five specific topics (only nineteen falling in the Other category). Whilst this is a reduction from the forty-one topics present in 1994–6 it appears to be an improvement from 1997 and 1999 (see Tables 8.2–8.6) when the number of categories of news involving Muslims fell substantially. However, as we shall see through an examination of the ten most frequently occurring topics from 1994–6, 1997, 1999 and 2003, although there may have been an increase in the variety of topics occurring, there is an increase in the percentage of articles occurring in the top ten topics, now amounting to 75 percent of coverage. There continues, therefore, to be a strong clustering around a few specific subjects that we will now examine more closely.

Table 8.2. *Significant Topics in 2003:* Guardian

Topic	Total number of articles
Terrorism	110
Politics	47
War in Iraq (reaction to)	45
Education	41
Discrimination	34
Race relations	23
Media	16
Relationships	12
Crime	11
Asylum	11
Total	**350**
Percentage of total articles in 2003	**75**

Table 8.3. *Significant Topics in 2003:* The Times

Topic	Total number of articles
Terrorism	147
War in Iraq (reaction to)	43
Politics	39
Education	30
Finance	18
Crime	17
Relations to Christianity	17
Rituals	14
Relationships	13
Belief	13
Total	**351**
Percentage of total articles in 2003	**74.8**

Table 8.4. *Significant Topics in 1999*

Topic	Times Frequency	Percentage	Guardian Frequency	Percentage	Total Frequency
Fundamentalism	42	21.9	55	25.1	97
Politics	19	9.9	12	5.4	31
Relations to Christianity	11	5.7	13	5.9	24
Relationships	12	6.2	10	4.5	22
Crime	14	7.3	6	2.7	20
Education	6	3.1	15	6.8	21
Immigration	8	4.1	11	5	19
Racism	6	3.1	9	4.1	15
Nation of Islam	3	1.5	7	3.1	10
Belief	7	3.6	3	1.3	10
Freedom of speech	4	2	3	1.3	7
Rushdie	2	1	3	1.3	5
Discrimination	0	0	6	2.7	6
Royalty	1	0.5	0	0	1
Sub-Total	**135**	**70**	**153**	**69**	**288**
Total articles on British Islam in 1999	**191**	**100**	**219**	**100**	**410**

Table 8.5. *Significant Topics in 1997*

Topic	Times Frequency	Percentage	Guardian Frequency	Percentage	Total Frequency
Politics	52	27.5	34	17	86
Criminality	27	14.2	40	20	67
Relationships	17	8.9	24	12	41
Education	20	10.5	11	5.5	31
Fundamentalism	9	4.7	19	9.5	28
Royalty	15	7.9	7	3.5	22
Censorship/Rushdie	14	7.4	14	7	28
Multi-culturalism	6	3.1	12	6	18
Christianity	12	6.3	5	2.5	17
Conversion	10	5.2	2	1	12
Discrimination	4	2.1	5	2.5	9
Sub-Total	**186**	**98.4**	**173**	**87.3**	**359**
Total articles on British Islam in 1997	**189**	**100**	**198**	**100**	**387**

Table 8.6. *Significant Topics 1994–6*

Topic	Total	Percentage
Education	128	15.2
Relationships	60	7.1
Fundamentalism	57	6.8
Politics	54	6.4
Crime	43	5.1
Prince Charles	41	4.8
Media	41	4.8
Belief	33	3.9
Freedom of speech	28	3.3
Immigration	25	2.9
Discrimination	21	2.5
Sub-Total	**531**	**63.4**
Total articles 1994–6	**837**	

It is clear from these tables that there is a consistency in the coverage of British Muslims over the whole period analysed. Whilst the frequency of coverage may alter slightly, five topics dominate. These are politics, relationships, education, crime and extremism (termed fundamentalism 1994–2000, terrorism in 2003 due to the shift in emphasis in coverage). I will now examine the most significant changes in the treatment of these topics in 2003 from that of previous coverage.

Terrorism

The most obvious and significant finding is not only the appearance of the category 'terrorism' but the amount of space given to it. I used the term fundamentalism previously to denote extremism, a term which was once used by the press but has been notably replaced by the more explicit categorisation since September 11. This shift occurred immediately following September 11 when coverage converged dramatically around three major topics: terrorism, counter terrorism measures and discrimination against Muslims (Poole 2002). We can see in the time that has passed since then that the association of Muslims with terrorism has concretised. Whilst this was clearly the prevailing image of global Islam previous to September 11, my own research found that, in particular, British Muslims were not attributed so blatantly with this label. Rather it was Muslims in Britain, exiles, who were categorised as extremists. Suggestions of covert activities, such as raising funds for political groups abroad, were made as were links to the wider Muslim community but the physical threat remained at a distance. There has now been a significant shift in the definition of British Muslims as terrorists.

Accounting for 24 percent of coverage in the *Guardian* and 30 percent of coverage in *The Times*, this corresponds with my argument that coverage in *The Times* has risen since the framework of representation fits more neatly with established perceptions of Muslims. This is also evident if we break down this category further. Table 8.7 shows how *The Times* focuses more on extremism, the cleric Abu Hamza and terrorism in general whilst the *Guardian* has less coverage of these subjects and more on counter terrorism and articles relating to September 11. These articles were more supportive towards Muslims as most focused on the plight of British Muslims held in Guantanamo Bay, Cuba. The articles questioned the legality of holding the prisoners without trail and featured interviews with the captives (on release) and their families.

Table 8 7: *Coverage of Terrorism, 2003*

Topic	*Times*	*Guardian*	Total	Percentage
Terrorism (general)	85	45	130	47.8
Directly related to September 11	14	32	46	16.9
Counter terrorism measures*	5	9	14	5.1
Cleric Abu Hamza	27	13	40	14.7
Other extremists	7	3	10	3.7
Raids on terrorists	4	16	20	7.3
Terrorism in mosques	5	—	5	1.8
Richard Reid, shoe-bomber	5	2	7	2.6
Total	152	120	272	100

* This was excluded from the overall category terrorism in Table 8.2 and 8.3 accounting for the different numbers in total seen here.

The number of articles featuring Abu Hamza al-Masri, who has now been detained charged with conspiring with terrorists and faces extradition to the USA, is also significant. Just becoming apparent in the press in 1997, he is now the most prominently featured British Muslim in the British press. He is regularly a feature of the tabloids front pages and his demonisation

parallels that of the media's global Islamic monster, Osa[...]
works to make the attributes associated with him easier [...]
these centre around his appearance (freak), expressi[...]
violence, and radicalism, this has significant implica[...]
British Muslims are perceived.

Of course, defining activities as 'terrorist' promotes a different kind of solution to responses to other crimes. It allows for the detention of people without trial. Asians have also experienced the largest increase in on the spot searches by police, from 744 in 2001–2 to 2,989 in 2003–4 (*Independent* 3 July 2004). This type of coverage also creates the conditions necessary for more repressive legislation apparent in acts such as the British Anti-Terrorism, Crime and Security Bill (November 2001).

War in Iraq

This was also a new category in 2003, referring to articles that covered the reaction of British Muslims to events in Iraq. Many of these articles feature the protests, campaigns and marches against the war and so construct Muslims positively and negatively. Positive articles sympathise with Muslims' perspectives and have a certain political expediency as they are used to criticise Government policy (mainly in the *Guardian*). However, coverage tends to assume one Muslim perspective as both interested and opposed to the war (the group categorisation homogenising a diversity of people and their opinions). These articles, therefore, place Muslims in a conflictual framework and, as with terrorism, associate Muslims with the more dominant global image. Representing them at odds with government policy also raises questions of loyalty, a feature of coverage in the last Gulf War (Werbner 1994). In fact, the strong ideological rhetorical approach to the 'war on terror', 'you are with us or with them' of the coalition's leadership functions to locate any opposition as verging on the criminal.

Previous analysis of coverage shows the tendency to link British Muslims to world affairs, in fact coverage often results in response to an international event as seen here (Poole 2002). It could be argued then that this is a way of offering space to Muslim voices whilst still representing then as troublemakers. It also has the effect of homogenising Muslims, linking hostilities abroad to Muslims in Britain and again raising questions regarding the enemy within. Foreign values and practices are seen to be transferred to British society through migration, whilst Muslims outside the UK dictate the agenda of those within it.

Examples of the positive/negative binary in coverage resulting from both the war in Iraq and September 11 include in the *Guardian* 'Muslims' ces: We must continue protesting' (3 April: 23). This article features the responses of a variety of Muslims to the war in Iraq, firmly positioning them as British Muslims (with their allegiances to Britain) whilst also opposing the policy. This approach is accompanied by providing space for Muslim writers. However, some of these articles, by highlighting issues affecting the community, also reinforce dominant ideas about Muslims in Britain: 'Young, British and ready to fight: New laws and the war have pushed our Islamist radicals underground' (Fuad Nahdi 1 April: 24). This more stable image is more likely to find a place in the coverage of *The Times*; 'The new enemy within' (6 December: 19) warns 'They were born in Britain, work hard, stay out of trouble and don't stand out in the crowd. And one of them may be the next suicide bomber' advancing the notion of 'home-grown sleepers' in the UK. Muslims are warned that they should be 'intolerant of intolerance' and welcome the greater surveillance of their communities (3 December: 21) hence providing a justification for this whilst appearing supportive. This article also gives the appearance of making the distinction between the vast majority of Muslims and the few whilst negating it in the same breath.

Politics

Politics, as with the categories above, has a high news value for the press in general terms so it is inevitable that coverage of this topic will be high whatever the subject under investigation. Previous stories reporting on Muslims' attempts to get selected for political parties and the substantial coverage, in 1997, of the fraud charges and trial of Muslim MP Mohammed Sarwar, still have a presence. However, most of these stories are about the loss of support for the Government from the Muslim community following the war in Iraq. They, therefore, operate as a way of undermining the government and its policies towards Iraq for the *Guardian* and more generally for *The Times*.

Education

Both politics and education are key areas of struggle for minorities wishing to be accepted within a wider conceptualisation of Britishness. Hence they are sites of contestation over what this means. I have illustrated previously how, for *The Times*, this has meant preserving a more traditional Christian ethos within education whilst the *Guardian* has adopted a more pluralistic approach, which can negativise Islam in its criticism of religion resulting in an exclusive liberalism. This has been played out through three prominent topics, the nature and role of religious education in schools (1994), the activities of Islamic groups (often constructed negatively) in Higher Education (1996) and the funding of Muslim schools (1997). All these stories continue to be featured in equal measure in 2003. This illustrates the continuing perception of the importance of education in the transmission of values (and the struggle over what 'British' values are) to all groups involved. Previously presented within a limited and comparative (ethnocentric) framework, the attention given by *The Times* in 2003 to Christianity, rituals and belief shows a continuing framework of representation whilst the space allocated to discrimination by the *Guardian* suggests a more supportive approach.

Relationships and Crime

I am analysing these two categories together because, in line with previous findings, the two continue to be closely related in coverage of British Muslims. Analysis of reporting 1994–7 showed that the relationships of Muslims were mainly featured when a non-Muslim converted as a result of this. This may feature a non-British Muslim with a British subject who then converted to Islam, or an illicit union between a British Muslim and non-Muslim without parental approval. They therefore focus on cultural difference. Increasingly from 1997 the focus shifted to arranged marriages and with this, the predominant story of 2003, honour killings where the relationship usually of a female Muslim and non-Muslim brings the family into disrepute and results in their murder. Whilst these incidences are rare the huge focus on honour killings in the press suggests to a reading public that Muslim families are dysfunctional, that misogyny is rife in Islam and that pride is more important than familial relations. This fits with a (mis)perception of Islamic cultural practices that are restrictive and abhorrent to a modern liberal society. Islamic law that governs relationships leads to illegal activities that are deemed cultural atrocities. Muslim values are represented at odds with 'British' values that question Muslims' ability to fit in. This locates the problem as emanating from within the community. These are dominant themes throughout coverage and are reinforced through a variety of topics. Coverage of crime is higher in *The Times* than the *Guardian*. Crime, like politics, has a high news value but its associations with deviance means that frequently it has been linked to different ethnic minority groups in British news coverage (Hartmann et al. 1974; Troyna 1981; van Dijk 1991). Its news value ensures that Muslims who are involved in crime will more likely make the news than other activities, promoting the idea of a criminal culture. It also makes stories such as relationships, with less news value, more salient. However, it is the particular types of criminal activity in which Muslims are involved that makes them newsworthy. This usually stems from an orientalist perspective (sexual deviance, domestic abuse etc.).

Coverage of crime *is* down on previous years but, of course, the focus on terrorism outweighs this change. It should be noted, however, that some of the articles on crime feature crimes against Muslims, the desecration of Muslim graves for example.

Discrimination

I have included discrimination (against Muslims) in the analysis (see Tables 8.2–8.7) even if coverage has been low to allow for a comparison with the reporting of other topics. What is most significant here is that a topic that has been relatively marginal before is now a topic of significance in the *Guardian*, as is its attention to race relations in the UK (when discussing Muslims in Britain). This is a positive development in representation given that previously the *Guardian*, whilst showing sympathy towards ethnic minorities in general, has often indirectly negativised and/or excluded Muslims from discussions of racism due to the specific religious identification of Muslims (resulting from its secular, liberal stance). It now more regularly debates issues relating to national identity and inclusivity. It should also be noted that *The Times'* coverage is also higher on this topic than previous years (ten articles on discrimination, twelve on race relations). The term Islamophobia, however, is barely visible in 2003 with only one article on this topic (there were forty from 1994–6).

Further Analysis of Coverage

We have seen that coverage in the *Guardian* in 2003 appears more supportive, with 149 articles (29 percent) reported within a positive framework (war in Iraq, discrimination, race relations). Articles about the media in the *Guardian* (Table 8.2), in the main, review the way the war in Iraq has been reported. *The Times* continues to focus more on faith, relating the beliefs and rituals of Islam to Christianity (Table 8.3). Articles on rituals, in this year, focused on government plans to ban ritual slaughter. A faith perspective sometimes favours the Muslim community, if the belief is in line with that of the paper. For example in 1999/2000 the Muslim community was represented positively, in allegiance with other faith groups, in the conservative press in their challenge to government plans to withdraw Clause 28 forbidding the promotion of homosexuality in schools.

In 2003, as representatives spoke out in favour of gay rights, this was represented favourably by the *Guardian*. However, previous research has shown how (Muslim) belief is used as a key to understanding all Muslim behaviour. This is seen to be the root cause of conflict and the difficulty of Muslims in adapting to majority culture. Hence the minority group's beliefs are problematised whilst dominant values remain unquestioned. The occurrence of the category 'finance' in *The Times* relates to a business focus reporting on Islamic banking and mortgages for Muslims launched by the bank HSBC.

Which topics have shown a decrease in coverage? The most substantial decrease, a topic which has been declining since 1999, is that of Rushdie and freedom of speech. Rushdie is no longer as topical especially since the fatwa was lifted in September 1998. Freedom of speech was barely covered, despite legislation on religious discrimination being passed in 2003. The two have been strongly debated together throughout the 1990s. I would argue that pressures of space means that if the themes that are often debated within one topic can be debated under a more topical event then this will be marginalised. In this case terrorism has overshadowed other coverage and issues of loyalty, democracy, threat and conformity can be raised (elsewhere) within the parameters of counter terrorism measures. For example, these themes can also be discussed from the different positions of the papers in the debate about ID (identity) cards which emerged after September 11. Royalty, which mainly focused on Prince Charles' support for Islam and where coverage was used to deride both him and his beliefs, also barely appears. This is again due to topicality but also relates to his greater credibility and management of his image since the death of Princess Diana in 1997.

Conclusion

So what conclusions can we draw from this analysis? It is clear that there is a continuation in the framework of reporting of British Muslims since 1994. The newsworthiness of Islam is consistent with previous frameworks of understanding and demonstrates how stories will only be selected if they fit with an idea of who Muslims are. Not only is there a consensus of news values but newspapers provide a particular interpretative framework for defining events. Unfortunately this means a continuation in the themes associated with the topics coverage. These being:

1   That Muslims are a threat to security in the UK due to their involvement in deviant activities.

2   That Muslims are a threat to British 'mainstream' values and thus provoke integrative concerns.

3   That there are inherent cultural differences between Muslims and the host community which create tensions in interpersonal relations.

4   Muslims are increasingly making their presence felt in the public sphere (demonstrated through the topics of politics, education and discrimination). (Poole 2002: 84).

The continuation of this framework represents the unresolved anxieties around these topics and the continuing struggle of all groups to establish hegemony.

Whilst the variety of coverage of British Muslims has to some extent been maintained – and there have been positive developments in the *Guardian*, with its attention to the increased discrimination Muslims experience due to September 11 – this oppositional interpretation has been marginalised by the dominance of the conservative interpretative framework. The huge shift to focus on terrorism now unifies coverage within the orientalist global construction of Islam. One image dominates, that of 'Islamic terrorism'. It would appear then that whilst Western/US-driven policy is now under question for various reasons, these powerful groups have been successful in maintaining a hegemony of ideas of Islam, sustaining 'the myth of confrontation' (Esposito 1992). For example, policy in Iraq has been under fire from various social/political groups and yet media coverage continues to offer us images of an anti-modern, political unstable, undemocratic, often barbaric, chaotic existence consistent with the now widely established foreign new framework (Dahlgren and Chakrapani 1982). The representations of Muslims in the UK are now closer to the undifferentiated global aggressor that theory postulates. The more persistent the framework, the more indicative it is of an essential Muslimness and is in danger of becoming fixed. These events then define for the public what it means to be a Muslim, and then Muslims worldwide can be managed through social and aggressive policies.

9. Who Gets to Speak? A Study of Sources in the Broadsheet Press

John E. Richardson

News Sources

The study of news sources involves a series of important questions that cut to the heart of contemporary journalism and its role in (re)producing inequitable social relations. First, and most logically, we need to consider who gets to speak in the news. As Cottle (2000: 428) argues, '[w]hose voices predominate, whose vie and contend, and whose are marginalised or rendered silent on the news stage' are questions of deep interest to the study of journalism. Simply put, who is allowed to speak and who is not; who is allowed to label others in the news and who is not, are important questions to ask. In the UK, Whitaker showed that there are only ten sources routinely monitored by the news: Parliament, councils, police (and the army in Northern Ireland), other emergency services, courts, royalty, diary events (e.g. Ascot), airports and other news media groups. Others such as corporations, trade unions, political parties, public service groups, pressure groups and 'experts' are monitored less regularly, with members of the public coming in a distant third (cited in Fowler 1991: 21). Therefore, because journalists rely on official or bureaucratic news sources, access to the news becomes a power resource *in itself.*

Second, we need to consider what effect this has on the content of news. As 'members of more powerful social groups and institutions ... have more or less exclusive access' to the news (van Dijk 1998: 5), we need to investigate the extent to which the news is dominated by elite versions of contemporary events. Further, repeated studies of journalism have shown 'how groups labelled as deviant within the news media can be dehumanised and even demonised, leading to both the depoliticisation and delegitimation of their claims for wider social acceptance or political change' (Cottle 2000: 429).

Muslims (British and otherwise) have been subject to a high level of suspicion, inequity and outright discrimination for a considerable period of time – practices that have increased since 11 September 2001 (see Fekete, this volume). A great number of publications have illustrated that the news media continue to be culpable for the creation and maintenance of racist sentiment and social practices, and for the maintenance of anti-Muslim racisms specifically (Poole 2002; Richardson 2004; Runnymede Trust 1997). It is therefore particularly important to investigate whose opinions are quoted in newspaper articles about Islam and Muslims and, specifically, the extent to which any patterns may be implicated in the (re)production or resistance to the prejudicial representation of Muslims.

The Sample

The sample under analysis is taken from a corpus of data, collected as part of a research project analysing the representation of Islam and Muslims in British broadsheet newspapers (Richardson 2001a; 2001b; 2004). The sample period covered four months (October 1997–January 1998) and included all five British broadsheet daily newspapers (*Financial Times, Independent, Guardian, Telegraph, The Times*) and two British broadsheet Sunday newspapers (*Independent on Sunday, The Sunday Times*). Any journalistic text that referred to Islam or Muslims in the headline, either of the first two paragraphs of the text or else the whole of a lower paragraph was included in the sample, thereby excluding passing references to Islam and Muslims.

Over this four-month period, 2,540 texts – news reports, editorials, letters, obituaries, etc. – were collected that referred to Islam or Muslims. A code book of 108 variables was applied to these texts, recording amongst other things: the reports' physical characteristics (newspaper, size, genre, pictures, etc.); topics and themes; citation and/or quotation of actors; the tone of the article; and the presence of certain words and phrases. The remainder of this chapter examines the presence and prominence of sources in these texts.

Who Speaks? Muslim and non-Muslim Sources

First, we need to consider the number of Muslim and non-Muslim sources in the sample and examine whether there are any differences between the type(s) of text they are included in. Table 9.1 below cross-tabulates sources 1 and 2 (the first two individuals or groups referred to in the text) with a variable that coded whether Islam was cited as a factor in explaining or contextualising the subject of the text. The results show clear differences between Muslim and non-Muslim sources.

Table 9. 1. *Muslim and non-Muslim Sources*

		Is Islam cited as an explanatory factor?						
		Yes			**No**		**Total**	
Source 1	**Count**	**Row %**	**Column %**	**Count**	**Row %**	**Column %**	**Count**	**Row %**	**Column %**
Muslim	454	92.7	34.4	36	7.3	3.0	490	100	19.4
Non-Muslim	866	42.7	65.6	1164	57.3	97.0	2030	100	80.6
Total	1320	52.4	100	1200	47.6	100	2520	100	100
Source 2									
Muslim	435	92.6	34.3	35	7.4	3.0	470	100	19.3
Non-Muslim	835	42.4	65.7	1134	57.6	97.0	1969	100	80.7
Total	1270	52.1	100	1169	47.9	100	2439	100	100

Table 9.1 shows that 19.4 percent of primary sources in the sampled texts were Muslim, a figure that is only marginally lower for secondary sources, about a fifth. This percentage corresponds quite nicely to the world population, about one fifth of which is Muslim, and is a positive finding for British newspapers. However this overall percentage hides a significant disproportion in the presence of Muslim sources: in the texts that did not cite Islam as an influential factor, only 3 percent (n= 36; n= 35) of sources were Muslim. Remember, these texts qualified for analysis – in other words they were *about Muslims* (for example, a Muslim country or a Muslim organisation) – but they were dominated by the actions and opinions of non-Muslim sources. In turn, Muslims are disproportionately present in 'Muslim articles': just short of 93 percent of Muslim sources appeared in texts that cited Islam as an influential factor.

Of course, Table 9.1 also begs a series of further questions about the inclusion of sources in this sample, not least, the proportion of these sources – both Muslim and non-Muslim – that were quoted.

Table 9.2 shows that Muslim sources are quoted less frequently and less proportionately than their non-Muslim counterparts. If 19.4 percent (n = 490) of primary sources are Muslim then you would expect the same proportion of *quoted* sources to be Muslim: in fact 16.9 percent of quoted primary sources are Muslim (n = 148). Similarly, just over 30 percent of Muslim primary sources are quoted (n = 148) compared to just over 35 percent of non-Muslim primary sources (n = 726). The comparative silencing of Muslims is even more marked for secondary sources (14.2

percent; n = 81) demonstrating that being cited in a newspaper is certainly no guarantee that your voice will be heard. Table 9.3 combines the two tables 9.1 and 9.2 to provide a sense of the context in which these Muslim and non-Muslim sources are quoted.

Table 9.2. *Quotation of Muslim and non-Muslim Sources*

	Is the source quoted?							
		Yes			No		Total	
Source 1	Count	Row %	Column %	Count	Row %	Column %	Count	Row %	Column %
Muslim	148	30.2	16.9	342	69.8	20.8	490	100	19.4
Non-Muslim	726	35.8	83.1	1304	64.2	79.2	2030	100	80.6
Total	874	34.7	100	1646	65.3	100	2520	100	100
Source 2								
Muslim	81	17.2	14.2	389	82.8	20.8	470	100	19.3
Non-Muslim	491	24.9	85.8	1478	75.1	79.2	1969	100	80.7
Total	572	23.5	100	1867	76.5	100	2439	100	100

Table 9.3. *Quoted Sources and News Context*

	Is Islam cited as an explanatory factor?							
		Yes			No		Total	
Source 1	Count	Row %	Column %	Count	Row %	Column %	Count	Row %	Column %
Muslim	136	91.9	30	12	8.1	2.9	148	100	16.9
Non-Muslim	318	43.8	70	408	56.2	97.1	726	100	83.1
Total	454	51.9	100	420	48.1	100	874	100	100
Source 2								
Muslim	73	90.1	25.2	8	9.9	2.8	81	100	14.2
Non-Muslim	217	44.2	74.8	274	55.8	97.2	491	100	85.8
Total	290	50.7	100	282	49.3	100	572	100	100

In keeping with Table 9.1, discussed earlier, Table 9.3 shows that Muslim sources are disproportionately quoted in texts that cite Islam as an explanatory factor: just less than 92 percent of quoted Muslim sources are in such texts; in texts that *did not* cite Islam as an explanatory factor, only 2.9 percent (n = 12) of quoted sources were Muslim. The quotation of Muslim sources stands as an index of wider societal inclusion. Sources quoted in newspaper reports are assumedly authoritative spokespeople, chosen by a speech community – journalist, newspaper, audience, society, etc. – for inclusion. From these results, it seems that Muslims are only thought to be an authority source when it comes to discussing their religion.

Who Speaks? Bureaucratic and non-Bureaucratic Sources

As summarised in the introduction to this chapter, previous research indicates that bureaucratic sources dominate the pages of newspapers. Is this also the case when in comes to news about Islam and Muslims?

Table 9.4 demonstrates that international government officials were the sources that appeared most frequently in these sampled texts (n = 1050; 41.3 percent), followed somewhat surprisingly by members of the general public (n= 290; 11.4 percent). This finding is produced by the manner in which I coded the sampled texts: *all* actors referred to were recorded, not just those whose opinions were reproduced, meaning that nameless victims were recorded as actors in the same way as quoted sources were. The third most frequently cited sources were illegitimate ('terrorist') groups. Such sources were referred to in 7.4 percent of articles (n = 189), rising to 12.2 percent in texts that cited Islam as an explanatory factor. Indeed 85.7 percent of their appearances were in articles that referred to Islam, contributing to the link often assumed between Islam and their activities and opinions.

Again, Table 9.4 begs a series of further questions, not least the proportion of these sources (for example, the corporate sources, the academics, etc.) that were identified as being Muslim. Table 9.5 explores this question, with the individual posts from the Table 9.4 collectivised as bureaucratic and non-bureaucratic sources.[1]

Table 9.5 reveals two significant characteristics of the sampled texts. First, the reporting of Islam is, as with other subjects, dominated by bureaucratic sources, with 70.5 percent of news actors originating from bureaucratic sources. Second, these bureaucratic sources are overwhelmingly non-Muslim: only around 11 percent of primary and secondary bureaucratic sources are Muslim; and only around 42 percent of Muslim spokespeople are from bureaucratic sources, compared with around 77 percent of non-Muslims. This absence of Muslim sources is the result of a combination of racist social

Table 9.4. *Post or Position of Source 1*

Cited Source		Is Islam cited as an explanatory factor?							
		Yes			**No**			**Total**	
Source 1	Count	Row %	Column %	Count	Row %	Column %	Count	Row %	Column %
International Government	441	42.0	33.1	609	58.0	50.4	1050	100	41.3
Adult citizen	196	67.6	14.7	94	32.4	7.8	290	100	11.4
Illegitimate/ terrorist group	162	85.7	12.2	27	14.3	2.2	189	100	7.4
Business/ corporate	35	28.5	2.6	88	71.5	7.3	123	100	4.8
UK Government	44	45.4	3.3	53	54.6	4.4	97	100	3.8
Public sector	54	56.8	4.1	41	43.2	3.4	95	100	3.7
UN	17	19.8	1.3	69	80.2	5.7	86	100	3.4
Armed forces	42	51.2	3.2	40	48.8	3.3	82	100	3.2
International legitimate opposition party	34	54.0	2.6	29	46.0	2.4	63	100	2.5
EU	36	63.2	2.7	21	36.8	1.7	57	100	2.2
Criminal	37	67.3	2.8	18	32.7	1.5	55	100	2.2
Other International	25	53.2	1.9	22	46.8	1.8	47	100	1.9
Media	38	77.6	2.9	11	22.4	0.9	49	100	1.9
Artist/Writer	41	93.2	3.1	3	6.8	0.2	44	100	1.7
Celebrity	26	65.0	2.0	14	35.0	1.2	40	100	1.6
Academic	19	61.3	1.4	12	38.7	1.0	31	100	1.2
Child citizen	17	56.7	1.3	13	43.3	1.1	30	100	1.2
Royalty	10	33.3	0.8	20	66.7	1.7	30	100	1.2
No source	11	55.0	0.8	9	45.0	0.7	20	100	0.8
Pressure group	13	68.4	1.0	6	31.6	0.5	19	100	0.7
Non-Muslim religious	11	84.6	0.8	2	15.4	0.2	13	100	0.5
Tribesman	6	66.7	0.5	3	33.3	0.2	9	100	0.4
Muslim religious	7	100	0.5	0	0	0	7	100	0.3
Other	9	64.3	0.7	5	35.7	0.4	14	100	0.6
Total	1331	52.4	100	1209	47.6	100	2540	100	100

inequalities that exclude Muslims from holding positions of social power and the reliance of broadsheet newspapers on these elite sources. In short, this research demonstrates, perhaps for the first time, the full implications of the dominance of bureaucratic sources on the exclusion of Muslim sources. News about Islam and Muslims is shaped and dominated by establishment and bureaucratic sources to the exclusion of Muslim sources.

Table 9.5. *Muslim and Non-Muslim Bureaucratic Sources*

Is the source Muslim?									
		Yes			**No**			**Total**	
Source 1	**Count**	**Row %**	**Column %**	**Count**	**Row %**	**Column %**	**Count**	**Row %**	**Column %**
Bureaucratic	196	11.3	40.0	1535	88.7	75.6	1731	100	68.7
Non-bureaucratic	294	37.3	60.0	495	62.7	24.4	789	100	31.3
Total	490	19.4	100	2030	80.6	100	2520	100	100
Source 2									
Bureaucratic	206	11.7	43.8	1554	88.3	78.9	1760	100	72.2
Non-bureaucratic	264	38.9	56.2	415	61.1	21.1	679	100	27.8
Total	470	19.3	100	1969	80.7	100	2439	100	100

Finally, in this section, what proportion of these bureaucratic sources is quoted?

Table 9.6. *Quoted Bureaucratic Sources and News Context*

Is Islam cited as an explanatory factor?									
		Yes			**No**			**Total**	
Source 1	**Count**	**Row %**	**Column %**	**Count**	**Row %**	**Column %**	**Count**	**Row %**	**Column %**
Bureaucratic	290	45.2	63.9	352	54.8	83.8	642	100	73.5
Non-bureaucratic	164	70.7	36.1	68	29.3	16.2	232	100	26.5
Total	454	51.9	100	420	48.1	100	874	100	100
Source 2									
Bureaucratic	213	47.3	73.4	237	52.7	84.0	450	100	78.7
Non-bureaucratic	77	63.1	26.6	45	36.9	16.0	122	100	21.3
Total	290	50.7	100	282	49.3	100	572	100	100

Table 9.6 shows that bureaucratic sources are quoted more often than non-bureaucratic sources: indeed, bureaucratic sources represent 76 percent of quoted sources. Table 9.6 also confirms findings described earlier in the chapter: Muslims are quoted more frequently in texts that cite Islam as an explanatory factor and these Muslim sources are predominantly non-bureaucratic. Table 9.6 shows that 70.3 percent of quoted primary non-bureaucratic sources (n = 164) are found in texts that cite Islam as an explanatory factor; similarly, non-bureaucratic (mainly Muslim) actors are quoted as the primary source in 36.1 percent of texts that explicitly cite Islam, compared to 26.5 percent of the total.

The next section explores a second set of questions relating to the content of the sampled reports: how are Muslims represented in these texts? And are there any relationships between such representations and the frequency and prominence of Muslim and non-Muslim sources?

Content and Representation

During data collection, I coded the evaluative tone of each piece along a five point scale, ranging from 'laudatory', through 'favourable', 'neutral', 'critical' and finally 'abrasive'. Specifically, this variable coded the paper's, or the journalist's or the reader's (in the case of letters) overall evaluation of Islam or of the Muslims represented. When the results of this variable are cross-referenced with the variable that coded whether Islam was cited as an explanatory factor, the results are interesting.

Figure 9.1 shows that stories in which Islam was regarded as unimportant are close to being 'normally' distributed: a 'neutral' evaluation is most frequent, with 'favourable' and 'critical' evaluations less frequent, and 'laudatory' and 'abrasive' evaluations returning almost identically low numbers of stories. In contrast, Figure 9.2 illustrates that stories in which Islam was viewed and hence *represented* as having an influential or explanatory role in the reported event are much more skewed towards a 'critical' evaluation of Muslim social actions: 63.5 percent of these texts are critical of Muslims (n = 632) compared with 36.5 percent (n = 363) of texts that did not cite Islam as a explanatory factor. In other words: when the actions of Muslims are perceived and represented as being especially 'Islamic', they are subject to a level of criticism that Muslims who keep their religion out of the 'public sphere' are not.

Thus, despite the high number of Muslims quoted in texts that cite Islam as an explanatory factor (see Table 9.3), the predominant argumentative thrust of these texts is *critical* of Islam and Muslims. Indeed these texts are significantly more critical of Islam and Muslims than the texts in which

Figure 9.1. Islam *not* Cited as an Explanatory Factor

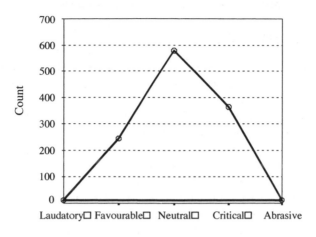

Articles' evaluative tone

Figure 9.2. Islam Cited as an Explanatory Factor

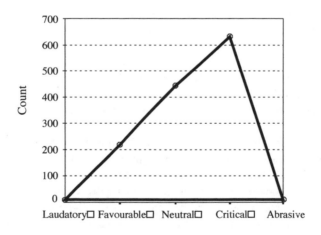

Articles' evaluative tone

only 3 percent of quoted sources are Muslim. This is a highly important finding and raises serious questions about how it was that these journalistic texts *include* Muslim voices and yet promote a 'global' argument that remains *critical* of either Muslims generally or these same Muslim sources specifically. To explore this question we need to examine in greater detail the way that Muslim sources are included in the sampled texts.

Presentation and Explication

First, exactly which sources are included, how are they described and how are their views introduced? Incredibly, in this sample of broadsheet journalistic texts, illegitimate ('terrorist') organisations are the most frequently quoted Muslim primary source (23.0 percent; n = 34) – quoted more frequently than even than the leaders of international governments (20.3 percent; n = 30). The views of 'Muslim criminals' are also frequently quoted (6.3 percent; n = 9), albeit usually in the form of indirect speech, described by other participants. For example, a report on anti-Chinese racist violence in Indonesia during a financial crisis ('Ruined Indonesians vent rage on Chinese minority', *Guardian*, 28 January 1998), included a source's description how 'a mob of stone-throwing Indonesian youths with knives, sickles and iron bars attacked [a] shop screaming "Kill the Chinese"'. The words of illegitimate ('terrorist') organisations are also included as second-hand speech, for example:

> Gangs armed with knives, axes, hoes and shovels slaughtered more than 400 peasants in four poor villages in western Algeria, the worst massacre in six years of Muslim fundamentalist insurgency. "We're almost done here", a gang leader was heard saying on a walkie-talkie during the killings in the hillside villages on the first night of the Muslim holy month of Ramadan. ('Survivors tell of worst Algerian massacre', *Independent on Sunday* 4 January 1998)

The opinions of 'terrorists' are occasionally quoted verbatim, recounted from direct interaction with the by-lined journalist. For example, in a news report headlined 'Holy Fighter hones the Hamas dagger' (*Guardian*, 22 October 1997) Sheikh Yassin is quoted as saying that Israel 'must disappear from the map'. The metaphor in the headline is developed in the first paragraph: the journalist declares that a 'bloody dagger plunged into a Star of David [painted] on the walls of Gaza's poorest streets announces the return of "the Holy Fighter"' from his exile in Jordan. Another report on this story, this time in the *Financial Times* ('Netanyahu defiant after Mossad failure', 7 October 1997) quotes Sheikh Yassin claiming that there would be 'no halt to armed operations until the end of the occupation'.

On occasion, the views of the quoted terrorist formed the subject of the report itself, as indicated by the article's leader. For example:

An Islamic extremist who masterminded the World Trade Center bombing in New York defiantly declared his devotion to terrorism yesterday as he was sentenced to life imprisonment. 'Yes, I am a terrorist and am proud of it,' Ramsi Yousef told a court in New York. 'I support terrorism.' ('New York bomb mastermind gets life in solitary', *Daily Telegraph* 9 January 1998)

Lower down the report, the journalist paraphrases an additional part of the declaration: 'Yousef was later to say that, had he known so few people would die, he would have planted a bigger bomb to bring down one of the towers.' Of course, such views from (people who claim to be) Muslims invite criticism, and understandably so. But the *prominence* of such views, combined with the relative absence of authoritative sources such as Muslim academics, religious spokespeople, writers and scientists (all n = 1), and the infrequency of texts quoting either non-terrorist Muslims or Muslims *criticising* violent activities, is misrepresentative, objectionable and needs to be rectified.

The frequency that Muslim sources are included in news reports is not the only significant issue when considering the representation of Islam. We need to bear in mind that the Muslim voice 'is made passive not only by those who want to eradicate it, but also by those who are happy to welcome it under some conditions they feel entitled to set' (Hage 1998: 17). Thus, we need to consider the manner in which Muslim opinions are explicated, elucidated or contextualised in reporting. For example:

'Coffee, tea, or headscarf?' *Kathy Evans lands in Tehran after six hours of austerity aboard the world's most Islamic airline.*
'You will please to put on your headscarf', said the matronly, heavily covered air-hostess. This was not a request, but an order to all women passengers, regardless of nationality, to adopt Islamic dress. (*Guardian* 5 December 1997)

The leader (in italics) provides the interpretive frame for the remainder of the article. This is a report of Kathy Evans' experiences of a stern, severe and sober *Islamic* (note: not Iranian) airline. This in itself is a fallacious strategy, since it makes an unwarranted over-generalising argumentative leap from part (Iranian airline) to whole (Islamic airline). However, it is the use of the source's words in this opening paragraph that I find most interesting. Ordinarily, ungrammatical quotes like this are 'cleaned up' by journalists – indeed, Malcolm (1990: 155) goes as far as to argue that 'Only the most uncharitable (or inept) journalist will hold a subject to his literal utterances.' So why, in this case, did Evans reproduce this quote in an (assumedly) entirely accurate way? By recalling *exactly* what the hostess said, Evans makes the *function* (or 'speech act') of her utterance unclear: going purely on what is reproduced, it is difficult to know whether the utterance is a 'request', an 'order' or some other speech act. Cleaned up, the quotation could have read: 'will you put on your headscarf, please?' (indicating a request); 'please, will you put on your headscarf?' (indicating a less direct request); 'you will put on your headscarf, please' (indicating a direction); or a number of other variations. However, by making the utterance ambiguous in the way she chose to, Evans was able to explicitly *dis*ambiguate the meaning of the statement in a way that supported her representation of this 'Islamic airline'. Only by interpreting, or 'clarifying' the pragmatic function of the quotation in this way – explicitly stating that it 'was not a request, but an order' – was Evans able to use the air hostess' utterance to support the broader argument of the article: Islamic *enforcement* of the veil.

Not all news reporters chose to use their sources' opinions in such a partial manner, nor did all the sampled newspapers. The *Financial Times* printed the most objective and dispassionate reporting, resulting in it being the least 'Islamophobic' newspaper in this sample (see Richardson 2004). For example, when covering the then thawing relations between Iran and the USA, the *Financial Times* wrote:

> President Bill Clinton, responding to an olive branch from Iran's leaders, said yesterday he would welcome a dialogue if it covered areas of US concern such as terrorism and destabilising weapons.
> 'I would like nothing better than to have a dialogue with Iran, as long as we can have an honest discussion of the relevant issues', said Mr Clinton, in a response which has surprised US experts on the region by its warmth.
> President Mohammad Khatami called on Sunday for a 'thoughtful dialogue' with the American people but stopped short of agreeing to meet the administration. ('US grasps Iranians' olive branch', 16 December 1997)

In contrast to the remaining sampled newspapers – who chose, first, to (re)present this story as an ideological disagreement between President Khatami and Supreme Leader Ayatollah Khamenei and, second, to imply that Khatami was 'Westernising' and therefore *improving* Iran (see Richardson 2004) – the *Financial Times* stuck to reporting the manifest events of the story. And, despite containing a number of the 'flaming' words commonly associated with derogatory reporting of Muslims – terrorism, weapons and, lower down, the 'peace process' – the report is even-handed and describes the reported event in a calm and detached tone.

Conclusion

The majority of research on news sources and of sourcing routines in newspapers are undercut by the assumption that, depending on the focus of research, more (Muslim, female, young, non-bureaucratic, etc.) sources will create more representative, and hence more positive, reporting. These data indicate otherwise, suggesting that while inclusion is undoubtedly important, it is certainly not the only significant issue when it comes to equal treatment. First, Muslim sources are overwhelmingly only included and only quoted in reporting contexts critical of their actions and critical of their religion. When Muslim activities are not criticised – or when reported activities are not labelled as *Muslim* actions – Muslim sources are, almost without exception, absent from journalistic texts.[2] Such an approach not only contributes to a popular association between Islam and negativity, it also distances Muslims from non-Muslims (since 'Their' opinions are often placed in opposition to 'Ours') and symbolically implies that Muslims are only qualified to speak in response to certain (negative) events.

Second, the data support Molotch and Lester's (1974) assertion that newspapers reflect the practices of those who have the power to determine the experiences of others. In the case of news about Islam and Muslims, this list is dominated by non-Muslim bureaucratic sources (particularly in stories in which Islam was not represented as playing a part in the reported action) and illegitimate ('terrorist') groups. This 'double act' of non-Muslim bureaucratic sources and terrorist-criminals ensures that the majority views in Muslim communities are excised from reporting.

Third, certain forms of news reporting – particularly the narrative approaches that centre the journalist as interpreter and not simply as reporter – appear to militate against fair and impartial treatment. Source opinions can only be included in an objective and fair manner if the 'voice' of the journalist is removed from news reporting. That is, the reporting of Muslims will be prejudicial until newspapers prevent reporters from evaluating the significance of the story they are reporting (including preferring verbs such as 'said' over more loaded verbs like 'claim') and maintain the traditional separation of factual reportage and editorial comment. Such an approach is still found in the *Financial Times*, which produces the least 'Islamophobic' reporting of the sampled broadsheet newspapers.

10. American Media's Coverage of Muslims: the Historical Roots of Contemporary Portrayals

Karim H. Karim

Muslims currently are fodder for front-page news in America. Johann Galtung and Mari Ruge (1965) demonstrated in their classic essay, 'The Structure of Foreign News', that the more closely a journalistic report reproduces the common stereotypes of a particular people, the greater the likelihood that it will be highlighted in a newspaper. Of the innumerable events in a day involving the one billion Muslims in the world, only those that dramatically break laws seem to appear on the front page and at the beginning of newscasts. Individual followers of Islam are occasionally presented in favourable lights in content such as scientific breakthroughs, innovations in socio-economic development or cultural performance, but in the rare cases when such items are given prominence the terms 'Islam', 'Islamic' or 'Muslim' are usually not mentioned.

Edward Said (1981) was among the first scholars to conduct an extended study of Western media's[1] constructions of Muslim societies. He attempted to demonstrate that events such as the oil crisis in the mid-1970s and the overthrow of the staunch American ally, the Shah of Iran, by Islamist militants were viewed by journalists within orientalist perspectives that have roots in medieval Europe. He showed that the correspondents reporting on Muslim countries were generally ill-equipped to provide adequate understanding about them. (Said did, however, make a distinction between American correspondents, who were usually moved around from one 'hot spot' to another and their European counterparts, some of whom tended to remain in the region for relatively long periods and were familiar with local languages.) 'Islam' was a timeless entity in much of the reporting, which was replete with stereotypical generalisations and clichés. Phrases such as 'the Islamic mind-set', 'the crescent of crisis', and 'the Shi'ite penchant for martyrdom' posed as standard explanations for events that most of the journalists did not bother to explore in meaningful ways.

Said's trenchant criticism appeared to have some effect on certain quarters of American media. Prominent dailies such as the *New York Times* and the *Washington Post* occasionally print articles that, while maintaining critical investigatory stances, provide informed insights into Muslim societies without pandering to stereotypes.[2] American media are also increasingly using local stringers to report on majority-Muslim countries, who perform with notable professionalism. Nevertheless, the dominant mode of coverage – especially on television – for the most part remains uninformed about the subtleties of Muslim life and, not too infrequently, hostile towards it. The lack of understanding about the histories and cultures of Muslim societies leads to failure in assessing contemporary trends. Just as the journalists from the US and other countries covering Iran in 1979 were not able to sense the impending revolution, those reporting the overthrow of the Taliban in Afghanistan in 2002 were too quick to predict that women in the country would all throw off the *burqa*.

Following the devastating attacks against American targets on 11 September 2001, Muslims have generally come to occupy the position in popular US imagery previously held by communists. Just as Cold War foes are being transformed into new-found partners in important Western organisations like NATO, militant Islamists are helping sketch out a portrait of the new collective enemy of America. Even though the entire 'Muslim world' is not always viewed as a singular threat in the manner that communism often was,[3] the overall idea about Muslims is that they are the Other against whom the collective Self should be on guard.

Commenting on the American government's contradictory positions on defining 'the enemy', Ronald St John (2004), a US foreign policy analyst, notes that 'The Bush administration emphasized from day one that the War on Terrorism was not a war on Islam; however, administration supporters and others have increasingly defined it in exactly those terms.' The tendency of the US media in adopting the president's declaration that 'You are either with us, or against us'[4] as an implicit frame for their coverage of the 'War on Terrorism' has generally constructed a polarised world in which anyone with the slightest connection with Islam comes under suspicion. When such frameworks are operative, Muslim Americans – even those with deep roots in the USA – are excluded from the collective Self. Despite the appearance of some print media articles and broadcast items that address the considerable differences in views held by Muslims on terrorism and relations with the West, the dominant discourses overwhelmingly present most followers of Islam as a threat (Hafez 2000; Karim 2003; Poole 2002; Richardson 2004).

The adjective 'Islamic' is frequently used by journalists to describe the criminal activities of terrorists in ways that would be inconceivable in referring to similar actions carried out by members of other religions, especially Christians and Jews (Karim 2003: 81). Headlines such as 'Islamic Terror Group: Hint of US Presence', 'Islam Versus the West', 'The Sword of Islam', 'The Dark Side of Islam' and 'The Roots of Muslim Rage' have appeared in leading American publications like the *New York Times*, *Newsweek* and *Time* (Karim 2003: 80). Since terrorism is termed 'Islamic', one does not have far to go before coming to see common Islamic forms of worship as illustrations of terrorism. Articles on terrorists claiming to act in the name of Islam tend to be illustrated with photographs depicting men bowing in prayer at a mosque (Karim 2003: 95).

Primary Images of Muslims

There has developed, particularly over the last few decades, a distinct, but not finite, set of visual signifiers in the transnational media's imaginaries of 'Islamic fundamentalism'. These include the hijab worn by some Muslim women and girls, the cloak and turban worn by Muslim *ulama*, the Arab head-dress and cloak, the figure and the face of Ayatollah Khomeini, people prostrating in Islamic prayer, a mass of people performing the hajj (pilgrimage) at Mecca, children at Quranic schools, domes of mosques, minarets, crescents with five-pointed stars, Arabic or Arabic-looking writing, Arabesque designs, scimitars, camels and desert dunes. Illustrations in the print media and television stories on the growth of 'Muslim fundamentalism' usually display such images that communicate a vast amount of information without verbalising it. A bearded 'middle-Eastern-looking' man wearing a black cloak and turban can trigger an entire series of images of a fanatical religious movement, of airplane hijackings, of Western hostages held helpless in dungeons, of truck bombs killing hundreds of innocent people, of cruel punishments sanctioned by 'Islamic law' and of the suppression of human rights – in sum, of intellectual and moral regression.

The primary frames for the portrayal of Muslims are deeply entrenched. They draw from cultural assumptions about Islam that were developed over many generations. Certain basic notions about the characteristics of Muslims, having survived hundreds of years, feed the dominant discourses of contemporary media. (The core stereotypes that Muslims have about the West similarly inform their current constructions of Europe and North America (Ahmed 1992; Clark and Mowlana 1978; Ghanoonparvar 1993; Mernissi 1992); however, Muslim societies have not institutionalised their imaginaries about Western societies to the extent that the latter have done of Islam, especially over the last two centuries (Said 1978).)

Several scholars have attempted to isolate specific core stereotypes (topoi) that characterise dominant Western representations of Islam. Certain 'essential thematic clusters' in the media coverage of the Middle East can be identified, according to Said (1987: 88–9):

1. The pervasive presence of generally Middle Eastern, more particularly Arab and/or Islamic, terrorism, Arab or Islamic terrorist states and groups, as well as a 'terrorist network' comprising Arab and Islamic groups and states... Terrorism here is most often characterized as congenital, not as having any foundation in grievances, prior violence, or continuing conflicts.

2 The rise of Islamic and Muslim fundamentalism, usually but not always Shi'i, associated with such names as Khomeini, Qadhdhafi, Hizballah, as well as, to coin a phrase, 'the return of Islam'.

3 The Middle East as a place whose violent and incomprehensible events are routinely referred back to a distant past full of 'ancient' tribal, religious, or ethnic hatreds.

4 The Middle East as a contested site in which 'our' side is represented by the civilized and democratic West, the United States, and Israel. Sometimes Turkey is included here, most often not.

5 The Middle East as a locale for the re-emergence of a virulent quasi-European (i.e. Nazi) type of anti-Semitism.

6 The Middle East as the *fons en origo*, the hatching ground, of the gratuitous evils of the PLO...

Whereas some of these themes may be receiving less emphasis since Said outlined them at a conference in 1986, they generally reflect the frames used in dominant Western modes of covering Muslim societies.

According to Jack Shaheen (1984: 4), television tends to perpetuate four primary stereotypes about Arabs: 'they are all fabulously wealthy; they are barbaric and uncultured; they are sex maniacs with a penchant for white slavery; and they revel in acts of terrorism'. Such core images have been the bases for dominant Western perceptions of Arabs/Muslims since the Middle Ages when they were viewed as being 'warmongers', 'luxury lovers' and 'sex maniacs' (Kassis 1996: 261). Although these topoi may vary from time to time in emphasis and in relation to the particular Muslim groups to which they have been applied, they remain the most resilient of Western images about Muslims. Variations of the four primary stereotypes of Muslims, having fabulous but undeserved wealth (they have not *earned* it), being barbaric and regressive, indulging in sexual excess, and the most persistent image of 'the violent Muslim', have not only been reproduced in newspapers and television, but generally appear as the representations of the Muslim Other in popular culture, art, music, literature, school textbooks, public discourse and in computerised formats. Some Muslims may indeed exhibit such characteristics, but it is grossly inaccurate to suggest that they are shared by significant proportions of Islam's adherents.

Reeva Simon (1989: 52–3) has traced portrayals of Middle Eastern characters in British and American crime fiction, indicating how – whereas the images of Arabs or Turks may change depending on the current political circumstances – the topos of the violent Muslim remains irrepressible.

> This perennial Western fear, that of a resurgent Islam, is part of the Western historical memory. The sword-wielding Muslim thundering across the Straits of Gibraltar or laying siege to Vienna, the Old Man of the Mountain's Assassins high on drugs launched to kill political leaders, white slavers, and Barbary pirates have been reincarnated as plane hijackers, embassy bombers, and nefarious creators of long gas lines. In the fiction of the 'paranoid' and 'vicious' categories, the conspiracy, the hero, and the villain are basic elements for thriller/spy novel success. One of the most popular conspiracies, the Islamic threat, has been a plot motif threaded throughout crime fiction since John Buchan's *Greenmantle* (1916).

The basic social myth of the Other, which allows the endowment of a range of negative characteristics upon the perceived rival, is superimposed onto the Muslim enemy whose evil status has been validated by the vast repertoire of the negative images she has acquired in European discourses over the last fourteen centuries. Consequently, the Muslim's depiction as a villain carries a high level of plausibility in cultural entertainment that portrays the struggles of the good against the bad.

Not only does the representation of the violent Muslim serve a propagandic purpose, it is also highly profitable. Apart from painters and writers of fiction, the utility of presenting Muslims in negative ways has been exploited extensively by producers of films, television dramas, advertising, comics and toys. Commercial and ideological purposes dovetail neatly in products that exploit the basic stereotypes of Arabs and Muslims.

> Viciously anti-Arab prejudices are moulded to serve contemporary imperial politics: like the Coleco children's toy Rambo and his enemy 'Nomad' with swarthy features, unmistakable head-dress, and Arabic writing on his cloak. The packaging tells us: 'The desert

is the country of the treacherous soldier Nomad. He is as unreliable as the sand, as cold as the nights and as dangerous as the deadly scorpions that live there. His family is a gang of assassins and wandering thieves. They are men without honour, who use their knowledge of the desert to attack innocent villages...' (Rachad 1992: 248–9)[5]

Children are thus socialised into identifying the Other in the form of an Arab or Muslim. Ritual fights can be staged in play between the 'good guy', who is the representation of the Western technological civilization, with the 'bad guy', who comes from a backward desert land. Television cartoons also frequently have villainous characters with cultural traits generally considered to be those of Muslims.

The 'Islamic terrorist' has come to be a major figure in the typology of characters who perform in Western dramaturges about Muslim societies. It does not appear to require much ideological labour to create such a role given the repertoire of Western images arising from the topos of 'the violent man of Islam'. The widely reported activities of the relatively few Muslims who practice terrorism also serve to strengthen this core image. For the propagandist, the generative framework of the violent Muslim becomes the matrix upon which to base the portrayal of the lives of people as distinct in character and in time as the prophet Muhammad, Saladin (Salah ad-Din), Rashid al-Din Sinan, Hassan-i Sabbah, Tamerlane (Taimur Lang), Jamal al-Din Afghani, Gamal Abdel Nasser, Muammar Qadhafi, Yasser Arafat, Abu Nidal, Ruhollah Khomeini, Saddam Hussein and Osama bin Laden. The latter two were linked together without much factual basis by George W. Bush's administration and supportive journalists to provide one of the main pretexts for the war against Iraq in 2003.

Reporting Hostage Situations

Cultural images of abductions of Westerners by Muslims have existed for a long time. Tales of 'White slavery' involving the kidnapping of European women by Arabs and Turks have gripped the European imagination since the Middle Ages. In the last century, there have been innumerable romances written about white women abducted by swarthy noble savages from the desert: Hollywood films such as *The Sheik* (1921) and *The Wind and the Lion* (1975) replicated this theme on celluloid. In the Elvis Presley film *Haram Scarum* (1965), the hero was kidnapped by an Arab group, whose chief was called Sinan – the name of a leader of the medieval 'Assassins'.[6] In such examples we have the manifestation of the American hero/victim suffering her trials as a hostage and eventually emerging triumphant over the violent and barbaric Muslim. News accounts of incidents in which Muslim groups take Westerners hostage appear to borrow from this cultural model.

The term 'hostage' has come to have a very specific cultural connotation following the highly publicised hostage-taking in Tehran in 1979–81, when fifty-two American members of the embassy staff were held prisoner by Iranian militants. Due to the length of the period (444 days), the poor handling of the incident by Washington and its intense media coverage the event had a strong impact on American public opinion. The episode was framed as 'America held hostage' by the US media, which depicted the entire nation victimised by 'Islamic terrorists'. The defeat of president Jimmy Carter in the 1980 American presidential elections was partially attributed to the inability of his government to bring the hostages home. The Reagan administration was aware of the consequences of giving a hostage situation too high a profile and attempted to downplay the subsequent kidnappings of Americans in Beirut.

From the mid-1980s to the early 1990s the kidnapping of a series of Americans and other Westerners by Islamist groups in Lebanon was a major running story in the transnational media. Narratives placed the abductions within the interlocking themes of the clashes between Islam and the West, terrorists and governments, and barbarism and civilization to make the long drawn out saga interesting for audiences. During this period there were a number of kidnappings around the world. However, the transnational media seemed primarily to be focused on the plight of the Westerners captured by Islamist groups in Lebanon – the captive Americans and Europeans came essentially to embody the notion of 'Hostage' in dominant discourses: the names of some of the captives became legendary – Terry Waite, Terry Anderson, David Jacobsen, Thomas Sutherland, Martin Jenco. Collectively and individually they represented the heroic Western victim of the 'Islamic terrorist'.

Included among the nationals of other countries reported kidnapped abroad between 1985 and 1991 were several Canadians; an Ecuadorean president; a former Belgian prime minister; a Colombian political leader; the daughter of an Italian industrialist; an Italian businessman and his grandson; an American missionary and a Swiss tourist in the Philippines; the daughter of a Lebanese millionaire; a Spanish millionaire in Spain; a French woman and her three daughters by Palestinians; a group consisting of Colombians, West Germans, French and Swiss officials and journalists in Colombia; and eight Israelis in Kashmir. But the occasional space given to these and other hostages paled in comparison to the transnational media's sustained coverage of the Lebanon abductions of Americans and British men.[7] Kidnappings of Westerners in other countries, even those by Muslim groups, did not seem to attract as much attention because they apparently did not provide the sharply outlined backdrop of Beirut's proximity to the Holy Land in which to portray the battle between good and evil.

There were occasional reminders that many non-Western people who had also disappeared from the streets of Lebanese cities were still unaccounted for and were probably also languishing as captives; however, the scale of this coverage was minuscule compared to that of the abducted American and European men. Also absent from the coverage of hostages were the thousands of Lebanese held in the 'detention centres' in Israel's 'security zone' in southern Lebanon. When lists of those kidnapped in Beirut were published in the print media they did not even make a passing reference to any Lebanese, reserving the term 'hostage' for foreigners – mostly from the West. Veteran British correspondent Robert Fisk (1991: 435), writing in an alternative vein, asked:

> ...why was it that Western hostages were called 'hostages' – which they were – while Lebanese Shia Muslim prisoners held in an Israeli-controlled jail in southern Lebanon were referred to by journalists simply as 'prisoners'? These Lebanese were also held illegally, without charge and – according to one of the militia leaders who controls their lives – as hostages for the good conduct of their fellow villagers in southern Lebanon.

Currently, individuals of Muslim origins are held by authorities for long periods in the USA and some other Western countries under anti-terrorism legislation, without being charged. Whereas occasionally they are mentioned by the media, there is not the steady coverage that was seen when Western hostages were held in Lebanon.

The reporting of airline hijackings is often conducted in dramaturgical frameworks, with specific types of individuals playing out the roles of heroes, villains and victims (Karim 2003). In the coverage of confrontations with Muslims, the latter almost always appear as villains. The role of hero is generally reserved for members of the Western military or police, who come to the rescue of victims – usually Western citizens.

During the 2003 war in Iraq, a particular incident involving a female American prisoner of war was given considerable attention by the US media. A small convoy carrying Jessica Lynch, a nineteen-year-old private, in a military unit had taken a wrong turning near Nassiriya and was ambushed. Nine of her comrades were killed by Iraqi soldiers, who took Lynch to the local hospital. Eight days later,

... just after midnight, Army Rangers and Navy Seals stormed the Nassiriya hospital. Their 'daring' assault on enemy territory was captured by the military's night-vision camera. They were said to have come under fire, but they made it to Lynch and whisked her away by helicopter. That was the message beamed back to [television] viewers [in USA] within hours of the rescue. (Kampfner 2003)[8]

This drama not only replicated an ideal rescue, in which the heroic members of military units saved an attractive, young blonde woman, but also featured the vanquishing of Iraqi Muslims who were her villainous captors. As the real story came to light, it became clear that Iraqi forces had long left the site and the dramatic 'liberation' had been staged by the Pentagon for propaganda purposes (Kampfner 2003). The American media, by and large, uncritically accepted the government department's version of the incident.[9] They had also left out awkward details such as the failed previous attempt to return Jessica Lynch by Iraqi doctors, who were fired upon by the US military (Kampfner 2003). The official 'rescue' story was overwhelmingly popular among the American media and public precisely because it reproduced the age-old script of interactions between Western and Muslim societies.

Covering the 11 September 2001 Attacks

When aeroplanes crashed into the World Trade Center, broadcast journalists who witnessed the event found themselves scrambling to provide coherent commentary on the disaster unfolding in front of them. In contrast to the normally well-rehearsed and controlled coverage of a scheduled live event, an unexpected disaster leaves reporters disoriented. The completely unexpected action of airliners deliberately being flown into one of the world's tallest and most symbolic buildings, followed by the massive loss of life, shook observers' cognitive foundations of reality. When faced with the unusual, journalists respond by falling back on set patterns of information gathering and reporting. The resort to routine involves carrying out a prescribed series of actions for accomplishing coverage, such as contacting institutions to obtain access to sites and persons, interviewing, attending press conferences and using documentary sources. The contingencies of the news-producing format such as meeting deadlines, as well as the necessity of obtaining 'facts', pictures and quotations from specific categories of people (eyewitnesses, authority figures) ensure that the procedures are followed in a systematic manner.

At the same time, attempts are made to place even the most atypical occurrences within cognitive scripts and models of behaviour shaped by the experience and the narration of previous events (van Dijk 1988). Dominant cultural and religious worldviews of society are critical in shaping these cognitive structures with which we make sense of ongoing events. Even though the events were extraordinary, their reporting – following the initial period of disorientation – was eventually put in frames that had been in place to cover such issues as violence, terrorism and Muslims. The dominant discourses about these issues shape the cognitive scripts for reporting the acts of terrorism carried out by people claiming to act in the name of Islam.

Following the 11 September attacks, there was only one story and generally one perspective on the multiple TV networks of the USA. Most experts interviewed responded to security matters and did not seem interested in the larger political, social and economic causes of the attacks. The focus was primarily on the immediate reaction rather than on the larger issues. After some initial fumbling, the government was soon able to establish the frames and the agendas according to which the unfolding story was generally reported. Indeed, most media, stunned by the events of the day, seemed all too willing to accept the government's lead. As the hunt began for the 'Islamic terrorists', journalists' narratives failed to provide a nuanced and contextual understanding of Islam, Muslims or the nature of the 'Islamic peril'.

However, there was a greater diversity of voices that participated in the discussions that followed the terrorist attacks. Karen Armstrong, who has written about religious militancy in Islam as well as in Christianity and Judaism, appeared on TV a number of times; however, her attempts at explaining the broader context of such conflicts were often brushed aside as interviewers sought confirmation for their perceptions about an endemically violent Islam. The dominant discourse's sheer ubiquity, omnipresence and manoeuvrability overshadows the presence of alternative perspectives (Karim 2003).

The terrorist attacks of 11 September, resulting in the deaths of some three-thousand people, revealed an overwhelming failure by the United States government to ensure the security of its citizens. However, for many months relatively few questions were asked by journalists about the multiple lapses of security that had permitted the network of terrorists to plan, prepare and execute the complex series of hijackings and attacks. The media spotlight was focused mainly on the incidents themselves rather than their broader causes. Instead of exploring how the American government's own activities abroad may possibly have laid the groundwork for the resentment leading to attacks against Americans, the media generally echoed the government's polarised narrative frame of good versus evil. The series of relationships between the US government and various Afghan groups, including the Taliban, over the preceding two decades also remained largely unprobed. Washington's support for the mujahedeen fighting against the Soviet Union in the 1980s, followed by an almost complete withdrawal as the country faced social and economic chaos in the 1990s, was hardly ever mentioned in the media, which instead presented the US as a saviour for the long-suffering Afghans. America's role as superpower and its involvement in and attacks on other countries were generally overshadowed. Instead, the righteous and moral stance of the USA became a key component of the dominant journalistic script for reporting 'the War on Terror' – a label produced by the government and accepted uncritically as the rubric for the coverage of the US's military actions in Afghanistan.

The coverage was not completely uncritical of the abuses of power and the infringement of civil liberties. Nevertheless, the dominant news discourses largely reflected government perspectives, which, besides completely disregarding the violence committed by the USA, also excluded the terrorism carried out by various groups in countries such as Ireland, Spain and Sri Lanka. Reporting within this frame seemed to imply that once the elimination of Osama bin Laden and al-Qaeda was accomplished the war against terrorism will have been won once and for all. Quite apart from the difficulty in eradicating all forms of terrorism from the world, the task of even identifying and locating individuals and cells of al-Qaeda was to be immensely arduous.

Enormous harm had been done to America, and the country was grieving. Many Americans were angry and vengeful. The most powerful government in the world did not want to acknowledge its failure to protect the nation – nor did it want to show defeat. American elites sought to ensure that no fingers were pointed at them. Criticism about any possible blame on US political and military actions abroad as even remotely being the causes for the attacks was strongly discouraged. The perennial theme of 'America the Innocent' came into play as representatives of the government consistently described al-Qaeda as 'evil'. Having created the bi-polar frame of the good Self and the evil Other, no further explanation was necessary in order to understand the reasons for the attacks. Most media proceeded to conduct their reporting within the broad parameters of this discourse. As with Ronald Reagan's singular characterisation of the Soviet Union as 'the evil empire' in the 1980s, there was no need to address the existence of any evil that may exist within the Self.

Opinion leaders in government, academia and media could have initiated a genuine search for answers to these and other questions. The rupture caused by the extraordinary and traumatic events had opened up space for innovative ways to understand the relationship between Western and Muslim societies. Unfortunately, the opportunity was lost and the ideological discourses shepherded people back to the set patterns of thinking about 'us and them'.

It is incumbent upon the users of media to act as citizens, rather than merely as consumers of news, by challenging journalists to provide reporting that questions the dominant frames. Given the failure of educational systems to provide an adequate understanding of Islam and Muslims, it behoves journalists to explore intelligently the currents that run through this religious community that is present around the world, including all Western countries. The vast diversity of belief and practice among Muslims as well as the intellectual debates that they are conducting on modernity, ethics and the good life, and as well as on their engagement with the West will provide valuable insights into contemporary global affairs. Abuses of power in Muslim-majority states also need to be reported; however, understanding the networks of influence that link autocratic governments around the world to Western elites should be key to this coverage. That most Muslim terrorists happen to have had training in the contemporary sciences seems to indicate that their terrorism draws inspiration from perverted conceptions of both Islam *and* Western modernity. They appear to seek the sources of power that make the West dominant in the world; they are replicating the violence that they see Western governments perpetrating around the planet. In order to make sense of the 'Islamic peril' the West will have to look carefully at the increasingly hybrid formations of its own Self and the Other.

11. Australians Imagining Islam

Peter Manning

Australian Muslims

Australians have found themselves traipsing around the Middle East in military garb for more than a century, fighting other peoples' wars. My grandfather didn't think much of 'the Gypos' he found in Cairo while he waited for transports to Gallipoli but he came away with respect for the Turks. Thirty years later, when Australian troops were fighting the Axis forces around Gaza, they found the company of the Jewish settlers more to their liking than the local Arabs. The Labor Foreign Minister, and third President of the United Nations, Herbert Evatt, later played a crucial role in dividing up Palestine to make Israel. Australian ships were blazing away at Iraq under Labor Prime Minister Bob Hawke, an Israel enthusiast, in 1991, when Saddam invaded Kuwait. And Australian troops and ships have been back there again, in Baghdad and Fallujah, when the United States called for help in an illegal pre-emptive war on false premises twelve years later.

So Australians do have a view of the Middle East, and it is largely about military engagement. As the Lebanese civil war raged in the mid-1970s, many sought refuge in Australia. Many were, for the first time, *Muslim* Lebanese. By 1981, 17,000 Muslim Lebanese had settled in Australia, three-quarters in Sydney. They were the first of many Muslims to find Australia home: most settled in Sydney, many in Melbourne, others around the country (Cleland 2001: 26). By the 2001 Census, Muslims were 1.5 percent (280,000) of Australia's population and many were congregated in Sydney's poorer western and south-western suburbs.

Having arrived in Australia, Muslims of the 1970s were to quickly find that their immediate political environment, while peaceful, was inhospitable. The Israeli invasion of southern Lebanon in 1978 received official sympathy in Australia. But it was as nothing to the official horror at the overthrow of the Shah in Iran in 1978 and the installation of the firebrand cleric the Ayatollah Khomeini as Supreme Leader of the new Republic of Iran. It was closely followed by the taking of hostages at the

128

Tehran embassy of the US and their release 444 days later. Suddenly, militant Islam was born in the headlines – with much of the Australian Press copy from British and American sources. The orientalist image of the Arab as, variously, magical, sleazy and oil-rich was replaced with the violent Muslim (Brasted 2001: 212–14). If you were a poor Muslim family from Tripoli, it was best to keep your head down.

Early Representations

The next twenty years of representations of Islam in the Australian media have been discussed by Australian historian Howard Brasted (2001: ch.10). The virulence of the imagery runs parallel to the growth in the size of the Muslim community. Brasted argues:

> Progressively, throughout the 1980s, the images inspired by Iran began to merge with images of Islam in general... the spectre repeatedly conjured up in newspaper headlines, archival photographs and cartoons was that of fanatical Muslims poised not only to 'cleanse' their own societies and restore their Islamic basis – but ultimately to 'Islamicise' the world along the lines established in Iran. (2001: 215)

Australia's national daily, *The Australian*, saw signs that the Muslim south Philippines was being financed by Libya (25 September 1980), the national newsmagazine *The Bulletin* saw Indonesia and Malaysia under threat (8 January 1980) and the prestigious *Sydney Morning Herald* said Indonesia was tottering 'on the edge' (27 January 1981). Brasted says Australia, entranced during the 1960s by the 'domino' theory of how states would fall one-by-one to communism in southeast Asia, was in fear again. Fear of Islam combined with the historic fear of Asia (Walker 1999).

Despite the growing Muslim community in Australia's two capital cities – increasingly made up of Australian-born Muslims and Muslims from non-Arab countries like Pakistan, Afghanistan and Indonesia – representations of Islam remained focused on Iraq (the first Gulf War), the Pakistani 'Islamic bomb', Muslim violence in Indonesia, the Taliban's practices against women and the generalised threat posed by the new mullahs of Tehran.[1]

Studies of Muslim representations in the Australian media during this period of the 1990s are few (Ata 1984; Shboul 1988; Jakubowicz et al. 1994; Brasted 1997 and 2001) and they tend to concentrate on Muslim responses to portrayals as reductionist models of internationalist constructions. In an earlier review of the 1990s in the south Asian journal *Manushi*, Brasted noted: 'For while scholars seem successfully to be freeing themselves from the straitjacket of orientalist depiction, journalism continues to retain strong resonances of it' (Brasted 1997). It is not until the late 1990s, when some criminals in the Lakemba area of Sydney began a violent shoot-up of the local police station, that a focus in the media turns to the Muslims within the Australian community. That response was fierce, confused race (Arabic) with religion (Muslim) – and, sometimes, anyone 'of Middle Eastern appearance' – and demonised a class and region of young males. Their alienated and confused reactions have been closely studied (Collins et al. 2000).

This *international* perspective on Islam, right up to the 1998 Lakemba shootings, raises several important issues. It must be remembered that Australia has had few real strategic self-interests in the Middle East unique to itself (maybe the live sheep trade) and yet this is the dominant space of constructing what it means to be Muslim during this period. If anything, Australia's interests are more closely tied to Asia and, specifically, to Indonesia (a constant refrain of former Labor Prime Minister Paul Keating). Unlike Britain, France or the United States, Australia has no imperial legacy or guilt about the pursuit of its interests. Yet so much of the imagery of the period is as though Australian journalists swallowed the orientalist rhetoric whole at the feet of Flaubert, Kipling and Kitchener. In *Covering Islam*, Edward Said speaks of how Islam takes the rap for any bad news the Americans seem to be suffering: 'Much of the most dramatic, usually bad news of the past decade, including not only Iran, but the Arab-Israeli conflict, oil, and Afghanistan, has been news of "Islam"' (1997: 83). This chapter explores how true this is of the Australian news media.

Muslim Representations: 11 September 2000–11 September 2002

Sydney's Olympic Games in September 2000, seem now to mark not just the turn of the century for many Australians, but the end of an era of innocence. For the next two years the nation's headlines, and especially Sydney's, would be dominated by international and domestic disasters, almost all of which involved Arabs or Muslims: the Palestinian second intifada exploded in September 2000 with the provocative visit of Ariel Sharon to the al-Aqsa Mosque; the numbers of asylum seeker arrivals (usually comprising Afghan and Iraqi refugees) on Australia's northern shores rising sharply in 2001; a series of gang-rape cases involving Lebanese-background young men in Sydney hit the headlines; planes hit the World Trade Center and the Pentagon on 11 September 2001, piloted by

Muslims; the federal government of the Liberal Prime Minister used the 'race card' to fight the federal election of November 2001, proclaiming he would 'stand up' to asylum seekers (including a claim, since proven wrong, that asylum seekers 'threw their children overboard') and protect Australia's borders; Australian troops left to fight in Afghanistan against the Taliban; David Hicks, an Adelaide loner who had travelled to Afghanistan to find out about Islam, and Mamdouh Habib, a Lakemba Muslim, both ended up in Guantanamo Bay; and the Howard Government encouraged talk of further Australian military involvement in Iraq. One year after the Olympics, the entire Sydney spring (September to November) was filled with daily headlines about Arabs and Muslims.

Impressed with and intrigued by this concentration on representations of one community and one religion, I applied for and received a research grant from the University of Technology, Sydney, to study them. I was interested in the kind of narrative that the journalists' texts represented and, as a former senior journalist of thirty or more years standing, I felt able to 'read' them with an informed eye. The bases for the study were the two local daily newspapers in Sydney, the more populist *Daily Telegraph* and the broadsheet *Sydney Morning Herald*. Some 12,000 such articles were sampled and the results were published in Manning (2003). As part of the grant, a textual software program – QSR NU'DIST[2] – was also used to take a random sample of the articles/texts to find patterns of word usage and to distinguish placement of various items of news. The results of this further study were published in Manning (2004a). The representations of Muslims in these reports were tested against Edward Said's 'orientalism' thesis (1995 [1978]; 1994). I used LexisNexis software, in the first instance to locate the 12,000 texts using keywords that were related to the concepts of being 'Arab' or 'Muslim'. However, the software biased these towards 'Arabic': that is, articles that report the Middle East over articles that cover countries with predominantly Muslim populations (e.g. Indonesia). The conclusion was clear:

Arabs and Muslims (and the terms appear coterminous in the articles) are seen as violent to the point of terrorism – especially Palestinians. Israel, the United States and Australia – 'us' – are seen to be under attack from such people and they are seen as both an external and internal threat. 'Their' violence is portrayed as without reason, humanity or compassion for its victims. Arab young men, in particular, are seen as especially threatening, wanting 'our' Caucasian women and not policed sufficiently by their own communities who lack either values (respect for women) or interest (accepting responsibility) for these men. The men, women and children seeking to come here 'illegally' from the Muslim Middle East are portrayed as tricky, ungrateful, undeserving (possibly well off), and often disgusting and barely human. It is a portrait of deep and sustained fear. It is also a portrait of an Australian Orientalism that has been successfully transplanted and developed on Antipodean shores. (Manning 2003: 69)

The QSR NU'DIST data has now been reconfigured for this paper with only three keywords, all around the concept 'Muslim'. This has meant using the LexisNexis base to cover other key areas with important Muslim populations such as north and sub-Saharan Africa and India. It has also meant including some domestic news reporting about Muslims that did not mention Arabic Australians.

Representing Islam: some quantitative data

Figure 11. 1 shows the number of articles/texts per week over the two-year period (September 2000–September 2002) in the two Sydney newspapers (their split was about 50–50) that mention the keyword 'Muslim' or synonyms ('Islam', 'Moslem').

Figure 11.1. Coverage in Australian Press September 2000–September 2002

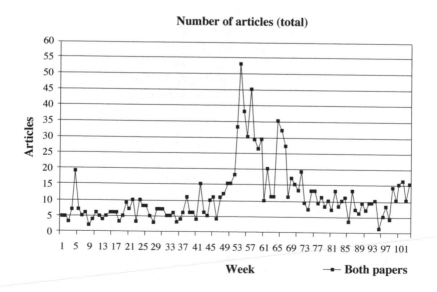

132

This graph reveals a great deal about the distribution of texts across the two year sample. Most notably:

- the shape of the graph reflects the crucial importance of the World Trade Center/Pentagon attacks in increasing the focus on Muslims in press coverage (week 52 onwards);
- the 'spike' in weeks 4–6 shows how the Palestinian/Sharon visit affected coverage;
- despite 11 September, the rise in coverage was already occurring, due to the federal government's refusal to allow a Norwegian ship, the Tampa, carrying asylum seekers, enter Australian waters (weeks 47–52); and
- the rise near the end of the sample (weeks 98–104) represents continuing mass coverage of the allegedly 'Lebanese' rape trials.

A number of questions were posed:

Question 1.
Of all articles, what proportion came from the following sections of the newspapers: international news, local news, opinion pages, leader (editorial), letters, other?

Figure 11.2 summarises data for this question.

Figure 11.2 Proportion of Coverage from Different Sections of the News

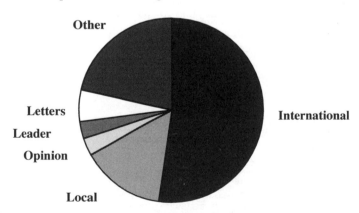

Figure 11.2 shows that, of 1,175 articles, 615 were from international news, 170 from local news, 39 opinion pages, 35 leaders, 64 letters and 252 other. This shows the dominance of international news (52 percent) as the major source of news.

I then explored the International section of the news pages in more detail.

Question 2.

Of these international articles (mentioning 'Muslim'), what proportion reference: (a) the Middle East (including Turkey and Iran); (b) Afghanistan, Pakistan or India; (c) North Africa (Algeria, Morocco, Libya, Tunisia, Egypt); (d) other Africa; and (e) Southeast Asia (Malaysia, Philippines, Indonesia)?

Once again, the results show the concentration of imagery outside Australia's immediate region – despite the large Muslim population in Australia's nearest neighbour. The Middle East was referenced in 55 percent of texts; Afghanistan, Pakistan or India in 48 percent; North Africa in 15 percent; sub-Saharan Africa in 3 percent; and Southeast Asia in 22 percent of sampled texts (with many articles overlapping references). This could be interpreted in two ways: either the newspapers have little concern about the large Muslim presence in Indonesia; or they follow the wider Western narrative about Muslims being defined by the actions of a few in the Middle East (especially Palestine and Iraq) and Afghanistan. I suspect the latter.

A further examination of the data provides a snapshot of the way that Islam is covered in these key international news pages of both Sydney newspapers.

Question 3.

Of international news articles, what proportion include the words: 'violent', 'death', 'attack', 'kill', 'bomb', 'gun', 'terror', 'suicide' or 'gunmen' whenever the words Muslim/Islam are used?

The answers overlap once again but the message is clear.

- violent/violence 28 percent
- dead/death/die/died 40 percent
- attack 59 percent
- kill/killed/kills 39 percent
- bomb/bomber/bombing/bombed/etc. 42 percent
- gun/gunmen/gunfire/gunned/etc. 17 percent
- terror 56 percent
- suicide 18 percent (though a few were not about suicide bombers)

The overwhelming image associated with the words Muslim/Islam is violence.

Domestic news accounted for 15 percent of all the articles mentioning the keywords around the concept 'Muslim'. (This compared with 24 percent from the Arabic/Muslim study, showing a major swing towards international news as the space for coverage of Muslims). What were the concerns of the domestic coverage? The following explores this question (including overlaps), by category keywords, in descending order.

Question 4.
   Of local news articles mentioning Muslims, what proportion mentioned the following categories?

* terror, 46 percent
* community/communities, 45 percent
* migrant/immigration, 21 percent
* crime, 19 percent
* Election, 16 percent
* Mosque, 15 percent
* Refugee, 15 percent
* Rape/rapists, 14 percent
* Detention, 11 percent
* Hicks, 10 percent
* Diplomat/diplomacy, 9 percent
* Asylum seekers, 8 percent

The two top categories, 'terror' and 'community' reflect, first, an association of Muslims with 'the War on Terror' (even though this is coverage of domestic news) and, second, at least in part, a persistent theme that the Muslim 'community' can and should take responsibility for its errant co-religionists. This second point will be discussed later.
   To investigate further the association of Muslims with violence in domestic news, the following question was asked, with special reference to the gang rape trials highlighted during this period.

Question 5.
   Of those local news articles mentioning 'rapist' and 'Lebanese', what proportion also mention the words 'Islam/Muslim'?

There were thirty-five local news articles mentioning 'rapist' and 'Lebanese'. Of these, twenty-one articles (60 percent) also mentioned Islam/Muslim. This finding again shows that, when it came to reporting the gang rape allegations against young Lebanese men, the religion of the accused was mentioned with great repetition.

Finally, to gauge the effect of 11 September 2001 on the amount of coverage and the link made with Muslims, I asked the following question.

Question 6.

Of all articles mentioning 'Muslim', what proportion mention the word 'terror' before and after 11 September 2001?

The total number of articles mentioning 'Muslim' was 1,175 and the number of articles that mention 'Muslim' and 'terror' over this period is 625. Therefore, over this two-year period, 53 percent of articles include the two words in the one article. However, prior to 11 September, only 11 percent of all articles mentioning 'Muslim' also mention 'terror', whereas after September 11, 89 percent of them did. This is a dramatic change of narrative.

2002: a Year to Remember

The reporting of the gang rapes in the western suburbs of Sydney in the second half of 2001 became extremely specific (Manning 2003: 59–63). These 'gangs' were Lebanese, they were Muslim and they came from the Canterbury–Bankstown area (western suburbs of Sydney). Despite the local police commander saying he knew of no evidence that Arabic-speaking people committed any more crime than Anglo-Saxon Australians, and the head of the New South Wales (NSW) Bureau of Crime and Statistics saying Bankstown had no worse record on sexual violence than many other areas of the state of NSW, the *Daily Telegraph* became increasingly hysterical. The mufti of the Islamic faith in Australia and the imam of the local Lakemba mosque, Sheik Taj El Din Al-Hilaly, was asked to 'show responsibility' (*Daily Telegraph* 21 August 2001:16) and stop washing his hands of these criminals. The next day the education writer of the paper made the connection between rape and Islam: 'A connection must be made between a religious attitude towards the demeanour of women and the taunts of slut and worse made to the Australian victims by their attackers' (*Daily Telegraph* 22 August 2001: 25). These victims were 'Australian' but presumably the attackers (also born in Australia) were some other breed. The taunts to their victims, too, allegedly were not because they were rapists, but because they were Muslim.

This narrative bounced along through 2002, as the trials of the young men came closer and they appeared before the courts. *The Australian*'s Janet Albrechtsen linked sexual violence and Islam in a column exposed by the Australian Broadcasting Corporation's 'Media Watch' programme. Albrechtsen quoted a French psychotherapist's research: 'Pack rape of white girls is an initiation rite of passage for a small section of young male Muslim youths, said Jean-Jacques Rassial, a psychotherapist at Villetaneuse University' (*The Australian* 17 July 2002). However, Albrechtsen had inserted the word 'Muslim' in the scholar's original passage. In a letter to the ABC programme, Rassial underlined his denial of Albrechtsen's quotation and linkage.

Hot on the heels of 11 September 2001, the debate about Islam in 2002 inevitably focused on the veiling of the Muslim woman – and not for the first time. Writing in the feminist journal *Hecate,* Binoy Kampmark, reviewing this period, says: 'This cultural, orientalist emphasis in Australia has similarly exaggerated the semiotic associations with the hijab and the chador with suggestions of terrorist infiltration and servitude. The female wearing the headscarf was oppressed while simultaneously dangerous' (Kampmark 2003: 93). The subject of sexual violence morphed into questions about Muslim women. A letter-writer to the Melbourne *Herald-Sun* asked why 'fundamentalist' Muslim women should be allowed into banks and post offices in chadors when motorcyclists had to remove helmets (*Herald-Sun* 17 June 2002). The ABC's *Media Watch* responded with a survey showing no Muslim women had robbed banks or post offices around Australia lately (*Media Watch* 9 September 2002).

On 13 August, the *Daily Telegraph* ran a story about a Muslim women's gym that had been granted an exemption from the provisions of the Anti-Discrimination Act and could be exclusively used by Muslim women. In the story, a non-Muslim woman complained about exclusion. Extensive talk-back radio, especially with 'shock jock' Alan Jones on 2GB in Sydney, pondered the question whether the Anti-Discrimination Board (ADB) was 'excluding others' – an echo of the line of Senator Pauline Hanson about grants and special privileges to Aboriginal people. Following the talk-back radio panic, on 15 August, the *Telegraph* ran its own 'vote-line' poll as to whether the ADB was 'discriminating' against others. In reply, 471 respondents said 'yes' (98 percent), while only 11 said 'no' (2 percent). A similar controversy, in August 2002, about Muslim schoolgirls using Auburn (public) Pool in a private session for an hour a day for swimming lessons saw the pool cancel these arrangements under the impact of talk-back radio commentary from Jones (2GB) and his competitor John Laws (2UE). This, despite public local pools often being closed for school-only sessions around Sydney (ADB 2003: 64–71) and the well-known Coogee Women's Baths (excluding Anglo men!) open since the Second World War.

On 10 October a series of bombs went off in a Bali nightclub, killing more than 200 people, including 88 Australians. The nation watched as the bodies of young holiday-makers, dead or injured, were flown back to emergency wards in Darwin and Perth. A madly smiling Amrosi was later arrested, truculent in his manner. Talk of an extremist group linked to al-Qaeda, and its leader Abu Bakir Bashir, filled the airwaves. More Australians died, proportionately, in Bali, than Americans in the World Trade Center. Violent Islamic fundamentalism now seemed very close to Australia.

In November, a conservative pastor-cum-politician, the Rev. Fred Nile of the NSW Christian Democrat Party, opened a new front: should Muslim women be allowed to wear the chador into public places? His comment followed Muslim women in chadors appearing in the Moscow theatre siege as Chechen guerrillas. A Channel Nine poll found 49 percent of respondents agreed with Fred. Prime Minister Howard, following his custom with Pauline Hanson, was ambiguous: 'I like Fred. I don't always agree with him, but he speaks for the views of a lot of people' (Kampmark 2003: 95). It was the classic 'dog whistle' of Australian politics at work (Poynting and Noble 2003; Manning 2004a).

The year closed with plans for a small Muslim prayer hall in Sydney's 'Bible belt', the northwest, being denied development approval. The local council, under pressure from 5,000 residents, found it difficult to state the reasons for its refusal apart from the fact that locals did not want it. The Mayor, talking to the ABC's *7.30 Report* nightly current affairs programme (18 December 2002 transcript), found it more difficult to explain why he had said local women would be in danger if the Muslim prayer hall arrived and why the small premises owned by the Muslim developer now had smashed windows and racist graffiti all over the walls (Lygo 2004: 171–4).

The Struggle for Control: 2003–4

The Australian involvement in the war on Iraq turned attention once more in 2003 to international affairs. Local reporters accustomed to writing on Muslims found the main story owned by foreign correspondents like Paul McGeough. A list of commentators, nevertheless, took on the role of sifting the intelligence available to Australians about the existence of weapons of mass destruction and Saddam Hussein's claims not to be involved in the attacks of September 11 (Manning 2004b). With Prime Minister Howard now one of George Bush's confidants (Woodward 2004: 183, 314), Muslim Australians could expect to feel as safe as Muslim Americans. Sheik al-Hilaly's strident anti-war stance, including appearances and speeches at anti-war rallies in the months leading up to the invasion in May 2003 led to his standing with the government falling fast in 2003 and 2004. Conservative media commentators like Andrew Bolt *(Herald-Sun)* and top Sydney radio talk host Alan Jones (ex-Liberal candidate) campaigned against al-Hilaly's survival as leader of Australia's Muslims throughout 2003 and 2004 (Jakubowicz, forthcoming 2006).

A host of mini-campaigns began around the country with the specific aim of changing the media narrative. The NSW Anti-Discrimination Board brought out its analysis in May 2003 of why media reporting was so prejudicial to Arabs and Muslims, but it was condemned by the media and the condemnation supported by the NSW Labor Premier, Bob Carr. Said Carr in Parliament: 'I treat with contempt any report that brands Australians as racists' (*Sydney Morning Herald* 2 May 2003). The ADB was soon abolished and its research division folded into another body, the Community Relations Commission for a Multicultural NSW. That body funded a study by the University of Technology, Sydney into practical ways to 'improve media practice'. In 2003, the Muslim Women's National Network of Australia began a campaign of meeting media executives (including those from the *Daily Telegraph*) and journalism students to explain the impacts of misreporting. In the same year, the South Australian Muslim Women's Association arranged a meeting with the editor and senior journalists of the only local newspaper, *The Advertiser*, to 'highlight their concerns'. All these comprised a reaction against the profiling of Muslims in previous years, especially since September 11 (HREOC 2004).

But would these pleas for understanding, recognition, fair and accurate reporting and consultation fall on deaf ears? Two incidents in 2004 suggested the negative stereotyping of Muslims was now a marketable commodity. In July 2004, an investigative report in the *Sydney Morning Herald,* by reporter Malcolm Knox, exposed novelist Norma Khouri's extremely popular book, *Forbidden Love*, as a fake (*Sydney Morning Herald* 24–5 May 2004). Published by Random House Australia, the book sold a massive 200,000 in Australia, was the subject of hundreds of tear-filled radio, press and television interviews and featured the friendship of the author with a Jordanian young woman who was later murdered in a Muslim 'honour killing'. But there was no honour killing, Khouri left Jordan when she was three, and owes $1m according to the Chicago police. Her book launched a series of other Muslim 'horror stories' in the birth of a new 'genre'. Khouri's books have been pulped and she is of interest to the US Federal Police. Nevertheless, the sales of the book exposed the appetite for lurid prejudice.

In September 2004, the ABC's *Media Watch* programme revealed that another retailer of orientalist commentary, Irshad Manji, was plagiarising herself. Manji was simply re-writing the top couple of paragraphs of her Op-Ed (opposite the Editoral) pieces and selling the same articles to different newspapers. Manji is the author of another Random House

Australia book, *The Trouble with Islam: A Muslim's Call for Reform in her Faith*. The ABC programme presenter said 'Running the same story every time there's a fresh outrage is cheeky, good business, and sloppy editing. But is it plagiarism?' (*Media Watch* 8 November 2004). Clearly, the 'good business' of criticising Islam strikes a chord in Australian newspapers, too.[3]

Conclusion

Australians seem to see Muslims through their press coverage of international affairs. However, it is skewed heavily towards conflicts in the Middle East rather than through their closest neighbour, Indonesia. This pre-dates September 11 2001, but was understandably, perhaps, focused by that event and its aftermath. The cast of the coverage overwhelmingly portrays Muslims as violent, irrational terrorists. It exists without context: no history, culture or social structures appear to inform the coverage. When it comes to domestic news coverage there is little difference. Again, Muslims are portrayed as violent people, possibly terrorist, and bent on maintaining their difference to an imagined 'mainstream' Australian culture. Their attempts at expressing their difference (particularly women, with their veils, women-only gyms, private swimming, etc.) are reported as deeply resented. The coverage panders to the Pauline Hanson fear of 'others' (usually Aborigines) getting 'special treatment'.

I suggest seven factors that explain this virulence, some peculiar to Australia, some not: (1) the basic frame of Australian international news coverage is Anglo-American (either news agencies or newspaper syndicated reports) and the outlook is as orientalist (in Said's terms) as these narrow sources; (2) September 11 2001 sent a shiver of panic and shock through the West, which reverberated not just in the United States but throughout Western media coverage and (further) demonising Islam became part of the response; (3) the suggestion that Muslims are more religiously observant than Christians in the West has challenged notions of secularism in a post-Christian West (Hassan 2002); (4) in Sydney, the peculiar event of gang rapists threatening victims with forced intercourse 'Lebanese-style' allowed press executives to suggest that a series of rapes in 2001 were 'racist' and inherently Muslim; (5) divisions within the Australian Muslim community, usually along ethnic lines, have enabled others to divide and play politics, weakening its leadership; (6) Western religious fundamentalist forces (especially in Christian and Jewish faiths) have grown and gained political power in Australia and elsewhere, partly in response to fears of Islam; and (7) Australian history is replete with racist scares, particularly of Asian invasion (Walker 1999) and Aboriginal resistance (Reynolds 1999), and the fears of Muslim invaders from across the seas fits a spectral vision.

Australian politicians pride themselves on the country assimilating wave after wave of post-war immigrants of varying ethnicities (*Sydney Morning Herald* 2 May 2003). Labor Premiers like Bob Carr and Liberal Prime Ministers like John Howard sing the same tune: the great Aussie melting pot. Yet neither want to acknowledge the dark racism of Australian history and its re-emergence in the public space today. Three recent surveys show Muslim Australians don't recognise that they are included in the public narrative. Many, especially Muslim women, live in fear (Ang et al. 2002; Dunn and Geeraert 2003). The latest report of the Human Rights and Equal Opportunity Commission has bleakly outlined how both the NSW Labor state and the Liberal federal governments have refused, since 1997, to pass laws outlawing religious discrimination affecting Muslims (HREOC 2004).

According to many, the representation of Muslims in the media has much to do with this overall lack of success in integration and acceptance of difference. Some governments live in fear of radio 'shock jocks' and their tabloid press allies; others work hand-in-hand with them in 'dog whistle politics' strategies (Manning 2003, 2004a; Poynting and Noble 2003). Few, if any, journalists on newspaper staff lists are Muslim; few live in the poorer areas where Muslims reside; few know Islam, have met Muslims or have gone beyond (Hindu) Bali in their holiday treks to Indonesia. Multiculturalism is yet to work for Muslims in Australia.

12. Joined Forces: the IDF and the Israeli Press Reporting of the Intifada*

Alina Korn

Introduction

The Palestinian uprising called the al-Aqsa Intifada broke out in late September 2000. The Israeli Chief of Staff at the time, Shaul Mofaz, boasted that the Israeli Defence Force (IDF) had foreseen this development and had even prepared for it. In the Israeli press, the mass insurrection in the Occupied Territories was greeted with 'surprise'; soon afterwards the press began constructing its 'disappointment'. Moreover, the explanation offered by official spokespersons, both inside Israel and in meetings with the international press, was based on the Intelligence Services's assessment, according to which Arafat 'is not a partner for peace' – an assessment highly compatible with the failure of the Camp David Summit in July 2000 (Laor 2001). The efforts invested in promoting this interpretation bore fruit, especially after the terrorist attacks of September 2001 (see Meital 2004).

This narrative gained popularity and developed in parallel to the army's preparations, but the IDF was not preparing to deal with a short burst of violence, nor to bring about an expedient cessation of the conflict in the Occupied Territories. Instead, the army prepared for war and aspired for the military defeat of the Palestinians (Shelah 2003). It is beyond the scope of the present chapter to discuss the various explanations for the violent outbreak in the autumn of 2000 and its escalation (see Klein 2003), but the views of Amos Malka, the former intelligence chief, are illuminating (*Haaretz* 11 June 2004). After retiring from his post, Malka raised accusations against the military and political elite, concerning the mistaken and misleading use of the assessments provided by Army Intelligence. According to Malka, the blame laid on Arafat should instead have been directed at the Israeli political and military leadership: it was this leadership that expected the outbreak of a new intifada, desired it and prepared for it, and when it indeed occurred, fanned the flames and caused an escalation of the violence.[1]

During the first days of the al-Aqsa intifada, more than a million bullets were fired while dispersing the demonstrations in the Territories, without any operational or professional justification if the aim was to curb or end the violence.[2] Following what the army learnt during the first intifada, the unrestrained use of gunfire on protesters brought about a decline in mass demonstrations and pushed more active members of the Palestinian organisations to turn to the use of arms (Reinhart 2002). The military means employed to suppress the protests were defined by the IDF from the start as 'the War on Terror', at a time when Palestinian terror attacks against Israeli civilians in the Territories or in Israel had not yet started. Consequently, during the first two months of the intifada, 228 Palestinians were killed by members of the security forces and by Israeli citizens, mostly settlers; thirty-three Israelis were killed, half of them soldiers. By late June 2004, 2,726 Palestinians had been killed by Israeli gunfire; about 20 percent of the dead were children. During this same period, 897 Israelis were killed in Israel and in the Territories.[3]

In this chapter I will argue that the Israeli news media took part in the construction of meaning during the decisive early months, and in the creation of a consensus, involving all of the Zionist parties, supporting military activity, of the kind impossible prior to this intifada. I intend to examine the construction of this public support with regard to two crucial issues: the coverage in the Israeli press of the IDF policy of assassinating specific persons suspected of involvement in terrorist activities, a policy implemented extensively in 2004; and the way in which the high number of Palestinians killed by the IDF in the Occupied Territories were reported (or not) in the Israeli press. These two issues, previously examined separately for the first months of the intifada (Korn 2004a, 2004b) combine to form the terrible story of the last four years: a huge army, one of the strongest in the world, doing as it pleases in the Palestinian Territories, breaking laws and international conventions, trampling basic human rights, destroying the landscape and imposing siege for months on thirsty towns.

The analysis includes Israel's main daily newspapers: *Yediot Ahronot* (hereafter *Yediot*), *Ma'ariv* and *Haaretz*. *Yediot* and *Ma'ariv* are both popular tabloids, whose coverage is characterised by exaggerated reports of terrorism and sensationalised, aggrandising, descriptions of Israeli suffering. Despite its low circulation, the influential daily *Haaretz* is considered to be Israel's foremost quality newspaper, due to its high journalistic standards and its readership among the ruling political, military and economic elites.[4] Despite the differences between them, all three papers embraced the IDF worldview, in light of which they continued justifying the policies adopted by the high command, which remained unchallenged after four years of conflict. Not only did the press not raise criticism or spark a public debate regarding the morality and benefit of an initiated policy of extra-judicial killings – it helped promote this policy.

'Their' Violence, 'Our' Reaction

From the beginning of the intifada the newspapers accepted the IDF's definition of its policy in the Territories as one of self-defence in response to the chain of violent events, initiated each time by the Palestinians. A pattern of coverage emerged that distinguished 'their' violence from 'our' reaction, constructed IDF actions as defensive reaction to terror and ignored the fact that Palestinian use of firearms and terrorist attacks against Israelis increased as IDF escalated its 'reaction' in the Territories.

Starting on 9 November 2000, the Israeli government launched a military strategy of assassinating Palestinian militants deemed to be security threats in the West Bank and Gaza, soon titled the 'liquidation policy' by the Israeli media (see Gordon 2004). In the first operation of this sort, Hussein Abayat, a Fatah activist in the Bethlehem region, was killed by a missile shot at his car. Two 52-year-old women standing nearby on a sidewalk were killed as well, and additional people were injured. Israel has not always admitted its responsibility for killings such as this, nor is every action deliberately undertaken with the aim of killing Palestinians termed by the press a 'liquidation' or an 'assassination'. However it is estimated that by November 2001, Israeli security forces had assassinated 46 Palestinians, and by the end of June 2004 at least 149 Palestinians were extra-judicially executed by Israel, 90 of them in assassinations carried out by the Israel Air Force and 59 in assassinations carried out by ground forces. In the course of these assassinations 100 additional Palestinians were killed, 90 of them minors (<www.btselem.org>). Among the people killed were political figures such as Dr Thabet Thabet, the director general of the Palestinian Ministry of Health and a leading figure in the Fatah, Abu-Ali Mustaffa, the leader of the Palestinian Popular Front, and Ismail Abu-Shaneb and Sheikh Ahmed Yassin, leading political figures of Hamas not belonging to its military wing. Both tabloids, *Yediot* and *Ma'ariv*, as well as *Haaretz*, fully accepted the narrative according to which the assassinations were justified 'targeted killings' directed against terrorists, and avoided discussing the connection between the Israeli 'reaction' and the escalation in Palestinian violence (Korn 2004a).

The first assassination gained sensational and extraordinary coverage.

Yediot announced on its front page in huge red letters: 'Senior Fatah activist liquidated'. The newspaper praised the assassination and described it as 'a targeted, surgical, and smart hit... which harms only the terrorists and not the general population' (*Yediot* 10 November 2000: 4). The leading *Haaretz* headline on 10 November 2000 used the term 'assassination' to refer to the killing of Abayat, with the term 'liquidation' appearing in a quote from an army spokesperson. The information and assessments supplied by the military spokespersons enabled the construction of reports around the assertion that Hussein Abayat was killed because he was responsible for many terrorist attacks aimed at IDF soldiers and settlers, and that the assassination took place in the course of such an attack. The inventory of activities attributed to him was not questioned. None of the reports or commentaries of the military correspondents – neither in *Haaretz* nor in the other papers – gave any clue as to the questions that could be asked, cross-checked, inquired into or given any kind of further consideration: is the list of activities attributed to Abayat reliable?[5] Does it justify his killing, the killing of the two bystanders and the injury of additional people?

By the end of December 2000, the reports of IDF assassinations had become a standard and routine feature of intifada coverage. The newspapers adopted the premise underlying the official policy, formulated by *Haaretz* in the following way: 'IDF sources say that the activity is focused on the most wanted activists, against whom there is concrete information regarding their involvement in terrorist attacks and in the planning of attacks in the near future' (*Haaretz* 19 December 2000). No questions whatsoever were posed to Israeli security officials regarding their decision to instate a policy that caused the conflict to escalate. The IDF operation was simply accepted and no mention was made of its repercussions, despite the fact that these assassinations provoked some of the harshest escalations of the conflict. Beyond the general assertion that the killings heighten the motivation of the terrorist organisations, the press never investigated the direct and terrible price exacted in terms of human lives, paid by Israeli citizens in retaliatory attacks carried out immediately after the killings.

Although the assassinations were carried out according to lists prepared ahead of time, and despite the fact that they required advance planning, a clear pattern could be identified, according to which most of the assassinations were performed on the same day, or within a few days after, a terrorist attack had taken place involving Israeli casualties. Thus, the assassination of Sheikh Ahmed Yassin and seven others was carried out about a week after a terrorist attack on Ashdod Port that claimed the lives of ten Israelis.[6]

The reports covering the deliberate killing of Palestinians underwent a process of normalisation, gradually becoming routine and laconic. In many cases, a report of a liquidation/assassination was not accorded particular prominence and was mentioned on the inside pages. The IDF only needs to attribute to its victims, in retrospect, an involvement in terrorist activities and attempts to harm Israelis, in order for the action to be justified. Often, it is enough to mention a phrase such as 'senior *Hamas* activist liquidated' or 'head of the military wing' to turn the killing into a 'military success story'. In cases where the IDF kills a high number of Palestinians in a premeditated operation, the terrorist record of the assassinated, or at least the most senior among them, is highlighted. The other Palestinian victims, aside from the 'senior' target, are barely mentioned.

All the events reported in the tabloids are interpreted in terms of a fixed, unchanging narrative, according to which the Palestinians are the aggressors and the Israelis are the victims. The temporal sequence of the reported events is of no significance: Palestinian deaths are mentioned only after the reports of attacks on Israelis; as part of the account on the IDF's reaction and its 'War on Terror'; and the terrorist attack always precedes the assassination, even when it takes place following and in response to it. Thus, on 26 July 2004, *Yediot*'s front page carried a close-up picture of the face of an Israeli child laid out on a stretcher. The headline above the picture read 'Missile fired on community centre' and the caption beneath it said '6 children were injured, one of them badly, when a missile shot by Palestinians hit a community centre in Neve Dekalim'. On pages 4 and 5, a headline spread over a page and a half read 'Missile against children', over a large picture of the child from the front-page picture lying inside an ambulance. At the end of the item, a single sentence made mention of the IDF's retaliatory fire on the source of the missile attack, but no mention was made of the fact that the missiles were fired on the settlement *after* the IDF attacked a residential building in Gaza earlier that day, in an attempt to assassinate a Hamas member. Part of that information appeared in a small sidebar: beneath the report of the missile fire on the settlement, an item reported 'another success in the war on terror' under the headline 'Five wanted terrorists liquidated in Tul-Karem'.

While the IDF widened its attacks in the Territories, killing more Palestinians, including many civilians, the tabloids continued to portray the Palestinians as terrorists rather than victims. On the few occasions that Palestinian casualties were reported, it was sufficient to report that they were terrorists or to add 'IDF sources said/believe/insist that they were Fatah members' or that 'they helped plan a terror attack last year'. Even the liberal *Haaretz* accepted the assumption that the IDF responds to an escalation in the level of Palestinian violence but, unlike the tabloids, it consistently published accurate reports on the magnitude of Palestinian deaths and the circumstances in which they were killed.

Killed in Confrontations and 'Exchanges of Fire'

A key difference between *Haaretz* and the tabloids can be seen in the coverage of Palestinian deaths. It seems as if the tabloids invest great effort in obscuring the killing of Palestinians. This camouflage is done in two ways: complete disregard, especially when the casualties in question are civilians; and coverage of the 'liquidation' of wanted militants and terrorists, in the course of which innocent civilians are killed accidentally, during 'exchanges of fire'. Below are some examples that shed light on the modes of reporting, published on especially bloody days.

- Sunday 25 April 2004, *Yediot* reported that 'The Border Police liquidated a squad in Jenin on its way to a holiday attack' (subheading, p. 1) and that a total of 'Nine terrorists [were] liquidated during a stormy weekend in the Territories' (kicker head, p. 9). On the same day, *Ma'ariv* reported that 'Border Police fighters worked hard: four *Fatah* and *Islamic Jihad* activists were killed yesterday in a joint operation of IDF, Shin Bet and Border Police forces' (p. 5). The two papers did not even hint at the accidental fatal shooting of Dr Yasser Ahmed Abu-Laimun, a lecturer at the Arab-American University in Jenin.
- 6–11 June 2004, six Palestinians were killed in the Territories: A Fatah activist and five civilians, including a man in a wheelchair, a mentally retarded youth, and a thirteen-year-old boy. None of these deaths were reported in *Yediot*.
- 2 July 2004, *Yediot* reported a 'Day of achievements for the IDF' (p. 6), in the course of which five terrorists were killed. The paper failed to report details of these 'achievements': three additional Palestinian deaths, including an 11-year-old boy.
- Sunday 4 July 2004, *Yediot* made no mention whatsoever of the seven Palestinians killed by the IDF during the weekend (two armed activists, two civilians and three children aged 10, 14 and 15).
- 7 July 2004, *Yediot* devoted a double spread to the coverage of the death in action of an officer from the Marine Commando special unit, during a raid in Nablus in search of wanted militants.[7] The heading of the small sidebar read: 'IDF operation killed two terrorists and two civilians'. The circumstances in which the two civilians were killed during the chase of the wanted activists were described as follows: 'A combat helicopter called in

for backup fired shots at the building – and killed two innocent civilians carrying American passports, Dr. Khaled Salah, a lecturer of electronic engineering, and his son Muhammad, 15.' The report also said that 'IDF officials expressed regret over the death of civilians', and the commander of IDF forces in the West Bank, was quoted as saying: 'Due to the conditions on the ground we had to employ a combat helicopter. We try not to use helicopters in residential areas, but in this case operational conditions required their use.' This apologetic formulation crops up when foreign citizens, especially Palestinians carrying American passports, are among the dead. In contrast, four additional Palestinians, including a 14-year-old boy, killed in other incidents in the Territories, were not mentioned in *Yediot*.

Casualty numbers are 'hard facts', and *Haaretz*, as a newspaper committed to a professional ethic of balanced, objective and impartial reporting, did not ignore them the way the tabloids did.[8] The paper reported on the number of Palestinian casualties in a consistent and reliable manner. Generally, its news items included personal details of the Palestinians killed, such as name, age and place of residence. Following days on which the number of casualties was especially high, and on occasions such as the end of the month or end of the year, the summary report of daily events was accompanied by a sidebar with the names and personal details of the Palestinians killed. In terms of Israeli journalistic outputs, one should not underestimate the significance of this practice.

However, a comprehensive scrutiny of the *Haaretz* reporting strategies reveals a more complicated picture. Despite the attempt to present a factual summary of events during which Palestinians were killed, the paper displayed a tendency to downplay their importance: as time passed, Palestinian casualties were less often mentioned on the front page, received fewer headlines and were relegated to inside pages (see Korn 2004b). Moreover, there was a growing tendency to highlight events in which Palestinians used weapons and to accept both the army's version of events in the Territories – an armed struggle between two combatant parties – and their justification for using of heavy weapons and collective punishment. The headlines reported the number of Palestinians 'killed in clashes', and often constructed a symmetrical equation comparing them with Israeli casualties. For example, 'One soldier and 7 Palestinians killed in clashes' (*Haaretz* 19 November 2000: 1). Frequent use of the term 'Palestinians killed in clashes' makes it possible to mention Palestinian deaths without ascertaining the circumstances in which they were killed, or to obscure the fact that most of the dead were unarmed civilians.

The narrative emerging from all three Israeli dailies is one of 'a nation under siege'. Reports centre on two principal issues: the besieged Israelis, in the settlements or in Israel, suffering under the threat of terrorism; and the intrusive operations of the IDF throughout the Territories, described in terms of a successful breach of the siege. The tabloids continue uncritically to report the IDF's policy, unquestioningly accepting that the IDF is obliged to react to the escalation of Palestinian violence, even when it is the one initiating an expansion of violent activity. Recently, the 'Qassam rocket launchers' have become a mantra used by the IDF to enlist public support for a major offensive in the Gaza Strip. The threat posed by the Qassam rockets has been inflated to demonic proportions, justifying the massive destruction of Palestinian lives, homes and property. Thus, during the month of July 2004 the IDF operated in the northern part of the Gaza Strip, taking control of areas from which Qassam rockets allegedly were fired on settlements in the western Negev, inside Israel. On 9 July 2004, *Yediot* reported that eleven Palestinians were killed in 'exchanges of fire' during an operation meant to uncover Qassam launchers, initiated after Qassam rockets were fired on the town of Sderot. The item reported that an IDF force progressed in the search for Qassam launchers and 'encountered a terrorist squad that opened fire on it'. The report made no mention of the fact that the encounter with the terrorist unit did not occur accidentally, but rather while the force was advancing on the home of a senior Hamas activist (and while a second force was surrounding the home of a senior Fatah activist). The report only mentioned that 'in confrontations with the Palestinians two senior local terrorists were killed: the leader of the *Fatah* military wing in Beit Hanun, Nasser Abu Harbeid, and the leader of the *Hamas* military wing in Beit Hanun, Mahed Abu Awda.' It was also added that 'Palestinian sources claimed yesterday that the casualties included three innocent civilians, one of them a woman' (*Yediot* 9 July 2004: 9).

Haaretz continues to report Palestinian casualties while accepting the IDF narrative. The paper reports 'the IDF's reaction' without noting that this reaction is a central element causing the escalation of the conflict. *Haaretz* distinguishes between 'armed' activists and civilians, and diligently reports the deaths of unarmed people, but downplays the fact that more 'armed' Palestinians are killed while being pursued by armed IDF forces than as the initiators of violent incidents. Further, the paper reports the killing of these 'wanted' and 'armed' persons as if its necessity were self-evident.

Discussion

One of the IDF's major achievements after four years of bloody confrontation is the wide support it has received in conducting the conflict with the Palestinians using military means, and the build-up of a consensus around its policy. As time passes, the press grows more committed to 'Israel's just war against Palestinian terrorism' and seems to have given up any attempt to raise questions, place the IDF's policy under careful scrutiny, or examine its implications for the future of the conflict. The structured relations between the press and the military establishment made it possible to construct the public discourse around the definitions prevalent in the military system, and provided a basis of legitimacy and a wide range of action, allowing Israeli governments and the IDF to persist in their policy and even expand it.

Various studies have noted that during periods of crisis and war, the press joins the war effort and a lengthy period can pass before it begins to raise questions and examine the official policy with a more critical eye (Philo 1995; Hammond 2000, 2003). The dependence of Israeli journalists on military sources and their tendency to follow official explanations is anchored in an ingrained bias according to which 'Israelis tell the truth' and 'Arabs are liars'. The tabloids clearly prefer the IDF's official version and no effort is made to engage with Palestinian reports. As the IDF intensified the level of fighting in the Territories, the tabloids grew more eager to fall in line with the official version and become instruments of propaganda, fulfilling the role accorded to the press by Israeli governments in the war they have declared on the Palestinian people.

Haaretz acts according to higher journalistic standards: it does not ignore the destruction wreaked on the Palestinians and reports consistently and reliably on the numbers of casualties in the Territories. Indeed, a careful reading of the Territories' correspondents' reports added many details, expanded the vague generalisations about Palestinians 'killed in clashes' and equipped the reader with vital information, which was frequently at odds with the official Israeli record of events. However, most of this information did not reach the front pages and headlines but was 'concealed' in the reports appearing on the less significant inside pages. Moreover, these reports typically appeared not as the 'official' version presented by the newspaper to its readers, but rather as alternative 'Palestinian claims' about events. Israeli military officials were over represented and their structured access to the newspaper enabled them to be the 'primary definers' of the topics (Hall et al. 1978). Yet, since *Haaretz* traditionally observes the 'strategic rituals' of balance and objectivity, reporting on 'both sides' of the story (Tuchman 1972), the priority it grants to the official version is not obvious. The 'Palestinian version' was in fact included mainly as testimony to a liberal standpoint, given as 'additional information', as part of the coverage of the Palestinian perspective and not as a 'competing account'. These reports hardly ever cast doubt on the dominant version and definition of reality, according to which the Palestinians initiated the violence and the IDF was forced to react.

The coverage of the killing of Dr Abu-Laimun exemplifies the problems inherent in the *Haaretz* mode of reporting. On 25 April 2004 the paper reported an incident in which Dr Abu-Laimun, a lecturer at the Arab-American University in Jenin, was shot and killed. A dog was set on two wanted Hamas activists pursued by IDF soldiers but the dog pounced on the lecturer. The soldiers killed him from afar believing the dog had attacked the suspect. The paper reported the IDF claim that intelligence information linked the academic to the two Hamas terror suspects. Three days later, on 28 April, an article was published on the editorial page in which Amira Hass, the *Haaretz* correspondent in the Territories, brought the facts as related to her by the Palestinian side. Following this article, the IDF was obliged to investigate and release an official statement concerning the incident, in which it admitted that Dr Abu-Laimun had nothing to do with terrorist activities. *Haaretz* reported this on 30 April. Yet here is the problematic aspect of the *Haaretz* coverage: beyond the reporter's account and the publication of the IDF's spokesperson's statement, there was no follow-up to this atrocious incident. The use of dogs to capture suspects was not discussed at all, shooting at people from afar was not criticised, and no legal or journalistic investigation was undertaken following this event. It was just another anomalous case swept under the carpet by the general rule that the IDF can inspect itself, monitor itself and be above suspicion, even in the eyes of *Haaretz*.

Conclusion

The sensational coverage of terrorist attacks, the focus on Israeli victimisation and suffering, and the disregard for the catastrophe we are inflicting on the Palestinians have all contributed to an increased fear and the presentation of Palestinian terrorism as a threat to the survival of the state of Israel (see Chermak 2003; Altheide 2003). The public panic constructed around the terrorist threat is an important element in the ability of the military elite to cross more and more red lines, mobilise public support, and convince the public of the necessity of 'extraordinary' means and operations to 'root out' terror and destroy 'once and for all' the 'terrorist infrastructure'.

The press had an important role, from the beginning of the intifada, in blunting the sensitivity of the Israelis and in the normalisation of reports of

Palestinian deaths. It took part in the dehumanisation of the Palestinians and the framing of significant portions of the Palestinian population as dangerous terrorists. The press granted a self-evident meaning to extra-legal military practices, and aided in establishing these practices within the Israeli political discourse. Furthermore, it helped construct exceptional and extraordinary IDF activities as a naturalised norm (Butler 2004).

The War on Terrorism is a war of images (Hammond 2003) and the most powerful and effective images are those of suffering victims and mourning families. Hence, as a rule, atrocities are always perpetrated against us, and the more brutal Israel becomes, the more it depends on our image as the eternal victim (Laor 2004). This is also why the suffering, death and mourning of the Palestinians are hardly represented in the Israeli popular press. The thousands of Palestinian casualties are not victims; their lives are not deemed worthy of living, their deaths not worth mourning. An uncharacteristic example may serve as an illustration to the 'hierarchy of grief' (Butler 2004) in the Israeli press. A dog that accompanied IDF soldiers and was killed during a military operation in Lebanon received an obituary, published in *Haaretz* (9 May 2004). The obituary dedicated to the bitch Tosca appeared on page 4, before the report on page 5 of five Palestinians killed in the Territories. In the tabloids, the latter were not even mentioned.

13. Towards an Islamic Information Revolution?[1]
Gary R. Bunt

Introduction

The Internet has potential as a tool for enhancing (many definitions of) 'democracy' and 'development' for Muslim societies, in a variety of contexts. Some have suggested that it may enhance the 'connectivity' of the *umma*, the paradigmatic global Muslim community. The Internet may also alter 'non-Muslim' understandings about Islam, being an obvious channel to consult when questions arise.

After the events of 11 September 2001 (henceforth 9-11) many 'Islamic' websites noted substantial increases in traffic, as people sought to understand Islam as a religion – and the possible motivation for the attacks. Whether simply typing 'Islam' into Google gave 'appropriate' results is open to question. A substantial number of sites from diverse perspectives have set themselves up to be *the* authoritative voice of Islam on the World Wide Web. Many present primers on Islam, chiefly aimed at non-Muslims, part of propagation strategies that encompass concise, multimedia, user-friendly introductions to the faith.

The Internet can highlight what is individual and distinct about different Muslim perspectives and communities. These facets may enhance dialogue and ideas of difference, countering those notions of homogeneity promoted on occasions both by non-Muslims *and* by Islamic 'authorities' as part of a singular path of Islam – which excludes marginalised groups, or alternative interpretations of Islam, including those that are traditionally less-political and more quietist in their outlook.

The term 'democracy' – along with 'human rights' – has many applications in Islamic cyberspace as a label of convenience for a myriad number of understandings of society and religion. If democracy relates to 'free speech', access to knowledge, influence in decision-making processes and political participation, then clearly the Internet *can* play a role as part of an overall 'democratising' process, not a solution in itself.

It cannot be assumed that higher levels of accessibility to the Internet in Muslim contexts will engender an increase in the creation of democratic

Islamic dialogues (however they might be defined), given the diverse expressions of Islam available online (Bunt 2000, 2003). Use of cyberspace in Muslim contexts should not be stereotyped. 'Islamic' content can constitute a small strand in general surfing habits, which may be dominated by popular culture, news, shopping and chatting – activities no different to Internet usage elsewhere. Some of these activities may have an overt or subtle Islamic edge. More research needs to be undertaken to 'join up' the religious and technological implications of Internet access: 'Very few Arab experts combine ICT knowledge with awareness of its social and cultural implications' (United Nations Development Programme, UNDP 2002: 75).

Whilst the term 'Arab' is not synonymous with 'Muslim', clearly this comment has implications for the Muslim populations. The focus in the following discussion is primarily on the Muslim 'Middle East' and the World Wide Web (although other Internet applications are referred to), in association with the theme of democracy.

The Digital Divide and Accessibility

Accessibility is a critical issue in any discussion of Islam, technology and democracy. The *Arab Human Development Report* (2003) reflected on the relatively low levels of Internet access and availability within Arab countries. Unsurprisingly, relatively wealthier nations such as the United Arab Emirates, Bahrain, Qatar and Kuwait had higher levels of Internet penetration – with Yemen, Sudan and Iraq having the lowest (UNDP 2003).[2]

The opportunity for access is significant, in terms of motivating intellectual enquiry and analysis – especially in relation to notions of democracy, and developing these intellectual tools. Whether the materials presented on Islam make a contribution to this development is a highly subjective and divisive issue. Certainly some sites provide critical Islamic opinions on political and religious issues in regional and global perspective, which some governments (and other authorities) seek to challenge and – in some cases – censor.

Improvements in Internet access can vary in different contexts, ranging from the establishment of a telephone line, enabling simple dial-up access, through to the establishment of high-speed Broadband and ADSL (Asymmetric Digital Subscriber Line) connectivity. For example, in 2003 the following developments would be seen as indicators of 'improvements' in Internet access in Muslim contexts: in Iran, news emerged of a private ADSL service being established; in Mauritania, a report suggested that its 'remoteness' was changing with the introduction of the Internet; Egyptian Internet access rose, in an unofficial estimate, to 6 million online users.[3]

Each of these developments could be described as information 'revolutions', depending on how the technology is applied. There may be wide-reaching implications, not necessarily in the areas Internet Service Providers (ISPs) intended. In the Iranian case, the opinion of one Information Technology (IT) company executive emerged from Iran in 2003: 'Chat and pornography have driven the whole technology sector in Iran,' said Massoud Bozorgi, CEO (Chief Executive Officer) of Chavoosh IT Development Co., the largest ISP in Esfahan, 'That's why most people buy computers. It's sad, but true.'[4]

Perhaps in reaction to such developments, the Basij (Iran's volunteer militia) announced the development of 'a chain of Internet cafes of its own, to provide religious families with access to sites upholding the Islamic values'.[5]

Accessibility in some cases clearly means – at least for some users – improved download times for 'un-Islamic' activities. A survey of cyber cafes in Sharjah in the United Arab Emirates revealed that 'many young Internet users spend most of their time chatting and searching "useless" sites. However, some do use Internet cafes for educational purposes.'[6] There are no suggestions here that the Internet was fuelling democracy; it was simply another form of entertainment or social activity. Quite how 'useless' sites can be defined scientifically is an issue for another time. However, for those seeking to bridge the 'digital divide', information about Islam may be just one strand in a broader tapestry. Even time spent accessing 'useless' sites may equip the user to tackle more significant objectives, through acquisition of practical and technical skills. Again, the theme is opportunity of access. Corporate access and software development may fuel economies, but does not necessarily trickle down to the broader population.

In some contexts, access is inhibited by language. The common language of cyber Islamic environments *was* English, reflecting the educational background of software and site developers. There has been an expansion of materials in (other) 'Muslim' languages, in minority and majority contexts, reflecting improved accessibility and software developments; for example, reliable browsers and email packages in various scripts and languages. However, many Muslim constituencies remain poorly served by the Internet. For example, Pakistan's minister of information and technology noted that '[W]ith more than 95 percent of Pakistan's literacy base in Urdu, the Internet is relevant to only the country's elite 5 percent.'[7]

The relative absence of materials in local languages – including Urdu and Arabic – may have inhibited access to the Internet. 'Scare stories' have dissuaded others from accessing the medium, or permitting members of their families from doing so. However, the Internet (in varying forms) is now an established presence in Muslim contexts.

Moving towards cheaper or free 'open-source' software could be one solution to enhancing access to the Internet in Muslim contexts. For example, the development of software based around the Linux Operating System, which is 'open' and free for users to develop (unlike systems such as Microsoft Windows), has been embraced in a number of relatively economically depressed contexts in Latin America, Asia and elsewhere. The potential availability of open-source Arabic software that was free or less expensive to install, use and develop offers one way of enhancing access to the Internet in Muslim (and other) contexts (UNDP 2002: 81). This development, in conjunction with an increase in the creation of Web software with 'Islamic' interfaces, may encourage Internet access (as well as economic and knowledge development) in some Muslim contexts. In terms of hardware provision, there has been limited development in basic and affordable computers for (and manufactured in) the developing world.

The absence of Internet access has been interpreted by some as being part of the 'problems' of Muslim societies, without consideration of the economic, cultural, social *and* religious factors behind that issue, or indeed any appropriate solutions. Others might ask whether these factors have anything to do with Islam. Does Islam need the Internet? 'Cyber-Islamic environments' have been accessible by Web browsers for over a decade on the World Wide Web (longer in other formats on the Internet), with content provided by 'established authorities' as well as individuals. The expansion of such content in languages other than English has been a significant development, reflecting improvements in software development and accessibility – together with recognition that there are audiences for such materials (UNDP 2002). These have been produced in Muslim minority and majority contexts, and one reflection of the phenomena has been the fluid transmission of thoughts and knowledge between diverse Muslim social and cultural contexts. Some focus on specific groups of Muslims, for example converts of Islam, or Muslims from specific cultural, ethnic or linguistic backgrounds.[8]

Accessibility has allowed marginalised and minority perspectives to network between themselves, and with affiliates throughout the world. Whether all such communication can be described as 'Islamic' is in the eye of the beholder, given the range of opinions this term can encompass. Clearly, in some extreme cases, the technology has permitted those without a manifest interest in 'democracy' to transmit their perspectives and agendas to a broad audience, including supporters, and to acquire new followers. Given that these perspectives (democratic and other) may be vigorously opposed to regimes in the Middle East, this leads to the question of censorship and control of the medium.

The Myth of Control

Any discussion of the Internet and Islam raises the issues of censorship and 'appropriate' website content, the demands of some states in controlling the media and explorations of how general readers approach textual sources (online and offline). For those with access and the knowledge to use the technology, there is no doubt that the Internet can provide a channel for alternative sources of information and interpretation, where consideration has been given to user-friendly (and culturally appropriate) design para-meters and content management. A good example of such channels is the substantial growth in sites providing fatwas (legal edicts) and sermons (in textual and, increasingly, multimedia formats). Some of these sites relate to government affiliated interpretations of Islam, while others provide alternative perspectives and ideas, not necessarily associated with local, cultural concepts of Islamic knowledge and religiosity (Bunt 2003).

Other sites provide opportunities for debating issues surrounding Islam, for example through chat rooms and email listings, in a way that might not be permitted in traditional and/or local settings. The content of some of these channels may be deemed divisive and contentious. Oliviér Roy[9] noted:

> I am struck by the homogenization of what is circulating all over the world under the name of Islamic religious literature. The ideas, the teachings – especially under the Wahhabi or Saudi influence – the media are more and more homogenous and transnational. If you go to the Internet – in English or in modern Arabic – you find all the literature which has been produced by the [radical] Salafis, the Wahhabis and so on. It's very important to the extent that young educated Muslims who are going to other countries for studying and so look at these websites. They exchange information. And I cannot say the same with liberal Islam, [whose ideas circulate] less.

The circulation of such ideas (whether deemed 'radical' or not) is one impact of the increased freedom of information engendered by the Internet, in conjunction with other technologies, including satellite television channels and mobile telephones. This has led to demands for censorship, as different Islamic perspectives vie for attention on the Internet.

The term 'Saudi Wahhabi' is frequently joined together in the discussion of Islam on the Internet, although its two elements are not necessarily always mutually compatible. Thus, some Wahhabi-influenced interpreta-tions of Islam are censored – where possible – by Saudi Arabian authorities because of their perceived incompatibility with national religious interests. Concerns are raised about uncensored chat rooms, or those out of the censorship reach of Saudi Arabia. Of course, censorship can take many forms: closing down (or closely controlling) a local ISP hosting hostile content may be easier than filtering content hosted abroad. Some content may require passwords to access or shift rapidly across different Internet locations – making it difficult to censor.

Defining what is 'hostile' and requiring censorship is another issue. In Saudi Arabia, it may be fatwas, sermons and/or interpretations that 'deviate' from state policy. In some cases, the original source of dissent may be beyond censorship control: the anti-American sermons of the late Sheikh al-Shuaibi continued to proliferate online after his death, causing his followers to be prosecuted in Saudi Arabia.[10] In other cases, 'dissident' opinions have been circulated through content masquerading as mainstream 'authoritative' sources, possibly damaging reputations in the process.[11] Saad al-Faqih, head of the London-based Movement for Islamic Reform in Arabia (MIRA), is one example of a 'dissident' who has drawn on the Internet to broadcast lectures and facilitate discussions on Islam, aimed against members of the Saudi royal family (see Bunt 2000: 93).

Another platform that has energetically applied the Internet to promote its views, directed against the Saudi regime, is that organised by Muhammad al-Massari (a former ally of al-Faqih) of the Committee for the Defence of Legitimate Rights (CDLR.). In February 2004, al-Massari's site hosted an English-language jihadi rap music track/video by Sheikh Terra and the Soul Salah Crew. Entitled 'Dirty Kuffar', this attracted considerable controversy, with the song's anti-Jewish and anti-American, anti-UK lyrics, and its montage of video clips eulogising Osama bin Laden and the events of 11 September 2001.[12]

More significantly, perhaps, CDLR and MIRA have provided online spaces where discussions (in Arabic and English) about different notions of 'democracy' and human rights can be discussed online. Saudi Arabia, through its Internet Service Unit, has developed an extensive filtering system for Internet content such as that provided by MIRA and CDLR.[13] This includes content filtering technologies, developed in conjunction with Western companies, which have raised the ire of anti-censorship organisations as well as 'hacktivists' promoting freedom of speech. Clearly, audiences in Saudi Arabia and elsewhere are still able to get around the censorship and access the CDLR and MIRA content online.

Blogging

'Blogging', the practice of posting a daily diary of web log (blog) on the Internet, came into prominence in Muslim contexts during 2002–3, with the emergence of 'Salam Pax'. His English language chronicle of life under Saddam Hussein, and the subsequent 'liberation' of Iraq, was produced despite the considerable danger the pseudonymous author was under (from all sides). Salam Pax eventually produced a book (2003) based on his blog and columns for the *Guardian* newspaper.

In Iran (and in Iranian communities abroad), the vibrant development of blogs has coincided with a vigorous discussion about web censorship that has reached the top levels of government. Demonstrations against Internet censorship by Iran took place at a United Nations 'digital summit' in Geneva in December 2003, and were also expressed online.[14] Censorship of web content by the Iranian government led to the United States' government sponsoring use of 'Anonymizer' electronic privacy software in Iran.[15]

Blogging has the potential to be a significant channel of 'democratic' (and other) discourse in Muslim contexts; basic software and hosting can be free. Subject to access, writers can instantly post their news and comments online, and hyperlink content with other sites. A significant turning point in blog discourse in relation to Muslim contexts was the development of Persian-script blogging tools in 2000. Hossein Derakhshan, an Iranian journalist based in Canada, was responsible for creating a blog compatible with Persian script (blogs had previously only functioned with Roman characters). Derakhshan's breakthrough creation resulted in an 'explosion' of Persian blogs, and their emergence caught the Iranian authorities off guard. Blogs were seen as instrumental in stimulating student protests in Tehran in June 2003. Derakhshan's own site, <www.Hoder.com> – along with pages such as Pedram Moallemian's <www.Eyeranian.net> – became focal points during the 2004 Iranian general elections, where Persian and English blogs provided 'eyewitness' commentaries. The concept of blogging also reached governmental offices, with the Iranian Vice-President Mohammed Ali Abtahi recording his daily activities.[16]

Derakhshan has stated that his software could be adapted for Arabic, and there has been some discussion on this issue online. However, at the time of writing Arabic language blogging was in an early developmental phase (in terms of content and composition software) compared with Persian blogs and associated services. Blogs and websites are closely related as regards technology, but they perform different tasks. Whilst Arabic writers are putting themselves online using conventional Web tools, these can lack the immediacy and ease of use of specific, popular, automated blogging tools such as 'Moveable Type' or 'Blogger'. These are not available in Arabic (or a number of other languages/scripts). In general terms, a basic web log in a 'journal' format requires less technical proficiency to update than a website. The development of freely available and user-friendly

Arabic blogging tools will lead to a substantial growth in Muslim expression online.

Digital Duels

Governments have applied the Internet as a means of observing 'dissident' activities online. However, sophisticated encryption programs have made control of many aspects of the Internet more problematic for government agencies in Muslim (and other) contexts, for example in censoring email exchanges. There are many ways of circumnavigating such controls of Internet usage.[17] States have been under attack from opponents, including hackers/crackers of varying grades of proficiency (including Muslims) seeking to compromise governmental online interests – for example through changing content of websites or accessing 'confidential' databases. These 'Muslim hackers' range from individuals to highly organised groups, not all operating with 'Islamic' agendas in mind – a small component in the global hacking and virus-writing phenomena.

During 2003, the Internet became a focus for 'dissident' activities associated with Iraq, with opposition groups utilising it as a medium for discussion. This included leaders of different religious interests. The organisation of Ayatollah al-Sistani applied the web to promote his interpretations of Islam to an audience that transcended Iraq's borders. His fatwas were made available in Arabic, English, French, Persian and Urdu.[18]

Other 'authorities', such as the Qatar-based religious scholar Sheikh Yusuf al-Qaradawi, have integrated the Internet into broader media strategies (al-Qaradawi also broadcasts on the al-Jazeera channel) giving themselves an international profile in the process. The online translations of al-Qaradawi into other languages, and the reproduction of his materials on affiliated websites, have been extremely influential, particularly following 11 September. His website statements on jihad, denouncing the targeting of civilians as contrary to Islam, were quoted in the international press.[19]

The emergence of 'online scholars' in part filled a vacuum that some traditional scholars were unaware of, or ill equipped to fill during the 1990s due to a lack of technical awareness. Now, Internet skills are being taught in Islamic seminaries, and 'conventional' national and trans-global authorities may reclaim some of the ground gained by Internet-based 'authorities'. However, it is difficult to generalise: those organisations, networks and individuals that have consistently been able to invest in developing their profile on the medium are in a good place to take advantage of improvements in accessibility, and changes in technology which are leading to new web interfaces being made available.

In terms of approaching notions of democracy, the availability of a broad range of online news sources has been significant. Al-Jazeera's influence is not exercised solely through the television set. The company invested heavily in its news website, initially in Arabic, and subsequently in English. Here it was able to compete with international news providers, competing in regional and global markets with the websites of established brands such as the BBC, CNN and NBC, all of which produce Arabic news content. Serious dangers of information overload have led to the development of news portals and aggregators, which help readers to manage the broad range of sources emerging from Islamic and Muslim contexts. Global brands for integrated 'Muslim' media (including Internet content and satellite broadcasts) have the potential to become influential.

Cyber Islamic Activism

Political-religious organisations have also become proficient news providers, with sophisticated and well-managed sites. Platforms such as Hamas, Islamic Jihad and Hizbollah have recognised that the Internet is an effective medium through which to present their perspectives. Al-Qaeda and related networks have also integrated the Internet into their propagation activities, as well as using it to mobilise their supporters. This has led to sustained attempts by their opponents to close these sites, through hacking, and through petitioning ISPs to stop hosting the sites. Al-Qaeda's affiliated al-Neda site has been attached illicitly to unsuspecting websites, and then rapidly publicised to supporters via email lists – before attracting the attention of ISPs, only for the cycle to commence again elsewhere (Bunt 2003). Hacking, cracking and other disruptive activities have been used to promote Islamic causes, and also to oppose them. This phenomenon became prominent during a 'cyber war' between pro-Palestinian and pro-Israeli supporters, which resulted in sustained disruptive activities on all 'sides'.

Given the investment of time and money in these sites, clearly their authors believe there will be a substantial return. This may take various forms, ranging from general support, through to logistical and financial assistance. Online platforms may interconnect diverse 'Islamic' campaigns. For example, Muslim sites focused on Palestine (which is not exclusively an 'Islamic' issue) may draw their readers to 'related' content on other issues and contexts, as part of a wider global dialogue on (their perspective of) Islam. Thus, opinions on, for example, Afghanistan, Algeria, Bosnia, Kashmir, Moros, Chechnya, Iraq and/or Kurdish campaigns are interconnected online. 'Real world' networking and the ideals of the umma are reflected, and in some cases created and facilitated, through the Internet.

Such application of the World Wide Web may be applied as a reason for preventing or limiting general access to computers and the Internet. This negates the potential of the medium as a means of facilitating other forms of dialogue, and also of presenting alternative perspectives of Islam to the wider world. Marginalised sectors of society can be empowered through the use of the Internet, whether this is Palestinian refugees networking with one another in dispersed camps, or Malaysian Muslim women using the Web to discuss perspectives on polygamy.

The Internet can be applied as a campaigning tool on issues of concern to Muslims, such as the sites highlighting the position of prisoners held at the Guantanamo Bay detention camp (by the USA). <www.Cageprisoners. com> produced a multimedia online video entitled 'The Forgotten Ones', and linked into human rights organisations such as Amnesty International. The campaigning potential of the Web in relation to global human rights issues has been exploited by a number of causes. The same potential has been used on domestic political issues, notably in Malaysia where the imprisonment of former deputy prime minister Anwar Ibrahim led to the creation of a plethora of 'reformasi' sites publicising his plight.

The nature of the Internet has encouraged marginalised Muslims, whose perspectives might not always be interpreted as 'Islamic' to develop a voice and a networking capability online: this includes gay, lesbian and bi-sexual Muslims between and within Muslim majority and minority contexts, whose application of sites such as <www.al-Fatiha.net> and <www.Queer Jihad> has attracted considerable attention (and at times negative comments). Irshad Manji has used her <www.Muslim-Refusenik.com> site to develop her profile as a 'lesbian feminist Muslim'.[20] In February 2004, a report suggested that – under pressure from American activists – access to gay Saudi websites was unblocked.[21]

In some Muslim contexts, the extent to which such developments will be interpreted as an indication of 'democracy' and/or one of the 'dangers' of the Internet, is open to question. Certainly, the Web also offers vehement denunciations of such sites, questioning their Muslim and Islamic credentials. The Web highlights the number of different notions of what Muslim identity really means, to individuals, groups and communities.

Islamic Web Applications

Other websites emphasise specific interests, with an Islamic angle. Away from the world of politics and community affairs, one significant and popular area of the Web is the development of marriage bureaux online, offering 'appropriate' matches based on established religious and cultural norms. A good example is the Iranian website/marriage bureau <www. Ardabili.com>, endorsed by several senior clerics, enabling its organiser Jaffar Savalanpour Ardabili to undertake his duties. He also answers email questions in relation to jurisprudence. However, in 2003 the Basij arrested users and operators of an Internet dating service in Iran, under charges of 'unlawful actions'.[22] London-based <www.MuslimMatch.com> 'boasts 47,648 registered members and 1,500 first-time visitors a day'.[23]

Such 'popular' sites can draw visitors to other cyber-Islamic environments, and may be seen as an appropriate or 'halal' application of technology. Other areas of the Internet, such as chat rooms, provide other forms of relationships online. These do not necessarily fall into an approved category, and have been the focus of fatwas from concerned authorities seeking to discourage or ban their use. Religious authorities have had to react rapidly to social changes caused by the Internet in this way, and provide advice and opinions on the appropriate use of technology.

Some previously reluctant sectors of Muslim belief have recognised the need to go online to meet the needs of their communities or networks. Through creating attractive portals and online services, they have sought to channel readers to their shade of the Islamic spectrum and to manage knowledge associated with their belief perspective. Broad-ranging sites may include Qur'anic translations and commentaries, (regulated) chat rooms, free email services, women's and children's sections and community services. These are often networked to a wider affiliated global constituency.

Information management has become a crucial area for some Muslim perspectives. At this key point in Muslim societal development, not all sites keep accessible archives of previous web pages or documents, nor do they preserve digital materials such as news services. There is also an absence of sophisticated central 'libraries' of Islamic knowledge online. These are areas that may see a change, reflecting the increasing sophistication of databases and their users, with materials preserved in accessible formats for future users.

One project in this area is the International Islamic Digital Library project, organised by the National Library of Malaysia, and collaborating with al-Azhar University in Egypt, al-Marashi al-Najafi Library in Iran, and other institutions.[24] Clearly, editorial control (and levels of censorship) will be critical issues. Such a development may also be seen as a democratising tool, contributing to an assertive Islamic knowledge economy online, perhaps in conjunction with more 'conventional' resources.[25] The new Alexandria Library in Egypt was presented in 2003 with a digital library copy of the Alexa Internet Archive, containing 10 billion web pages.[26] However, the extent to which libraries in Muslim contexts will seek to develop an organised archive of websites relating directly to Islamic expression online (including sites referred to in this chapter) is open to question.

Conclusion

An Islamic information revolution, based around the Internet, could have profound implications for Muslim societies. Some would say that this revolution is already occurring, opening up societies to new influences and forms of knowledge. The truth of this assessment depends on the measurement criteria. Developments relating to Islam and the Internet have to be seen in relation to issues of accessibility to the medium, as well as Islamic content and context. The ideals and clichés associated with 'freedom of expression' in Muslim contexts should be evaluated in the context of Internet controls and censorship, which have been enabled with varying levels of success in different societies. These are complex issues, associated with diverse macro- and micro-cultures and contexts, not all of which have been approached here. Several future possibilities emerge, potential models of Islam and Muslims interacting with the Internet to a greater or lesser degree. This might not constitute a 'revolution', but a gradual integration of Internet technologies and Islamic expectations, in which manifestations of 'democracy' may form a vital strand.

Part 3
Audience Practices

14. The Media Consumption of Young British Muslims

Sameera Ahmed

The representation of Islam and Muslims in the Western media has been the subject of much debate amongst academics, media institutions, Muslim organisations and the general pubic alike.[1] This interest and concern has become more significant following the events of September 2001 (Bunglawala 2002; Allen 2001). The impact of this representation has often been analysed in relation to the perceptions and opinion formation of non-Muslims.[2] However, also of considerable importance are the reactions and media consumption habits of Muslims themselves.

The salience of media in the development of attitudes, perceptions and 'received wisdom' is increasingly evident in contemporary society. The media occupy a more prominent position in our social and cultural landscapes and its ubiquity has become a normal part of our lives. In addition, community or particularistic media (Dayan 1998) are becoming especially important in providing minority groups with their own voices and alternative sources of information. Their conscious avoidance of certain media and consumption of alternative media is a reflection of the developments that are taking place within the communities themselves.

Having analysed the context and history within which much of this representation exists in previous chapters, as well as the media production practices and output itself, this chapter examines audience practices by considering the consumption of media by a selected group of young British Muslims.[3] In describing their audience practices, the concept of 'media' is extended beyond the traditionally recognised print and electronic forms to include social and cultural activities, religious learning and knowledge acquisition, and new methods of information exchange. Consequently, the consumption of this broader range of media appears to be developing a sense of British Muslim identity amongst its readers. The various ways in which this identity is manifesting itself will be explored in this chapter. Furthermore, in order to illustrate the potential Muslim media landscape that these young Muslims have access to, and to provide a context in which this consumption takes place, a brief overview of the Muslim press is given, including the opinions of selected publication editors.

Britain's Muslim Press

The existence of the Muslim press[4] in Britain is a relatively recent phenomenon. Although a small number of publications have been in circulation for many years,[5] the majority of publications have a shorter history. The events of late 1989 onwards with respect to the Muslim community, specifically the reaction to Salman Rushdie's book, *The Satanic Verses*, and the first military action in the Gulf, were the background events during which the beginnings of much of the Muslim press can be framed. The demand for media in English grew as this became the preferred language for an increasing number of Muslims. Historically, newspapers were often written in the mother tongue (for example *The Jang* and *Awaz* in Urdu), effectively cutting out many second-generation Muslims[6] who, while having a basic command of spoken Urdu, Punjabi or Bengali, for instance, were often not fluent in reading or writing it. As Muslim communities developed a more distinctly religious identity, alternatives to mainstream media were sought through which to express this identity. In addition the Muslim media became an important means by which information was obtained and ideas developed. Those with a desire to maintain and strengthen cultural and religious identities saw a strong and vibrant media as one way to help achieve this.

Editors interviewed stated that their intention was to produce a publication – title, content and outlook – that strongly reflected the Muslim or Islamic identity both of its producers and its readers. They were conscious about distinguishing themselves from the British *Asian* media and though the nature of the British Muslim population meant that a large proportion of Muslims were South Asian, the producers wanted a strictly *Muslim* identity and this was also encouraged by the readers. Thus a combination both of the demand from within the Muslim community as well as editors' own conviction brought about the realisation of Muslim media.

> We were aiming our magazine at young second generation British Muslims and these are the people who have made up their mind that Britain is their country, who want to come to terms with their lives and the fact that they are British and they are Muslims and we wanted to capture the day-to-day struggle about each aspect of their lives. (*Q-News*)

When the editor of *The Invitation* was asked to describe the magazine he said:

> We started [in 1989] to run a study circle... with the idea to attract young Muslim boys and to also support them with their school work and with that came other *dawah*[7] opportunities like holding regular

quarterly youth camps and from that sprang the idea of actually putting things on paper... the idea was really to reach the young people who couldn't read Urdu... our priority has always been Muslim youngsters.

Similar to mainstream media the range of issues covered by the publications varies. Editorials, news, book and conference reviews, profiles, regular contributors, spiritual sections, question and answer, matrimonial, jobs and advertising are amongst some of the regular features. Most publications (excluding specialist ones) tend to have a combination of current affairs, social and 'religious' issues. The latter category comprised of faith or belief issues, explanations on the Qur'an[8] and *Hadith*,[9] 'how to' guides on certain practices in Islam and reminders of special dates in the Islamic calendar. Social and cultural matters relating to Muslims in Britain and dealing with problems in the community were also a focus. Frequency of publication (weekly, monthly, bi-monthly etc.) automatically influenced the currency of topics.

The diversity of Muslim media is illustrated by the different kinds of publications available. In a way this diversity represents the variety of opinions, organisations and perspectives amongst the British Muslim population. Identifications with various ways of thinking and approaches to Islam such as different political inclinations, *dawah* oriented outlooks, academic or spiritual Islam, are facilitated and reinforced by different publications. Certain fundamental aspects of identifying oneself with Islam are shared by almost all the publications, but there is also diversity amongst them which is a reflection of the community itself.

The role of the Muslim press appeared to be of particular significance after the attacks of 11 September 2001. Muslim media were particularly concerned about covering the issue because of the immediate focus on Muslims that resulted from the attacks. They provided a platform for discussion not only within the established readership but arguably opened new avenues for debate amongst those who would not normally access ethnic or religious media. The exchange between mainstream and alternative press was also clear as writers from the Muslim press were invited to write in mainstream press, not only about the attacks on the USA but on other matters relevant to Britain's Muslims.

Consuming British Muslim Publications

In recent years British Muslim publications have evolved considerably and increased in number. There are now a variety of media including newspapers, magazines, journals and community publications. The production and demand for these publications was fuelled partly by dissatisfaction with mainstream media as well as the desire to seek alternative perspectives, not only on issues relating to Muslims but other issues too. Research has shown that the role and use of alternative and community media amongst minority ethnic communities is considerable under 'normal' circumstances (Dayan 1998; Husband 2002). However, in recent years and especially following the extraordinary events of September 2001, the importance of these media not only as a source of information but also as a channel through which minority communities express their views and anxieties has increased substantially. In this research several reasons were given for reading Muslim publications[10] (see Table 14.1).

Clearly the most frequently stated reason, Muslim current affairs, would have increased considerably at the time of September 2001 and in subsequent days. In view of recent world events affecting Muslims, including the military operations in Afghanistan and Iraq, ongoing concerns such as Palestine and Kashmir and more recent incidents involving Chechnya and Sudan, this interest in current affairs will continue. For many of the reasons cited above, including mistrust and cynicism towards mainstream media, young Muslims actively sought alternative sources of information about the events linked to September 2001.[11] This included not only domestic sources but also international news media and satellite channels, including al-Jazeera. As well as questioning the news media and their coverage of both pre- and post-September 11 issues, Muslim readers were critical of government reactions to the event. In addition, the number of non-Muslims accessing Muslim media would also have increased at this time, including the use of Muslim publications by the government to communicate its views and responses to the Muslim public.[12]

Table 14.1. Reasons for Reading Publications

Reason[1]	Frequency
Muslim current affairs (national and international)	47
Religious knowledge	21
Interesting news/articles	9
Supporting Muslim media	7
News from alternative perspective	5
Sense of community/unity	4
Disillusionment with mainstream media	3
Reviews	2
Academic study	2

1　Respondents often gave more than one reason.

Accessing Muslim media facilitates the desire to keep informed about fellow Muslims, feel part of a larger group and keep in touch with what is happening in the rest of the Muslim world. All of these lead to a greater sense of belonging to the global *umma*. The importance of this belonging and identification with the global community was noticed by Jacobson (1998) and Vertovec (1998) in their studies of young Muslims. Also, Anderson's (1983) concept of an 'imagined community' is evoked in people's reasons for using the media, and increased awareness means identification with other Muslims is stronger. In this way the media appear to provide a focus that gives a sense of belonging to British Muslim communities. Though the experiences of community and belonging are facilitated by other aspects of people's lives, the media have enhanced these to a considerable degree.

In general, there was a consensus amongst the young South Asian Muslims interviewed in this study that Muslim media had great potential to develop further, encompass more information and appeal to a larger number of people. There was an appreciation of what already existed and it was seen as a positive way to initiate debate amongst Muslim communities that potentially could extend to mainstream society. However, most respondents commented that the current media, particularly the press, need more publicity. The purpose of setting up Muslim publications was seen to be to educate the Muslim community about Islamic issues as well as giving information about what was happening in the *umma* across the world. Another reason stated was to counteract the negative portrayal of Islam and Muslims in the mainstream Western media. They considered some publications better than others, but the overall feeling was that mainstream media is biased against Islam and Muslims and generated negative perceptions amongst the general public about the religion. Conversely, their use of Muslim media stemmed from the need to understand issues and events from an alternative viewpoint and they saw gaining Islamic knowledge and increasing awareness of issues relating to Muslims as a more 'serious' aspect of their media intake. Though scepticism about mainstream media has encouraged the use of alternative sources, in some ways the diet of media for young Muslims was similar to young people from other ethnic and religious groups. It included mainstream television shows, soap operas, comedies, dramas, news and sports programmes as well as ethnic and religious media.

Many of the Muslim publications are written and edited by Muslims who were born in Britain. This made them more accessible and the issues they report on easier to relate to for younger British Muslims. The appeal of these publications to young Muslims seemed greater because people from their own generation, with similar experiences and aspirations, communicated to them in an engaging manner the problems and challenges they face. Indeed, Muslim media reflect the changing culture and demographics of Muslims in Britain and the views it represents, the issues it discusses and the way it does so differ from the first generation of British Muslims. As such it is pivotal in constructing a discourse on contemporary British Muslim life.

Muslim Media – More Than Just a Good Read

It is clear from this research study that Muslim media are facilitating various functions for its readers. It is evident that Muslim media (defined in the broadest sense) are contributing to local and global community and identity; Islamic knowledge and learning; family and gender issues; and the formation of new cultural habits.

The notion of being *British* and *Muslim* has become an issue that is widely debated amongst academics, policy makers, the general public and the media. Following September 2001 this concept has gained significance, whereby the loyalty of Muslims and security of Britain are constantly being questioned. In order to say how Muslim media are being used to articulate a Muslim identity, the survey in this research asked specific questions on the sense of belonging gained through media and how this helps readers to think about their own identity. Many respondents noted how the media enabled them to identify with and feel part of a Muslim community and helped strengthen their identity as Muslims – locally, nationally and going beyond simple diaspora connections to the global *umma*. In some responses there was a clear distinction between feeling part of a British community and a global *umma*. The sense from some responses seemed to be that there was more of a feeling of a global *umma* rather than of local or national community.

> Muslim media has immensely developed my sense of belonging to an '*umma*' as articles on Islam are unifying as they entail Islamic beliefs. I don't think the sense of belonging to a *British* Muslim community is all that evident, as Muslim media is too intent on showing the pitfalls of young Muslims living in Britain. [original emphasis]. (Female, age 19. *Trends*)

> There are a number of Muslim newspapers I've seen and I feel they strengthen the Muslim community here and inform people about what's happening and what they should do. (Female, age 24. *Trends*)

172

The concept of identity linked very strongly to knowing about other Muslims and their condition. Being informed about Muslims around the world seemed to have a direct link to how people identified themselves as Muslims.

I certainly feel part of an active community. I feel less isolated, better informed about Islamic issues. (Male, age 25. *Q-News*)

It has helped me to understand a Muslim perspective on issues and made me more confident to be a Muslim and has reinforced my identity as a result. (Male, age 30. *Muslim News*)

For many, their identity has been directly influenced by the existence of Muslim media. Muslim media are indeed playing a role in establishing and developing a sense of being a British Muslim, a sense which encompasses beliefs and practices and various elements of socio-cultural, political and economic issues. As the concept of British Muslim identity is specifically discussed within most publications, readers are automatically focused on this issue and can relate to the experiences of others in their community.

Muslim media are also playing a key role in developing and disseminating Islamic knowledge to Muslims, particularly in diaspora communities (Mandaville 2001). Not only have young Muslims utilised Muslim media as an alternative to mainstream media but they are actively seeking out Muslim 'media' to fulfil the obligation of obtaining religious knowledge. Almost every Muslim publication is concerned with imparting Islamic knowledge to its readers, though the specific outlook of this varies between publications. For some respondents the presence of Muslim media was essential in providing them with Islamic knowledge, and the easy access to and the informal style of many publications made obtaining information more flexible than through structured learning. Actively seeking knowledge through literature, electronic sources, events or more traditional styles of learning is a strong symbol of the assertion of Muslim identities. Thus, the emphasis placed on seeking knowledge in Islam manifests itself through this proactive attitude towards learning. This focus on Islamic learning is also visible in academia, with organisations emerging to deal with the roles and responsibilities of Muslim academics, researchers and students.

Apart from reporting on events around the country and globally, the Muslim media work to influence and shape the way Muslim communities themselves develop. Not only does their content set a particular agenda but the way in which this is written also has an influence on how the readers frame issues. For those readers who are actively looking to the Muslim media as their main source of information and as a way through which to measure their own opinions, its presence is vital. Using the media as a stimulus for discussions with other Muslims is one way of developing concepts and issues in the community. Cases of discrimination, relevant political activity, issues of education, employment and similar concerns are shared, and the media highlight these experiences to reflect the reality of living in Britain as Muslims. The shared experiences portrayed in the media encourage a perception of shared identity as Muslims in various parts of Britain are tackling similar issues and facing the same challenges. So whilst raising awareness amongst its readers, the Muslim media are also contributing to a sense of belonging to a particular community and are thus enhancing a British Muslim identity.

It is apparent that certain groups of young Muslims are placing great emphasis on adapting their behaviour, including their media habits, to facilitate their affiliation to Islam. Not only are their reading and watching habits influenced by their religion but other aspects of their lives are also affected. Conferences, lectures, seminars, study circles, camps and gatherings as well as books, other publications, audio-visual media and the Internet are some of the components that can be placed within a broad definition of media. There are numerous topics discussed at these events and some of the common themes include living as Muslims in the contemporary Western world; issues relating to *dawah*; unity amongst Muslims; concerns of Muslim students; the essentials of belief and practice such as praying, fasting, giving alms and performing the pilgrimage. Exhibitions of Islamic art and crafts, calligraphy, spiritual music and religious poems are also available at these gatherings and new outlets have been set up for the distribution of such materials.

By using this concept it can be seen that media consumption is a very important aspect of the 'active identity' of young Muslims. They have made conscious decisions to replace many social and educational elements in their lives with those of an overtly Islamic nature. Thus, an entire social, cultural and educational infrastructure appears to be developing amongst young Muslims that provides 'Islamic' alternatives in areas of entertainment and social life, but more importantly in news and the acquisition of knowledge.

Summary

The emergence of a distinct Muslim media has provided a focal point through which Muslims, and particularly young Muslims, can find expression of their concerns and aspirations. Enthusiasm for Muslim media demonstrates the need for a public discourse on Islam and Muslims and Muslim media. The press in particular at this stage have articulated a British Muslim-ness that readers find increasingly relevant to their lives. The numerous forms of community media, both new and old, are enabling Muslims to explore new ways of expressing their conviction to Islam and what it means to be Muslim, as well as creating new hybrid cultures which merge together aspects of Islam, South Asian culture and British cultural norms. These in turn are being complemented by increasing information about Islam at a global level and giving rise to new relationships between young British Muslims and their international associates.

The role of Muslim media in articulating the concerns of British Muslims and serving as an apparatus through which to voice the diverse opinions within the Muslim communities looks set to increase in significance. At the same time as helping to develop and sustain new identifications with Islam and forming 'British Muslim' identities, with increasing attention now on Muslim publications and other channels of information dissemination, their role as 'spokesperson' for Muslim communities will also increase in significance. In light of the events of September 2001, and indeed more recent events, the new 'spaces' that are being created by Muslim media are crucial. These spaces are enabling Muslims to express their views and debate those issues that are of concern to them, whilst also anticipating that some of the discourses present in Muslim media may filter through to mainstream media audiences.[13]

British South Asian Muslims, especially the younger generations, are using various media channels, including not only new information technologies but also social and cultural activities, to exchange information and disseminate knowledge about their experiences of living as Muslims in Britain. Some of these activities are aimed at including the non-Muslim population with the sole objective of trying to dispel the myths and inaccurate information about Islam and Muslims, which have circulated as a result of irresponsible and sensationalist media representations. The perceptions and attitudes held by their non-Muslim counterparts, the impact these have had on their relationships, Muslims' own experiences and expectations of living as a religious minority in the West and the future of a multi-religious coexistence, are all issues that will continue to be of concern. The media will undoubtedly be one of the most significant arenas in which these concerns are debated and recorded and the Muslim media occupy the primary position in articulating the standpoint of British Muslims.

15. Arab Public Opinion in the Age of Satellite Television: the Case of al-Jazeera

Mohamed Zayani

Until not long ago, there was a perception that Arab public opinion did not matter. As such, it did not seem to affect the policies of governments in the Middle East and North Africa or alter their behaviour in any significant way. When it comes to foreign policies, Arab governments did not need to take into account what people thought or heed their wishes, which is tantamount to saying that power politics and public opinion in the Arab World did not usually spin on the same axis. According to Joseph Farah (2001), Arab public opinion does not drive action by Arab leaders because of a democracy deficit in Arab nations. In the same way Arab leaders do not submit themselves to the will of the people, 'the public is not free to express opinions that might run counter to the official government line' (Farah 2001). Because of the profoundly undemocratic and authoritarian nature of governments in most if not all Arab countries, public opinion hardly makes any difference: 'Since meaningful free elections are largely unknown in the Arab world, public opinion is worth nothing' (ibid.). Writing about the Arab public's reaction to the war against Iraq, Illin, Thorn and Burton (2003) put forth the same line of argument: 'As for claims to be able to discern Arab or Muslim public opinion, either in general or within any one country, they must all be regarded as highly suspect ... There is no genuine Arab public opinion to be discerned, and not much in most other Muslim countries.'

While for some observers Arab public opinion is a figment of imagination and a myth, for political scientists like Mohammed Oifi (2003), it is a variable that is hard to ignore, particularly since managing a transnational public space is increasingly becoming a constraint which the American administration as well as Arab governments have to integrate in their strategies. According to Telhami (2002), Arab public opinion has always existed but was largely kept under control, as was public displeasure. Even when on occasions it made itself heard, Arab public opinion had a somewhat limited effect. A case in point is the relevance – or lack thereof – of Arab public opinion during the Second Gulf War:

> In 1990, even though the 'Arab street' was generally opposed to the US-led war against Iraq, that did not prevent several Arab governments from cooperating strategically with the United States. Indeed, the ability of the United States and its allied Arab governments, especially Egypt and Saudi Arabia, to increase their influence in the region after the Persian Gulf War in 1991 was an indication to many analysts in Washington that Arab public opinion was not especially relevant. They concluded that the way to do business with the Middle East was by building relations with rulers through a strategy of incentives and threats, and then relying on rulers to bring their peoples along. (Telhami 2002)

All things considered, Arab public opinion may have had a felt presence, particularly during times of war or periods of turmoil in the region, but was not a force to contend with or a variable that decisively could sway things in a particular direction. States were largely successful in pacifying the public mood during times of crisis and reining-in public demonstrations when they grew large: 'Because demonstrations do not occur in [most Arab] countries without the written consent or, at times, the prodding of the authorities, it is clear that Arab governments have found a way to exploit antiwar sentiment, rather than suppress it, for fear it will ultimately turn against them' (Schanzer 2003). This is not to undermine Arab public opinion. Noting that there is often an interaction between Arab publics and their governments, David Pollock (1992) suggests, in one of the few works on Arab public opinion, that Arab politics is far from being confined to a thin and brittle upper crust and, further, that Arab governments usually pay attention to the views of their public and respond to them differently. Although in most cases Arab public opinion did not matter much, in some cases it mattered a little, while in a few instances it mattered considerably.

Increasingly, however, Arab public opinion has acquired a certain relevance, particularly as attempts to contain 'the Arab street' have become a challenge. In more recent years, however, Arab public opinion has managed to register a more imposing presence and to reflect more assertively the frustrations and aspirations of the people. A number of factors have contributed to the consolidation of the role public opinion plays in Arab societies and Arab politics. These include the succession of wars and crises in the Arab and Islamic world in general, and the Middle

East in particular, as well as the advent of globalisation, the interconnectedness of local and global issues and the influence of the discourse on democracy. Likewise, the eminence and spread of satellite television in the Arab World have played a role in consolidating a pan Arab public opinion. The fact that Arab governments were able to control their people was to a certain extent facilitated by control over the media. At the turn of the century, however, it has become increasingly hard to control what people watch and think. Over the past decade or so, the Arab media scene has witnessed the rise of a wide spectrum of satellite channels, many of which were keen on addressing issues of common concern to all Arabs across state boundaries. The emergence of a vibrant mediascape in the Arab World is not without effects. According to Telhami (2002), in the age of satellite television the Arab public started to matter more in challenging the wisdom of their governments:

> In the era of globalization, public opinion in the region may have even a greater impact on the policies of Arab governments. An information revolution has overtaken governmental media monopolies... The information revolution has empowered the public in the region on a scale that has never been seen before. The Arab public opinion can no longer be disregarded.

Nowhere is the issue of the impact of Arab media on public opinion more insistent than in the case of al-Jazeera – an all news channel beamed out of the tiny peninsula of Qatar. Catapulted to international prominence since 11 September 2001 and more specifically during the war in Afghanistan, al-Jazeera has in no time managed to acquire a leading role in the Arab media scene. According to a recent report on Middle East communication (Spotbeam Communications 2002), al-Jazeera has become 'centre-stage in the modernization of Arab-language broadcasting', so much so that it developed the potential to influence Arab public opinion and Arab politics. The rigidity of the political establishment in most Arab countries has made al-Jazeera – with its bold and daring coverage of a variety of political, social and religious topics which strike a cord with Arab viewers – a relatively more credible, albeit controversial, alternative. By projecting an undeclared reformist agenda, best epitomised by the network's institutionalisation of the right to have access to the media for the representatives of the region's various voices, al-Jazeera has in a way succeeded in aligning itself with 'the people', in fact, with a large section of Arab society which has been disenfranchised. Breaking away with the culture of political restrain, the network has helped instill what loosely may be described as a 'culture of accountability' as political figures and policy makers have seemingly become answerable to their public. With its motto 'the view and the opposite view', al-Jazeera has even earned itself the reputation of a parliament on the air.

Although the information available about the number of al-Jazeera viewers is anecdotal and, at best, amounts to rough estimates, the large viewer-base of the network is hard to deny. According to a 2002 Gallup poll conducted in nine Arab or Muslim countries (Kuwait, Saudi Arabia, Lebanon, Jordan, Morocco, Turkey, Iran, Pakistan and Indonesia), al-Jazeera is widely watched (Saad 2002). Part of the appeal of the channel is its ability to expand what people in the Arab Middle East can talk about. The network's profile, as well as the make up and diversity of its personnel, have also contributed to its success. With staff from a range of Arab countries and broadcasting in standard Arabic from within the Arab Middle East (during times when eminent Saudi media ventures like MBC and Orbit were broadcasting from European capitals) the channel is often perceived as toeing a pan-Arab line and 'promoting an Arab nationalist discourse' (Al Shammari 1999: 45) which many viewers identify with. Watched by scores of Arabs both within and outside the Arab Middle East, this transnational Arab channel is often seen as providing the context for an Arab unity impulse. By tapping into the Arab identity, al-Jazeera gradually evolved from a transnational broadcaster to a potential opinion maker that cannot be ignored. By providing instant access to news and discussing issues that matter to Arabs most al-Jazeera has gradually developed the potential to influence public opinion. Of course, Arab media cannot be reduced to al-Jazeera, nor can Arab public opinion be said to be implacably moulded by this channel; to argue otherwise is to run the risk of homogenising Arab viewers. Still, one can venture that, occasionally, the sense of political awareness al-Jazeera has been nurturing in ordinary Arab viewers translates into signs of popular pressure on Arab governments to step up their efforts to act on certain issues and to alter their tame policy. This is particularly the case with the coverage of the Palestinian intifada, the war in Afghanistan and the invasion of Iraq. In some instances, al-Jazeera allegedly has sparked demonstrations, prompted occasional protests and inflamed public opinion, so much so that some Arab governments are finding it more and more pressing to keep pace with popular opinion.

If the network has been a thorn in the side of Arab governments, many of whom have filed official complaints with the Qatari Foreign Ministry about some of al-Jazeera's practices or programmes, it has also proven to be a *bête noire* for the American administration. During the so-called War on Terrorism, al-Jazeera has particularly infuriated American officials. It came under close scrutiny and harsh criticism from the United States for its coverage of the war in Afghanistan and the invasion of Iraq. Upon transmitting the controversial Al Qaeda videotapes, al-Jazeera was accused of serving as a mouthpiece of Al Qaeda, providing bin Laden with a platform from which to preach jihad on 'the West', in general, and the United States, in particular. al-Jazeera was also criticised for its tendency to air grisly footage and graphic pictures of killed children, wounded civilians and destroyed homes, for no other reason than to 'to drum up viewership or else to propagandize against the United States' (Hume 2001). Afraid of losing the information war, the USA tried to muzzle al-Jazeera. In official circles, the network was often criticised and characterised as being vitriolic and irresponsible. It was also demonised in the press, its offices in Kabul and Baghdad hit by American missiles, its website hacked and some of its journalists detained for a while.

The United States' obsession with al-Jazeera is curious to say the least. For all practical purposes, al-Jazeera could well represent virtually all that went wrong in the Arab and Muslim world. In spite of al-Jazeera's claim to unbiased news, the channel has often been blamed for its sensational approach and for its tendency to air what viewers want to see. For some critics, al-Jazeera's 'success with audiences has caused a strident and highly politicized tone to creep into some of its programming' (*The Economist* 13 October 2001: 46). In the words of Thomas Friedman (2001: 31), the channel sometimes 'goes over the edge and burns people unfairly'. There is a perception, common among many Western critics, that the channel has a distinctly anti-Western orientation that makes it a platform for demagoguery. Not surprisingly then, al-Jazeera has been heavily criticised for galvanising Arab radicalism. While for Friedman (2001: 31) the kind of journalism al-Jazeera engages in deliberately 'fans the flames of Muslim outrage', for Makovsky (2001:26) it insidiously 'reinforces existing prejudices'. Overall, al-Jazeera is perceived as a maverick media outlet 'moving the masses in uncontrolled ways' (Hammond 2001: 22). For Poniwozik (2001: 65), it is one of three institutions that have the power to influence people: 'Among all the major influences on Arab public opinion – the mosque, the press, the schools – the newest and perhaps most revolutionary is al-Jazeera.'

The foregoing analysis points to a number of insistent questions: can and does alternative Arab media mobilise the masses? Does al-Jazeera have the ability to influence the Arab public opinion? Does it really sway people to think in a particular way? Can it frame issues in ways that shape the views and opinions of its viewers? Answering these questions, which are of paramount importance, requires an analysis of Arab public opinion and an understanding of a number of variables that affect public opinion formation, particularly in the Arab–American context.

More than ever before, the United States has become fixated on the question of Arab public opinion for obvious reasons. Public opinion polls conducted in the Arab and Muslim world reflect an unfavourable and even negative view towards the United States. Still, it is hard to claim that such an attitude bespeaks a deep-seated cultural chasm. According to a 2002 poll conducted by Zogby International, the unfavourable opinion towards the United States is far from being merely an anti-Western feeling or antagonism towards Western culture per se as impressions of France and Germany tend to be relatively favourable (Zogby 2003). As Tessler and Corstange (2002: 29–31) point out, many of the surveys investigating the Arabs' attitude towards the United States reveal a constant pattern, namely a generally positive and more favourable attitude towards American society and culture but a strong dislike of the US foreign policy.

Although arguable, such reasoning does not do justice to the complex and intricate nature of Arab public opinion. Brumberg (2002) recognises the politicised nature of the issue but finds such a framework inadequate for understanding the intricacies of Arab public opinion. In his view, the negative attitudes of Arab public opinion towards the United States cannot simply be relegated to the failure of the latter, under the Bush administration, to play an effectual and impartial role in seeking a long-lasting settlement for the Palestinian issue or its faltering policy in the Middle East. Accordingly, Brumberg proposes to depoliticise the issue by enacting a vivisection of Arab public opinion. In his words, Arab (and Muslim) public opinion is made up of three circles of influence – the ideologues, the professional elite and the broad populace. At the core of these circles are political activists as well as Arab-nationalist and 'illiberal'-Islamist ideologues whose hostility towards the US is informed by an 'ideology of resentment'. Their ideology of alienation is about identity and power rather than any pragmatic problem. The second circle is made up of the immediate audience of these ideologues, namely students and professionals. The outer circle encompasses the overwhelming majority of Arab society. Although the latter group has an anti-Western attitude that does not necessarily emanate from the 'ideology of resentment' that is espoused by the members of the first circle, it can be mobilised by the members of the first circle during times of national or international crises. The economic condition of the third group makes it particularly vulnerable to the demagoguery of the first group. According to Brumberg (2002), the combined effect of economic despair in Arab countries (as evidenced by the rate of unemployment) and failed political systems (as epitomised by the absence of participatory forms of government that give young people a sense that they can control or at least influence their futures) makes many young people vulnerable to demagoguery:

> The potential universe of recruits to the ideology of resentment espoused by Islamists and Arab nationalists is very large indeed. Young people who are frustrated, bored or angry, and who tend to get their news from satellite TV stations rather than a responsible, professional press, are particularly vulnerable to the simplistic slogans of Islamist demagogues, and to the daily images of strife in various quarters of the Islamic world. (Brumberg 2002)

However, such mobilisation, Brumberg points out, comes at irregular cycles and its sudden cresting cannot be sustained for a long time. Whether they take the form of street protests, university demonstrations or mass marches, such 'spontaneous outbursts are difficult to sustain and can be suppressed' (Brumberg 2002).

Although insightful, Brumberg's exegesis is not without problems. To start with, the attempt to depoliticise the notion of 'Arab public opinion' tends to drain it from its dynamism. Arab public opinion operates in dynamic interaction with Arab government policies as well as regional, and to a certain extent international politics. Likewise, the author does not emphasise enough the internal diversity of Arab opinions. As David Pollock (1992) points out, Arab public opinion is not static, uniform or monolithic; rather it is dynamic, diverse and complex. Furthermore, the typology of Arab public opinion Brumberg puts forth seems unable to dissociate or distance itself enough from earlier formulations about Arab public opinion that are inherent in the very terminology used to designate it. In the 1950s and 1960s, the common terminology was the 'Arab masses'. During the heyday of Arab nationalism, Gamal Abdel Nasser, who was well served by radio *Sawt al Arab*, succeeded in capturing the hearts and minds of the 'Arab masses'. Gradually, this term – which has Marxist overtones (namely the notion of the proletariat, class struggle and angry protests) – gave way to the 'Arab street'. For John Kifner (2001), the idea of the street, which denoted a shared, cohesive body of views and values, was not a fixed idea. Since the wave of nationalism that threatened to topple down governments, 'the street's sentiments have been by turns nationalist, socialist, Baathist, Palestinian, and now increasingly Islamic'. The 1979 Islamic revolution in Iran and more specifically the role the Iranian people played in such a historical moment has crystallised the power of the street. The vast participation of people has contributed greatly to the success of the revolution that was inspired by the Imam Ayatollah Khomeini, and which in many ways changed the dynamics of the Middle East. Over time, the term 'Arab street' – being often associated with the vulgarised image of angry protests – has come to be perceived as derogatory. For James Zogby (2003), the concept of Arab street is a misnomer as it 'appears to be demeaning almost like a faceless rabble'. With the pressure for political reform in the Middle East region and the call for democratisation, the term 'Arab public opinion' acquired a particular relevance. For Mohammed Oifi (2005: 74), the shift in terminology is interesting as it gives the impression of change more than it reflects real change:

> After the 1991 Gulf War, a number of elections were held in the Arab world. The main purpose behind these elections was to bestow some legitimacy on a power that was strongly contested by the Islamist parties. It is in the framework of this 'transition towards democracy' that the term 'public opinion' acquired a particular pertinence, giving the illusion that citizens can choose among several competing projects in society and that they do play a role in a process which in reality aims at depriving them from their will.

Finally, and no less problematic in Brumberg's formulations, is the contention that Arab satellite television channels like al-Jazeera are shaping what the public thinks:

> This is why Arab satellite stations, particularly al-Jazeera, have played an important role in shaping the consciousness of young Arab people ... [H]aving watched hours of al-Jazeera, I have no doubt that this station has framed the news in ways that portray black and white, evil versus good images of complex conflicts such as the Israeli–Palestinian dispute. Moreover, by regularly hosting extremist ideologues whose racist views merit no more attention than do the racist or anti-Muslim views of 'White Power' or extreme-right wing Christian groups in the USA, al-Jazeera has muddled the boundaries between fact and fiction. (Brumberg 2002)

Inherent in Brumberg's discourse is the belief that media in the Arab World has a tremendous and decisive effect on opinion formation. But this is not necessarily the case. Al-Jazeera's coverage of the Palestinian–Israeli conflict is a case in point. The passion with which al-Jazeera has been reporting the Al Aqsa intifada, which broke out in September 2000 at the provocation of Ariel Sharon's visit to Al Haram Al Sharif, is hard to deny.

Day in and day out, the network has been providing instant coverage of the events and airing detailed reports on the latest developments, shedding an unpleasant light on the practices of Israel in the Middle East, airing raw footage and images of incursions, death and demolition in the West Bank and the Gaza Strip. The impact of the network's intense on-the-ground coverage of the suffering of the Palestinians under the weight of the Israeli war machine is profound to say the least. For James Drummond (2001: 4), 'The station's role in propelling the Palestinian uprising in the Arab public consciousness – and keeping it there – is considerable.'

However, al-Jazeera's effect should not be exaggerated. One may even argue that it has a moderating effect that is hardly noted. What is interesting is not only the way al-Jazeera charges up and heightens the viewers' emotions, but also the cathartic role it plays. The channel's numerous interactive programmes afford the viewers the ability to call in to vent their anger live on the air and express their frustration both with Israel's violations and the official Arab silence vis-à-vis what is happening in the Occupied Territories in particular and the Middle East, in general. It is true that viewers are fed a daily staple made up of images of death, suffering and victimisation. As these images keep recurring, however, viewers risk becoming numb as a result of experiencing what Keith Tester (2001: 13) calls 'compassion fatigue', which leaves them exhausted by the spectacle of violent events and reports about misery and suffering. As such, they become used to graphic pictures and dreadful incidents, so much so that the event loses its eventfulness in the daily routine screenings of violence. If anything, many of the images that find their way to al-Jazeera are tragic and in that sense tend to sap the energies and hopes of the Arab viewer. The fact that the continuous airing of images of victims and victimisation, of expulsion and demolition cannot only incite the Arab masses but also affect them negatively suggests that al-Jazeera, and for that matter new Arab media as a whole, may not have the power, influence or impact it is often believed to have on Arab public opinion. It is interesting that Israel has tolerated al-Jazeera when even the Palestinian authorities closed down the network's office in the West Bank after al-Jazeera broadcast an unflattering image of Yasser Arafat in a promotional trailer for a documentary on the Lebanese Civil War.

The foregoing analysis suggests that public opinion formation in the Arab world is far from being a purely 'media effects' issue and is far from being a matter of TV moulding. Developing this point, Lynch (2003) provides a more nuanced conception of the interaction between new Arab media like al-Jazeera and Arab public opinion. In his view, elites in general and intellectuals in particular play an increasingly important role in the growing influential mediascape, and have the proclivity to influence public opinion. The 'elite Arab public' (such as intellectuals, politicians, journalists and other public or political figures) who appear in new Arab media are key to understanding Arab public opinion – in fact they are instrumental in shaping Arab public opinion (Lynch 2003). The key to Arab public opinion lies neither in the ideologues (whether they be radicals, Islamists or nationalists) nor in the broad populace. Away from a simplistic cause and effect paradigm, Lynch (2003) maps out a social group whose growing influence often goes unnoticed. In his view, the key to Arab public opinion is a broad and diverse educated group of intellectuals who, to a certain extent, constitute the interface of Arab media with the public at large:

> Arab public opinion is a more complex phenomenon than conventional notions of a cynical elite and a passionate, nationalistic 'Arab street' suggest. The street, or mass public, is real, and its views (expressed or anticipated) can indeed affect government policies. But what now matters more than the street, and sometimes even more than the rulers, is the consensus of elite and middle-class public opinion throughout the Arab world. Articulate and assertive, combative and argumentative, this nascent public sphere increasingly sets the course for the street and the palace alike. It is here that the battle of ideas about internal reform and relations with the United States is already being fought. (Ibid.)

The new Arab media is not only shaping the terms of the debate but also providing views and opinions about news and developments that affect the region the most:

> These new Arab media increasingly construct the dominant narrative frames through which people understand events. In some ways, the absence of real democracy in the region makes the new media outlets even more powerful, since they face few real rivals in setting the public agenda. An effective approach to Arab public opinion today should therefore focus less on the street and the palaces than on the participants in and audiences of these new public forums. (Lynch 2003)

Lynch's formulations are particularly relevant because they help us enact a slippage between public opinion and public sphere. For Habermas (1989), the bourgeois public sphere of his model was institutionalised through rational critical debate that was shaped in centres of criticism and then carried over to the political sphere *per se* through such instruments as freedom of opinion and speech, freedom of the press, and freedom of assembly and association. In this manner, the new public sphere of civil society asserted itself through public opinion, prompting private people to relate to each other as a public (Habermas 1989: 37).

Habermas's theoretical formulations afford us the opportunity to think differently about Arab public opinion. Away from the reductive cause and effect paradigm that posits that satellite TV channels like al-Jazeera have a direct and decisive effect on Arab public opinion, one can venture a more subtle understanding of the dynamics new Arab media set in place. One has to be sceptical about the revolutionary impact of transnational Arab media like al-Jazeera on Arab public opinion. Certainly, it would be reductive to assume that al-Jazeera is a network that brainwashes its viewers and decisively channels them in a particular direction. Being at the forefront of pan-Arab satellite TV, al-Jazeera strikes a chord with many Arab viewers, particularly because it has been able to capitalise on a field of interaction which favours the flow of information and the circulation of ideas in a society characterised by its communal nature and the politicisation of its viewers (Ayish 2002: 151). What is new and revolutionary about al-Jazeera is not the discourse it promulgates as much as it is the 'publicness' of such a discourse in a culture that is marked by political restrain. In this sense, al-Jazeera, along with a number of prominent Arab satellite channels which have been sprouting over the past decade or so, has not really mobilised or bolstered Arab public opinion. In fact, Arab public opinion has always existed: these new channels have made it more visible, more pronounced and more public.

However, channelling the energies of a public opinion that the media is making more pronounced poses noteworthy challenges. At least in Western democracies, the news media are part of a political process that both enriches it and keeps it in check; the media have the potential to enhance the interconnectedness between citizens and their government, make the process of governing more transparent, promote citizen participation in government, lead to greater public awareness about public policy debates, strengthen civil society and project democratic values. Not so in the Arab Middle East. The wide appeal and growing influence that a channel like al-Jazeera is believed to have point to a fragile equation. The more open and forthcoming it is about the state of affairs in the Arab world, the more likely it is to create discontent, the roots of which cannot be properly addressed if the democracy deficit persists in the region. Media can be an integral part of political life and political institutions, but it can also breed extremism. If al-Jazeera gives the impression sometimes that it is 'the bin Laden channel' it is not because it broadcasts Al Qaeda tapes or toes an anti-Western line, but primarily because the political institutions in the Arab world are largely deficient and do not allow for real participation or promote a governing system based on checks and balances. Not surprisingly then, media democracy in Arab autocracies often results in a media mobocracy. To ignore this point is to risk treating the symptom of the problem as the problem itself and, in the process, reduce a complex institutional political problem to a purely 'media effects' issue.

16. Framing the Other: Worldview, Rhetoric and Media Dissonance since 9/11[1]

Lawrence Pintak

There exists today a fundamental disconnect in communications between the USA and Muslims around the world. At its root lies an essential truth: each side sees the world through a very different prism. This perception gap is exacerbated by an increasingly polarised media who do little to counter what columnist Paul Krugman (2003) has called 'a willful ignorance'. For example, a Pew survey (2002) found that more than 40 percent of Americans said they 'do not have the background' to understand international news, so they simply tune out. The US president himself has admitted that he does not read the newspapers or watch television news. 'I glance at the headlines just to kind of [*sic*] a flavour for what's moving. I rarely read the stories, and get briefed by people who are probably [*sic*] read the news themselves,' President Bush told Fox News (Hume 2003). 'The best way to get the news is from objective sources. And the most objective sources I have are people on my staff who tell me what's happening in the world' (ibid.).

This blinkered view of how others perceive the USA not only contributed to the implementation of policies that angered much of the world but, perhaps just as significantly, meant those policies were presented and packaged in ways that were deeply offensive to the majority of Muslims. Meanwhile, many words and actions by Muslim leaders have had a similar polarising effect in the West, as exemplified by the furore over the comments about the political power of Jews made by outgoing Malaysian Prime Minister Mahathir Mohamed. This polarisation is exacerbated by news media, on both 'sides', eager to create controversy.

Rhetorical Borders

Beginning within hours of the horrific acts of 9/11, the Bush administration framed the struggle against terrorism in absolutist terms that painted the world in black and white and ignored all shades of grey. 'Freedom itself was attacked this morning by a faceless coward' the president told a shocked nation (Bush 2001c), laying the rhetorical borders that would soon protect palaces of suspicion and hate. Terror itself became the enemy, rather than a weapon used by an enemy, firmly shutting the door on any discussion of root causes or motivations. Those who questioned any aspect of US policy were instantly 'Othered', for, as the president sternly proclaimed, in this 'war between good and evil' (Bush 2001b) every nation had a decision to make: 'Either you are with us, or you are with the terrorists' (Bush 2001a).

Bin Laden could not have agreed more. He too had long been preaching that the world was divided into two camps: 'The Hypocrisy-free camp of Belief and the camp of Unbelief from which latter may God protect us and you' (bin Laden 2001). The views of those who inhabited the vast grey no man's land between these two black and white poles were eclipsed as the media in the USA and the Middle East, South and South-East Asia reflected the absolutist rhetoric of leaders with worldviews blinkered by religion, nationalism and ignorance. Understanding was replaced by cliché, empathy with stereotype.

Even so, in the immediate aftermath of 9/11, many Arab and non-Arab Muslim commentators saw opportunity in tragedy. 'As America prepares to retaliate and as it prepares for more possible strikes against it, the world wishes that America would tackle the root causes of terrorism rather than merely fight against its tools', wrote Rafiq al-Khuri in Beirut's *al-Anwar*. The Bush administration had no patience for such introspection. Nor, for the most part, did the US media. Instead, a series of myths were created upon which all subsequent policies and actions were based. Central to these was the myth of terror, elaborately sketched in the president's address to a joint session of Congress:

> Americans are asking: why do they hate us? They hate what we see right here in this chamber – a democratically elected government. Their leaders are self-appointed. They hate our freedoms – our freedom of religion, our freedom of speech, our freedom to vote and assemble and disagree with each other. (Bush 2001a)

It was a memorable sound-bite that played upon the nation's sense of manifest destiny, fed American prejudices about Arabs and Muslims and firmly shut the door on further discussion. But, as audiences across the Middle East, Asia and elsewhere knew, it was a portrait of terrorism that was fundamentally flawed.

Despite the clichés endlessly repeated in the speeches of Bush administration officials, numerous studies have found that most suicide bombers do not hate American freedoms or values, as President Bush would have it (see Atran 2003). Their motivations are complex. But, when it comes to anti-American terrorism, what unites them all is opposition to a US Middle East policy that supports the very regimes that deny them those freedoms. Post-9/11 US policy largely ignored that fact. It also actively denied what was obvious to anyone watching from the Arab Middle East: at the foundation of that resentment was a deep and abiding anger at what was, to Arabs, America's unquestioning support for 'the ultimate Other': Israel.

The Bloodshot Lens

'Us' and 'Them', 'Self' and 'Other' – fundamental dichotomies of human existence; concepts embedded in psychology, anthropology, political science, communications and a host of other disciplines. Since 9/11 this division has been the defining characteristic of global affairs. For Americans, Islam has emerged as the quintessential 'Other', replacing the Soviet Union as the touchstone against which US citizens measure their collective sense of Self. It has become a cliché to say that the attacks of 9/11 'changed everything'. On one level that is true: America's illusion of security was shattered; its relationship with terror as something that happened 'somewhere else' was unalterably changed. But on another level 9/11 simply made overt a worldview that had long been present but little acknowledged: since a *keffiyya*-clad Rudolph Valentino first strode across the silent screen, Arabs and Muslims have been 'Othered' in US society, the subject of stereotype and differentiation.

While the image of the United States among Arabs and non-Arab Muslims has been shaped by a variety of factors, the overarching element has been the perception that the USA is intrinsically linked to, and responsible for, the policies of Israel. In a meeting in 1985, Ali Akhbar Mohtashamipur (then Iran's Ambassador to Damascus) told me: 'We think that as long as America as a superpower looks to Israel in a special way and prefers it to all countries, and until the US can be non-aligned in the Middle East, there will be difficulties' (Pintak 2003: 232). Very little has changed in the intervening years. In a study of polling data from the Arab world, Mark Tessler found that 'anti-Americanism is for the most part a response to perceptions and judgments regarding our foreign policy' and 'all aspects of our Middle East policy were judged very unfavourably' (Tessler 2003: 180). Similarly, a Gallup poll concluded that 'the perception that Western nations are not fair in their stances toward Palestine fits in with a more generalized view that the West is unfair to the Arab and Islamic worlds' (Gallup 2002). Twenty years to the day after the bombing of the US Marine

Corps barracks in Beirut, President George W. Bush met with Indonesian Muslim leaders on the island of Bali. Afterwards, the *New York Times* reported, Bush turned to aides and, shaking his head asked, 'Do they really believe we think that all Muslims are terrorists?' (Sanger 2003). 'He was equally distressed,' *The Times* reported, 'to hear that the United States was so pro-Israel that it was uninterested in the creation of a Palestinian state living alongside Israel, despite his frequent declarations calling for exactly that' (ibid.). It was a moment reflecting the yawning gap in worldview, perception and communications that fed the rise of anti-Americanism in the post-9/11 era.

In the immediate aftermath of 9/11, there existed a broad level of sympathy for the USA across the Muslim world. Formal polls showed that only a tiny percentage of Muslims approved of the attacks (see Morin and Deane 2002; Haddad and Khashan 2002). Two years later, a report to Congress on public diplomacy concluded, 'hostility toward America has reached shocking levels' (Djerjian 2003: 19), while Pew (2003) noted that 'the bottom has fallen out of Arab and Muslim support for the United States', reflecting 'true dislike, if not hatred' of the USA (Kohut 2003). Take Indonesia, the world's most populous Muslim country, for example: after 9/11, Gallup found that only 5 percent of Indonesians surveyed said the attacks were justified (Morin and Deane 2002). In the year 2000, Pew had reported that 75 percent of Indonesians had a 'favourable view' of the USA; in the spring of 2002, that figure stood at 61 percent. But by the May of 2003 the situation had essentially reversed, with 85 percent of Indonesians reporting an unfavourable view of the USA (Pew 2003). Significantly, by 2003, in a country where the Israeli–Palestinian conflict had never been more than a tertiary issue, 68 percent of those polled listed Yasser Arafat as the world figure in whom they had the most confidence, with bin Laden coming in third at 58 percent. King Abdullah of Jordan, a major player in the Israel–Palestine dispute, came in second (ibid.).

The question is: what happened? A host of complex factors had influenced the relationship between the USA and the world's Muslims. These included:

- The conflicting worldviews of Americans and Muslims that led each to perceive post-9/11 events in fundamentally different ways
- The polarising rhetoric of leaders on each side that was shaped by, and reinforced, those contrasting worldviews
- The prevailing worldview in the Bush White House – and the USA at large – which produced an elemental failure to understand the impact of US policy statements and actions among Muslims

- The framing of coverage by media in the USA and in Muslim countries in a manner that reinforced the dichotomy and inflamed opinion
- The impact of 'the al-Jazeera effect', the growth of more aggressive non-traditional media outlets in the Muslim world and a resulting liberalisation in traditional media outlets

These factors contributed to the emergence of an imagined transnational community of Muslims – or *umma* — that was far more psychologically cohesive and politically engaged than ever before.

The perception gap between the USA and the world's Muslims was epitomised by the very definition of terrorism. Each of the main US government agencies had its own definition, but they were all built on the language enshrined in US law that described terrorism as 'premeditated, politically motivated violence perpetrated against non-combatant targets by *sub-national* groups or clandestine agents' (CIA 2002; my emphasis). Their failure to acknowledge that state-sponsored terrorism was, to much of the world, a far greater threat to human life exemplified this perception gap. This difference in definition sparks a cascade of other essential questions: Who is a 'terrorist' and who is a 'freedom fighter'? When does a 'freedom fighter' become a 'terrorist'?

Needless to say, from the US side, this discussion left no space for the notion that many in the world considered actions of the US – and Israeli – military to fit precisely the definition of terrorism. Rather, the rhetoric from the White House was deeply rooted in the language of American exceptionalism – the paternalistic notion that the USA somehow knew what was best for the world. It was a perspective articulated in the ageless lines of John Winthrop's 1630 poem, *City Upon the Hill*, about the first settlement in the New World, and reprised by Ronald Reagan in his now-famous speech of the same name:

> We cannot escape our destiny, nor should we try to do so. The leadership of the free world was thrust upon us two centuries ago in that little hall of Philadelphia. In the days following World War II, when the economic strength and power of America was all that stood between the world and the return to the dark ages, Pope Pius XII said, 'The American people have a great genius for splendid and unselfish actions. Into the hands of America God has placed the destinies of an afflicted mankind.' We are indeed, and we are today, the last best hope of man on earth. (Reagan 1974)

Sardar and Davies depict this contrast between America's self-image and the image of the USA held by many Arabs and Muslims, in the terms of the quintessential Hollywood western:

> American political rhetoric may circle its wagons around old familiar idea of national self-identity, with clear and certain recognition of the need for self-preservation and security. But beyond the comforting wood-smoke and firelight, outside that circle, the meaning is plain: other people will have to die. (Sardar and Davies 2002: 172–3)

The 2003 invasion of Iraq is a case in point. In a wave of self-examination since the invasion, US journalists have come to the belated recognition that they fell victim to what the *Washington Post*'s Bob Woodward has called a 'groupthink' mentality that marginalised voices sceptical of the march towards violence. 'The result,' the *Post* concluded in a front-page *mea culpa*, 'was coverage that, despite flashes of groundbreaking reporting, in hindsight looks strikingly one-sided at times' (Kurtz 2004). The *New York Times* (2004) likewise acknowledged that its editors and reporters were 'too intent on rushing scoops into the paper' to see through 'the pattern of misinformation' they were being fed by sources in the administration and the Iraqi opposition.

While US news organisations engaged in a hawkish patriotism that helped pave the road to war, Muslims were exposed to images and language no less polarising. Coverage was built on a host of pre-existing stereotypes of the USA and effectively leveraged by Osama bin Laden in his own rhetoric. Central to these stereotypes was that of the 'crusader-Zionist conspiracy' in which 'the Western demon [was] bent on the eradication of Islam' (Haddad 1996: 491). In short, the media on both sides were 'weaponised', transformed from channels of understanding to tools of violence. As Rami Khouri (2003), a political scientist and editor of Beirut's *Daily Star* put it, 'For different reasons, Arab and American broadcasters provide a distorted, incomplete picture of the war in Iraq – while accurately reflecting emotional and political sentiments on both sides.'

For example, while US correspondents covered the initial phase of the US assault on Kabul from 'listening posts' hundreds of miles away in Pakistan and northern Afghanistan, concentrating on the 'defensive' nature of the American assault, al-Jazeera's team was on the ground in the Afghan capital, providing coverage that 'conveyed far more of the human truth of a massive bombing attack and its effects at ground zero' (Hickey 2002). And where the US media presented a bloodless view of the Iraq conflict, concentrating on the technological 'shock and awe', al-Jazeera and its imitators, al-Arabiyah and Abu Dhabi television, focused on the suffering of civilians, with graphic, close-up images of casualties that have become their signature style (Ayish 2002).

Reviewing media coverage in the world's Muslim-majority countries post-9/11, certain key themes are readily detected: the USA as an imperialist power; the USA as cover for Israel; and the USA as enemy of Islam – each theme built on existing attitudes and stereotypes. Likewise, the US media fell back on an historic orientalist portrayal of Arabs and Muslims characterised by stereotype, distortion and cliché. In short, journalists reported through the prism of their own worldview. As CBS News anchor Dan Rather told CNN's Larry King, 'When my country's at war, I want my country to win; there is an inherent bias in the American media' (Krull 2004: 65). That sentiment was echoed by one Arab reporter covering events at the United States military command headquarters in Doha, Qater, who told an American journalist-scholar, 'he put his duty to his people, to the Arab nation, above his duty as a journalist' (Schleifer 2003).

Urban Renewal in the Global Village

The question 'Why do they hate us?' and its corollary, 'Why is the US losing the war of ideas?' have been the centre of debate in the USA since 9/11. The Bush administration argued that it was because a biased media in 'the Muslim world' skewed its message. But was it that simple? In an examination of data gathered in North Africa by the Gallup organisation, Nisbet et al. (2003) compared the anti-Americanism of al-Jazeera viewers with the attitudes of those who watched CNN International and the BBC. They concluded that the source of news had only a 'slight buffering effect' on anti-American sentiments among viewers (Nisbet et al. 2003: 26). More importantly, they found that 'for both types of networks, increasing levels of attention to coverage of the US leads to stronger anti-American attitudes' (Nisbet et al. 2003: 32). In other words, the more those Arabs questioned watched television, no matter which network, the stronger their anti-American views: For the Muslim public, 'the difference in media effects for receiving news through either Al Jazeera or a Western network is a matter of degree, not direction' (Nisbet et al. 2003: 32).

The clear implication is that anti-Americanism arose not from *the way* in which Bush administration policies and actions were portrayed, as the White house claimed, but from the policies and actions *themselves*. Precisely because the world is seen through diametrically opposed prisms, the impact on audiences in the USA and 'the Muslim world' of the same words, TV pictures and political actions is very different. As Nisbet et al. (2003: 25) surmised:

> The extreme anti-American predispositions that are endemic to individuals living in Muslim countries are likely to channel any opinion response, with these pre-existing views of the US serving as perceptual screens, enabling individuals to *select considerations from TV news that only confirm existing anti-American attitudes.* (my emphasis)

In short, Arabs and Muslims perceive US policy statements and actions in the context of their worldview, no matter who is doing the framing. So when President Bush claimed 'the Middle East is where you find the hatred and violence', as he did in a US television interview (*Meet the Press* 2004), Arabs had no doubt he meant *they* were violent; when he couched those comments within the frame of Judeo-Christian values, Muslims saw it as proof he was targeting their faith; and when President Bush made a casual comment about a 'crusade' against terror, it reopened wounds that had festered for a millennium. The impact of this fundamental disconnect in worldviews was exacerbated when such comments were mediated through the new fragmented information sources, which themselves were subjective in their choices of words and pictures.

To return to Indonesian attitudes toward the USA: the dramatic shift that occurred between May 2002 and May 2003 was the cumulative effect of a series of watershed events – or episodic frames – that resonated across 'the Muslim world' between early 2002 and the capture of Saddam Hussein, which built and reinforced a Muslim perception of America as 'the Other'. Taking place against the backdrop of the invasion of Afghanistan a few months earlier, these events were portrayed very differently through the bloodshot lens of the media on each side, thus exacerbating polarisation, confirming stereotypes and underlining the perception gap. These watershed stories included:

- Israel's spring 2002 invasion of the West Bank and Gaza Strip, a conflict that would leave more than 600 Palestinians dead, 3,000 injured (Palestinian Red Crescent 2004), and thousands more homeless, and lead to charges of 'war crimes' from Amnesty International (2002)
- President Bush's April 2002 characterisation of Israeli Prime Minister Ariel Sharon as 'a man of peace' (Bush 2002b), and his subsequent meeting with Sharon, even while Israeli forces were laying siege to Palestinian cities

- Bush's June 2002 declaration that Arafat must be replaced by 'a new and different Palestinian leadership' (Bush 2002a) at a time when the PLO leader's Gaza headquarters was ringed by Israeli armour
- The March 2003 invasion of Iraq

A critical driving element in this perception gap was the arrival of al-Jazeera and the broader era of media reform it heralded. Previously, viewers in the Arab world and beyond had to rely on brief clips on CNN or the BBC, or coverage provided to their terrestrial TV stations by Western news organisations. Now al-Jazeera and its rivals supplied 'hours and hours of uncut footage that was never available before', notes Salwa Kaana, the Internet editor of the Palestinian daily *al Quds al Arabi*.[2] The impact was particularly notable in the non-Arab Muslim world. Where the conflicts of the Middle East were once distant events, al-Jazeera literally brought them into the living rooms of non-Arab Muslims at a time when they had already become more politicised by the 'War on Terror'. It wasn't even necessary to have a satellite dish: one terrestrial TV station in Indonesia simply rebroadcast the al-Jazeera feed twenty-four hours a day during the height of the violence, while others made extensive use of coverage of the Intifada and the US invasion of Iraq by al-Jazeera and its clones in their own newscasts.

As al-Jazeera and the other cross-border Arab channels brought the wars of the Middle East and South Asia into the living rooms of Muslims from Morocco to Malaysia, they increased the appetite for more, which meant that newspapers across the region ratcheted up their coverage as well. In Indonesia, this rise in interest coincided with the emergence of an independent media following decades of muzzling in the Suharto era. My own study of Indonesia's largest newspaper, *Kompas*, found that while coverage of the first Intifada was paltry, the paper carried extensive reporting on the more recent so-called al-Aqsa Intifada (Pintak 2006).

The implications of these changes are profound. Even as the administration and many others in the USA were downplaying the connection between US support for Israel and anti-Americanism in 'the Muslim world', the psychological impact of that conflict among non-Arab Muslims was being amplified by the media, turning it into a marker of Muslim identity. So, while President Bush was welcoming Sharon at the White House and praising him as a man of peace, Muslims were watching Palestinians being killed in Ramallah and Jenin on the orders of the man they knew as the 'Butcher of Beirut'. While the administration was trying to disabuse Muslims of the notion that the 'War on Terror' was some Zionist-Christian conspiracy against Islam, the US president was adopting Sharonisms like 'homicide bomber', endorsing the Israeli leader's notion of a 'shared threat' posed by Islamist militants, and failing to condemn the inflammatory remarks of a fundamentalist Christian Army general who called the God of Muslims 'an idol' (Associated Press 2001). And even as the White House insisted it was taking a new even-handed approach to the Israel–Palestinian conflict, President Bush was calling for the elimination of Yasser Arafat, whom Ariel Sharon had labelled 'my bin Laden' and who, at that very moment, was appearing beleaguered and besieged on TV screens around the world.

Shifting the Psychological Centre

In an earlier era, the proclivity of successive US administrations to say one thing and do another was, to a large degree, masked behind a veil of media silence. This silence was a legacy of the fact that in the Middle East and many Muslim-majority countries – where the media was (and still is) government controlled – reporters toed the government line, had few resources, and 'the concept of television journalism ... was virtually nonexistent' (Ayish 2002). With the arrival of al-Jazeera and its clones, independent websites and loosened restrictions on print media in some countries, all that changed. An open, cross-border public sphere arose, freed of dependence on the Western media lens. Now, what America said *and* what it did – in Afghanistan, Palestine and Iraq – were right there for the world to see. In the process, America 'Othered' *itself*; inadvertently creating among Muslims both a heightened sense that Islam was under threat and a greater sense of Muslim solidarity. Fallujah and Najaf became epic confrontations, twin rallying points for Arab nationalism and Islamic identity. Abu Gharaib was, meanwhile, the inevitable result of America's dehumanisation of Arabs, a systematic policy of humiliation and abuse both shocking and – to many in the Middle East – unsurprising. Each new event fuelled more antipathy and hatred. By the summer of 2004, a pair of polls by Zogby International found that America's 'favourability rating' in the Middle East was effectively zero (Zogby and Zogby 2004).

In short, the USA had achieved precisely what Osama bin Laden set out to do: polarised opinion in the Muslim world. However, this polarisation may only be skin deep and, again, Indonesia provides a useful case study. Prevailing wisdom in 'the West' is that Indonesian Muslims, long among the least doctrinaire practitioners of Islam, have been radicalised since 9/11. That would seem to be borne out in the increased presence of *jilbab* headscarves among Indonesian women, the growth of Islamist political parties and the rise of Jemaah Islamiyah, a home grown al-Qaeda affiliate responsible for various terrorist actions across the region. But a 2003 survey of attitudes towards Islam and politics found that 'while many Indonesian Muslims appear to be Islamists on the broadest construal of the term (they believe that laws should somehow be basically in accord with Islam), relatively few support policies advocated by Islamist activists' (Mujani and Liddle 2004: 110). Although 67 percent of Indonesians surveyed said they wanted a government led by Islamic authorities and based on the Qur'an and Sunnah, and 71 percent thought *shari'a* should be obligatory, the numbers dropped dramatically when they were asked if they favoured specific aspects of Islamic law. Only about a third of Indonesians favoured requiring women to wear headscarves or cutting off the hands of thieves, 21 percent thought only Islamist parties should take part in elections, 26 percent opposed a woman president, and that number dropped to just eight percent when asked if women should be banned from serving in parliament.

These findings were matched by the modest support Islamist parties received in Indonesia's April 2004 parliamentary elections (approximately 20 percent of the vote went to overtly Islamist parties, much of that attributed to their anti-corruption stance) and would seem to indicate that while there is an increased sense of Muslim identity and politicisation, the historically moderate approach to Islam among Indonesians has not fundamentally changed. The election in Malaysia that same year, in which Islamist parties were largely vanquished, carried a similar message.

Together, the Indonesian and Malaysian elections were vivid reminders for Americans that not all Muslims are extremists and not all democracies need be 'Made in America'. Equally important, many within the news media – in both the USA and the vast arc of nations from West Africa to South-East Asia – are regrouping, reassessing and reconsidering their respective roles. This reflective mood creates a glimmer of hope that in the future the news media may aspire to a borderless journalism that shatters today's bloodshot lens, broadens world views and gives voice to the silenced majority who seek to replace diatribe with dialogue.

17. Bad News and Public Debate about the Israel-Palestine Conflict
Greg Philo and Mike Berry

This chapter brings together the key findings of an extensive study of TV news coverage of the Israel–Palestine conflict and the impact of news on public understanding.[1] It also examines the wide-ranging public debate in this country and abroad that was engendered by the publication of the study. We show that this debate both mirrored and developed wider arguments about the nature of the conflict and its representation in the media. Between September 2000 and April 2002 the Glasgow University Media Unit analysed nearly two-hundred news bulletins from BBC and ITV news and questioned some eight-hundred individuals in Britain, Germany and the United States about their knowledge and understanding of the conflict. The research indicated that many viewers were so confused about the origins and underlying political dimensions of the conflict that it would be difficult to have an informed public debate about how it might be resolved. The research strongly suggested that the gaps in public knowledge were related to a lack of context and explanation of key issues in news bulletins.

Television news is the most important site in the formation of public knowledge about world events (Committee on Standards in Public Life 2004; Philo and Berry 2004; ITC 2003). Approximately 80 percent of the population relies on it as their main source of world news. Broadcast journalism retains a relatively high degree of public trust compared to other media and public institutions. A September 2004 survey found that that television news is considered significantly more trustworthy than broadsheet journalism and seven times more so than the tabloid press (Committee on Standards in Public Life 2004). In an area such as the Israel–Palestine conflict where so much is disputed, the attainment of balance is made especially difficult.

Context/Background

The events of 1948, when the Israeli state was created, and 1967 when Israel conquered the Occupied Territories, remain highly controversial. Part of the reason why the historical record is so contested is because it is intimately linked to the justifications given by Israelis and Palestinians for their actions. However, it would be very difficult for viewers to understand why the conflict had been so bitter and prolonged without some knowledge of the events of 1948 and 1967. One of the most striking findings of our research was the almost complete lack of any information within news bulletins on the region's history. In our first sample we found that out of more than 3,500 lines of transcribed news text only 17 mentioned any aspect of the conflict's history. Since so many people rely on television news as their main source of information on the conflict it is not surprising that such absences were closely mirrored in audience understandings. Few could name any of the region's wars and less than a fifth of viewers were aware that Palestinian refugees had lost their land and homes during the creation of the Israeli state. Many viewers felt that they were not being given enough background to make sense of the conflict, and some went further to argue that this was characteristic of most television news. One young male from Glasgow expressed the view that:

> I've not heard any historical context from the news at all. They don't tell us that – they don't say – they leave it on the short scale. 'This fighting was due to yesterday's fighting which was due to the day before'. But they don't go back to all that, I don't know anything about that [history]. The reporter will say 'The Israelis fired into a Palestinian refugee camp today in response to a Palestinian suicide bomber yesterday,' but they won't say why the Palestinians are fighting or why the Israelis are fighting – it doesn't go back any length of time. (Student group, Glasgow, cited in Philo and Berry 2004: 216)

Because viewers lacked key information about the conflict's history it was very difficult for them to make sense of the central issues separating the parties. For instance, a number of viewers suggested that 'land' was an issue, but appeared confused about the territorial dimensions of the conflict. A common perception was that the conflict involved two states fighting over a coveted piece of land, as in a border dispute. One viewer expressed his surprise that the Palestinians had actually lost land to the Israelis:

The impression I got was that the Palestinians had lived around that area and now they were trying to come back and get some more land for themselves – I didn't realise that they had actually been driven out, I just thought they didn't want to live as part of Israel and that the places they were living in, they decided they wanted to make self-governed [*sic*] – I didn't realise they had been driven out of places in wars previously. (Student group, Glasgow, cited in Philo and Berry 2004: 216)

In another focus group, we noted the following exchange:

Female speaker: I just thought it was disputed land, I wasn't under the impression that the Israeli borders had changed or that they had taken land from other people. I just had the impression it was a nice piece of land, that both, to put it simplistically, that they were fighting over and I thought it was more a Palestinian aggression than it was an Israeli aggression.
Moderator: Did anyone else see it this way?
Answers: Yes, yes [five out of ten people in this group assented].
    (Student group, Glasgow, cited in Philo and Berry 2004: 217)

Journalists told us that part of the reason for the lack of historical context was they were under pressure from news editors to produce dramatic reports with strong visuals that would catch the attention of viewers. The BBC correspondent George Alagiah claimed that he was constantly being told by his editors that the 'attention span of our average viewer is about twenty seconds' and that if they failed to 'grab' these viewers there was a danger that they would switch channels to one of the BBC's competitors. This view was confirmed by another BBC journalist who told us that his editor had encouraged him to produce reports heavy on 'bang bang' and to avoid 'explainers'. However, our audience research indicated that viewers' appetite for coverage of the conflict was directly related to how much they understood of it. Viewers who felt they were watching an incomprehensible and irresolvable litany of death and suffering turned away from news reports. As one female student put it, the news, 'never actually explains it so I don't see the point in watching it – I just turn it off and just go and make a cup of tea or something. I don't like watching it when I don't understand what's going on' (cited in Philo and Berry 2004: 240). Conversely we found that when viewers gained even a very brief historical understanding of the conflict it could lead to a dramatic increase in levels of interest. There was a feeling that understanding the reasons behind the fighting allowed viewers more fully to engage with the story. One viewer remarked that 'I wouldn't have switched off if I'd known the historical context. I would probably have had an emotional tie to it and got into it a bit more' (cited in Philo and Berry 2004: 242).

Viewpoints/Use of Sources

Another finding to emerge strongly from our research was that Israeli perspectives on the conflict were featured more prominently than those of the Palestinians. We found, for example, that the Israeli security perspective, that they were fighting a 'War on Terror' was heavily featured, sometimes so much so that the Palestinian viewpoint, that they were resisting an illegal military occupation, was excluded from coverage. Previous research carried out before the al-Aqsa Intifada found a similar pattern that suggests that this is a consistent feature of coverage across time (Berry 2004). Part of the reason for this imbalance was that Israeli representatives were given twice as much time to speak (as measured by lines of news text) as Palestinian sources. The imbalance in this area was magnified by the prominence given to American sources who tended to support the Israeli position. These received more than twice as much airtime as even British politicians.

There was very little reference to the military nature of the occupation and its social consequences for Palestinians or to the large number of United Nations resolutions condemning the occupation. The exploitation of Palestinian land and water resources is widely seen as a violation of international law. Again we found that such absences were closely replicated in viewers' knowledge. Only 9 percent knew of the control of water and 11 percent knew of UN resolutions. Some viewers were confused over who was actually occupying the Occupied Territories and what this signified. In our first major sample only 9 percent of viewers knew that the Israelis were occupying the Occupied Territories and that the settlers were Israeli. Many participants did not see the occupation as being military in nature and were surprised to learn that there are checkpoints and restrictions on movement. A teacher in a group from Paisley commented that:

> I think you sometimes get the impression from the news that these are people [Israeli settlers] who happen to want to live there ... and the military back-up is in pursuit of their peaceful wish to just go and live there, and I think that's the impression I get from the news, rather than that it is a military occupation. (cited in Philo and Berry 2004: 219–20)

Sometimes journalists did mention some of the central Palestinian grievances, but without actually explaining their significance or role in the conflict:

> There is also the question of millions of Palestinian refugees that lived in neighbouring countries. Will they ever be allowed to return home? And what will be the fate of the Jewish settlers, who now live on the West Bank, land the Palestinians say must be part of their future country? And there other seemingly mundane issues like access to water which are so important in the Middle East and that are still eluding negotiators. (ITV early evening News, 2 October 2000, cited in Philo and Berry 2004: 115)

The problem here is that our audience research suggests that few viewers possessed the background knowledge to make sense of such statements. There is no explanation about how the Palestinians became refugees, the strategic role of Israeli settlements or why water is a vital issue. This brings us to a more general point about how reporters write for their audience. There was a tendency, exemplified in the extract above, for journalists to speak in a kind of shorthand that assumed that viewers possessed a level of background knowledge that is often simply not there.

We also found that television news presented a very limited picture of Israeli settlers living in the Occupied Territories; yet the settlements have a key role in the occupation. As the Israeli historian Avi Shlaim put it, they were part of a policy of exerting strategic and military control, which, for example, involved 'surrounding the huge Greater Jerusalem area with two concentric circles of settlements with access roads and military positions' (Shlaim 2000: 582). Many were built on hilltops to give them a commanding position, with the explicit encouragement of Ariel Sharon. Established settlements were strongly fortified and their occupants were often heavily armed. But we found that even people who were sympathetic to the Palestinians could absorb the message of the settlers as small embattled communities. A middle-class male from Glasgow expressed his surprise that the settlements controlled over 40 percent of the West Bank: 'I had absolutely no idea it was that percentage – I was gob-smacked when I heard it. I saw them as small, embattled and surrounded by hostile Palestinians – that's entirely thanks to watching the television news' (cited in Philo and Berry 2004: 220).

Without history or context, news reports tend to focus on day to day events, and in reporting these we found a familiar theme whereby the Palestinians are seen to initiate the trouble or violence and the Israelis are then presented as 'responding' or 'retaliating'. Between October and December 2001, for example, on BBC1 and ITV news, Israelis were said to be 'retaliating' or in some way responding to what had been done to them about six times as often as the Palestinians. Phrases such as 'Israel's retribution', 'Israel responded', 'Israel has hit back' and 'Israel's payback' were used. This pattern of reporting clearly influenced how some viewers understood the conflict. As one young woman put it: 'You always think of the Palestinians as being really aggressive because of the stories you hear on the news... I always think the Israelis are fighting back against the bombings that have been done to them.' Another wrote: 'The Palestinians trigger every incident which makes the Israelis retaliate.' It is interesting how closely this language parallels that of the news: 'Palestinian suicide attacks *trigger* more Israeli raids' (BBC1, late news 5 January 2002), and 'The *trigger* for the Israeli offensive was a massacre on the West Bank' (ITV, early evening news, 13 December 2001). There were other differences in the language used on the news to describe the two sides. The word 'terrorist' was used to describe Palestinians, but when an Israeli group was reported as trying to bomb a Palestinian school, they were referred to as 'extremists' or 'vigilantes' (ITV main news and BBC1 lunchtime news, 5 March 2002). We also found differences in the language used for the casualties of both sides. Phrases such as 'mass murder', 'atrocity', 'brutal murder', 'lynching', and 'savage cold blooded killing' were used only to describe the deaths of Israelis and not Palestinians. The emphasis on the deaths of Israelis was very marked in the coverage. In March 2002, when the BBC had noted that the Palestinians had suffered the highest number of casualties in any single week since the beginning of the intifada, there was actually more coverage of Israeli deaths on the news. This again apparently had a strong influence on the understanding of viewers and only a minority questioned in these samples knew that Palestinians had substantially higher casualties than the Israelis. The following comment is from a viewer who believed that the Israelis had suffered around five times as many casualties as the Palestinians:

> Well basically on the news coverage they do always seem to make the Palestinians out to be the ones who are the suicide bombers, so it's like, I would imagine it's going to be more casualties on the Israeli side, but it's purely from television, that's where I'm getting my info from, that's how its been portrayed to me on television. (cited in Philo and Berry 2004: 234)

It was not our intention to justify any killings or violence in our research but it was clear that the killings of Israelis were treated in a very different fashion to the killings of Palestinians. This was part of a general trend in which Israeli perspectives were featured more prominently than those of Palestinians, and there was an almost complete absence of coherent information about the conflict's origins. The result of this was that most viewers lacked the necessary information to understand the conflict or to debate how it might be resolved.

Reactions to the Research

The publication of this research attracted a great deal of media attention. This included articles in the British broadsheet and tabloid press and interviews on BBC radio. The findings of the research were also reported in France, Germany, Greece, South Africa, Australia, New Zealand, Canada, the United States, Israel, Lebanon and across the Middle East. Publication of the study's findings also triggered a large number of letters and emails from members of the public. Some of this correspondence came from supporters of Israel and was very critical. Some argued that the British media was in fact heavily biased against Israel and that our research (like much of the British media) was anti-Semitic as in these examples:

> I have known for many years that you are a mouth-foaming Fascist-left propagandist. I must admit I never realised that you are also a rabid anti-Semite (though I might have guessed). Only an utter idiot or someone totally ignorant of Middle East realities could accuse the BBC of 'pro-Israel' bias: in truth, they are institutionally anti-Israel, which of course is a fundamental breach of their charter. They repeatedly broadcast Islamo-Nazi lies about Israel as though facts. You need treatment. (17 June 2004)

> I read your article in [the] *Guardian* – let me tell you Mr Philo what we get in 20 seconds with your so called 'research' – we get nothing, but an anti-Israel and anti-Semitic (O YES! anti-Semitic) British media gets a fig leaf to its extreme anti-Israeli bias and the license to pile more anti-Israeli and anti-Semitic garbage trying to dehumanize Jews and to vilify Israel. (14 July 2004)

And this from Australia:

> You clearly do not understand the difference between your arse and your elbow... Go and spend a bit of time in Israel. Tour around a bit.

Have a look at things. Try to get your feeble brain round a few facts. Get a life. (5 July 2004)

We also received responses from pro-Israel writers that were more considered. One writer from New York wrote numerous letters to us, some extending to thousands of words on aspects of this and other world conflicts. For instance, he attempted to justify European colonialism as a 'complex phenomena, sometimes but not always or even usually an evil' that had made an important contribution to 'civilisation'. Much of the correspondence we received from the general public was actually supportive and expressed the view that the research confirmed what they suspected about media coverage of the conflict.

There were also attempts to criticise the work by those writing in the mass media. Andrew Neil writing in the London *Evening Standard* commented that:

> The methodology of this quasiacademic stuff is of course flawed. Israel gets a better deal, say researchers, because more of its official spokesmen get airtime. But no one believes spin doctors and pictures of Palestinians taking on Israeli tanks with sticks and stones are worth a thousand Israeli officials... When 'plucky little Israel' was regularly invaded by Arab armies, the media was pro-Israel. Now that the Palestinians are perceived as the underdogs, the media naturally sympathises with them. That sympathy comes through even in the most objective reporting. (23 June 2004)

Our reply which the *Evening Standard* did not publish, went as follows:

> In his comments on our book *Bad News from Israel* Andrew Neil says that academics can reach any conclusions they choose. If this is so why would we spend three years on such an exhaustive study? Some of the most serious criticisms of TV news in the book actually come from journalists. He also thinks that the public will always support the underdog stone-throwers against the people in the tanks. But is this true of troops in Iraq or Northern Ireland? It all depends on public understandings of the reasons for a conflict – which is what we show in the book. What a shame he didn't bother to read it before reviewing it.

Another critique of our work was made by Dan Shaham, the director of public affairs at the Israeli Embassy in an article published in the *Scotsman*

(28 July 2004). Shaham did not discuss our findings but instead accused us of 'disguising the prejudice to which Israel is treated'. He also attempted to conflate our research with those who tried to 'delegitimise' the Israeli state, and had compared the fighting in Jenin in 2002 with the events of 9/11. At no point had we made such a comparison, nor had we at any time questioned the legitimacy of the Israeli State. We also wrote about the anti-Semitism prevalent in parts of the Arab Middle East and have spoken out against it publicly.

The critical responses to our research were in fact outnumbered by positive reviews. Will Hutton described it as 'scrupulously researched', whilst the investigative reporter John Pilger suggested that 'every journalist should read this book; every student of journalism ought to be assigned it' (*Observer* 4 July 2004; *New Statesman* 28 June 2004). Pilger particularly emphasised that the research demonstrated the need for journalists to stand up to those with economic and political power and not be bamboozled or intimidated by 'spin'. The same point was made by the former BBC Middle East correspondent Tim Llewellyn: 'Spin doctors and media bullies' he argued 'must be seen off whether they are in Westminster or West Jerusalem' (*Observer* 20 June 2004). This issue of journalism's relationship with power was also raised by the academic and environmental campaigner George Monbiot, who argued that the research illustrated the pitfalls of journalism's heavy reliance on official sources (*Guardian* 13 July 2004). Emphasising an issue that has long been stressed by media academics, Monbiot noted that journalists 'who are favoured with special information are those who have ingratiated themselves' with the powerful, whilst 'the US, British and Israeli governments can make life very difficult for media organisations that upset them'.

Other commentators took the view that the research illustrated a wider problem in that news broadcasters were structured in a manner that failed properly to explain important issues to audiences. The journalist and academic Roy Greenslade, writing in the *Guardian*, suggested that the study raised 'serious questions' about broadcasters' responsibilities to inform the public:

> The study shows the crucial importance of TV news in informing public opinion and the powerful influence it can have on how we see and understand our world. It also shows how news can fail to inform, and the researchers do suggest different and innovative approaches to improve the quality of news. The study also raises serious questions for broadcasters – indeed all journalists – about their responsibility in trying to tell the truth while maintaining impartiality. (21 June 2004)

The issue of journalism's responsibility to inform viewers was also highlighted in an article by Molly Watson that appeared in the *Mail on Sunday*. She suggested that the study illustrated how news increasingly was being 'dumbed down' because of its emphasis on 'sound bites' and 'bang bang' at the expense of more informed analysis:

> There's no doubt that even the Beeb has dumbed down its news programmes. It may not have fallen to the level of ITV, which, on the night of last month's European summit in Brussels to discuss an EU Constitution, led its broadcast with details on the fight in the *Big Brother* house. Nevertheless, night after night millions of us are treated to PowerPoint presentations that reduce issues to half a dozen sound bites as the anchor repeats the phrases flashed up on the screen. (25 July 2004)

Tim Llewellyn argued that part of the problem was that too much of the BBC's news output was 'glib' and assumed that viewers understood the background to stories, a view that many members of the general public we interviewed agreed with:

> I know a lot about the Middle East, but I was watching BBC World the other night, which is supposed to be better on foreign coverage ... I remember one story was about presidential elections in Brazil. Now I watched very closely on this, I don't know much about Brazil, I knew there were elections but I haven't been following it in the newspaper – what the background is, who's running for office and why. I thought [the item] was dreadful. You were given no background information, it was extremely glib, it took a lot for granted on the part of the viewer. (Philo and Berry 2004: 214)

Other journalists took a different view and argued that the limitations of the medium precluded the possibility of including more context in news bulletins. Roger Mosey, the Head of BBC Television News, writing in the *Guardian* argued that 'a transcript of the Ten O'Clock News would not fill one page of a newspaper like this: it is, inevitably, a brief digest of the day's events with as much analysis as we can manage' and that 'for the complete background you may need to go to a website or a newspaper or a book' (*Guardian* 28 July 2004). Mosey also brought up the problem of attracting young viewers, 'a notoriously difficult group for BBC television news to reach' and the 'responsibility for schools or colleges to teach about the Middle East'. We would certainly agree with the last point as we have argued that the educational curriculum in this country fails to equip young people with the necessary historical knowledge to make sense of contemporary world events (see, for instance, Philo 2004). The BBC journalist Brian Hanrahan, who had collaborated with us in the research, agreed that context was important but stressed it was a challenge to 'drip feed' it into bulletins when journalists were under many constraints:

> News programmes aren't good places to keep recapitulating history, not least because I think audiences would rebel against it, but few other programmes have their reach or accessability. The best solution I can see is to keep reports which move away from the daily news agenda and so can create space to drip feed in more context into the output. The challenge is to find, and find time for, pieces which are visually strong, intellectually astute, and sufficiently novel to hold their place in the schedule (*Ariel* 29 June 2004)

This raises a central question on the structure and future development of news. It is not possible for television news to give a history lesson every five minutes. Yet it is possible to contextualise stories and to insert brief explanations, which radically can transform both the understanding and levels of interest of viewers. The challenge for academics and broadcasters is to develop innovative forms of news in which this can be done, and thus to enable television to play a proper role in developing an informed public debate.

Notes

Chapter 3

1   Quoted in Amnesty International US, Questions and Answers on Racial Profiling at <www.amnestyusa.org/discrimination/racial_profiling/qanda. html#security>.

2   The SUS law ('stop under suspicion') gave the police the right to arrest someone on the suspicion that they were about to commit an offence. It was finally abolished in the 1980s.

3   See *European Race Bulletin* nos 43 and 44.

4   *Deutsche Welle* 18 May 2004, *IslamOnline.net* <www.islam-online.net/ English/News/2004-05/19/article01.shtml>.

5   *Reuters* 8 July 2004.

6   *Deutsche Welle* 16 February 2004.

7   See *European Race Bulletin* no. 41.

8   *Expatica News* 22, 24, 26 September 2003.

9   *Deutsche Presse Agentur* 17 March 2004.

10   *Statewatch* November–December 2003 (vol. 13, no. 6).

11   See Arun Kundnani, 'Stop and search: police step up targetting of Blacks and Asians', at <www.irr.org.uk/2003/march/ak000015.html>.

12   The Stephen Lawrence Inquiry: report of an inquiry by Sir William Macpherson of Cluny, The Stationery Office, CM 4262-1, February 1999.

13   Statewatch at <www.statewatch.org>.

14   *Guardian* 10 August 2004.

15   *The Bulletin* 4 Septemnber 2003.

16   See *European Race Bulletin* no. 41.

17   *Copenhagen Post* 10 July 2003.

18   *Aftenposten* 29, 30 January 2004.

19   Ibid.

20   Ibid.

21   *European Race Bulletin* no. 41.

22   *Frankfurther Rundschau* 10 September 2002.

Chapter 4

1   Hansard, Written Answers, 'Iraq' 9 July 2003: Column 818W <http://www
.parliament.the-stationery-office.co.uk/pa/cm200203/cmhansrd/
cm030709/text/30709w09.htm>.

2   <http://www.ukresilience.info/role.htm> accessed 20 September 2004.

3   <http://ukresilience.info/mefreport.htm> accessed 20 September 2004.

4   From: Dr Pat Troop, Deputy Chief Medical Officer, Department of Health
'CONCERN OVER RICIN POISON IN THE ENVIRONMENT' 7 January
2003, Ref. CEM/CMO/2003/1, joint statement from the Metropolitan Police
and the Deputy Chief Medical Officer, <http://199.228.212.132/doh/
embroadcast.nsf/0/2344372825A05AFC80256CA7005727CE?Open
Document>.

5   Interview with the author, the Cabinet Office, 17 July 2003.

6   Email to the author 25 February 2003.

Chapter 5

1   Thus when the *Mail* and *Standard* mounted a strident campaign to try to
pressurise the British Board of Film Classification into banning *Crash*, I wrote
to the PCC to complain that the numerous articles which constituted this
campaign were factually wrong on just about every conceivable count. But
although repeatedly I pointed out that I was specifically *not* complaining about
these papers' editorial stance, the PCC mulishly insisted on treating my
complaint as if that's exactly what I was doing, inevitably rejecting it on the
grounds that: 'The Commission acknowledges the right of newspapers to take
a partisan stance on such matters', thus rejecting a complaint I'd never made,
and had indeed been very careful not to make, in the first place (Petley 1997:
72).

Chapter 6

1   The Society of Editors report was edited and written by the author of this
chapter, Peter Cole. Robert Cockcroft, Sean Dooley, Chris Elliott, Liz Griffin,
Tony Johnston, Doug Melloy, Marc Reeves, David Rowell, Bob Satchwell,
Keith Stafford and Richard Tait, all members of the Training Committee,
contributed material.

2   Information provided by Roger Borrell in interview with the author.

3   *Coronation Street* – a British soap opera set in Manchester.

Chapter 7

1   Oumma.com, the first French-speaking Muslim website, was created in
September 1999 and has 120,000 subscribers. OummaTV has broadcast on the

same website since June 2003. Aslim-taslam.com, a more conservative website, has been online since November 2000. The women's magazine *Hawwa* has also been produced since 2000. Using the new technologies of information and communication, these media are led, presented and consumed by the young generation of French Muslims.

2   In September 2003, Sarah Joseph also launched the Muslim lifestyle Magazine *Emel*, a magazine she continues to edit.

3   The List Euro-Palestine was an anti-Zionist political organisation that ran in the 2004 European elections. Constituted by a range of celebrities and public figures (including the singer Princess Erika and the humorist Dieudonné) the group attracted the usual accusation that its criticisms of Israel, and support for Palestinian rights, were anti-Semitic.

Chapter 8

1   Although because of the visibility and associations with Muslims made in articles on September 11 and the war in Iraq, people are increasingly making connections between these articles and Muslims without the explicit signifier.

2   Global refers to total coverage of Islam and Muslims in these papers.

Chapter 9

1   The bureaucratic sources were taken to be: UK Government, UK Opposition Party, Other UK Political, Pressure Group, UN, EU, NATO, Other International Group, International Government, International Legitimate Opposition, Business/Corporate actors, Public Sector, Armed Forces and other Media. The non-bureaucratic sources were taken to be: Illegitimate and/or Terrorist Group, Tribesman, Criminal, Academic, Non-Muslim Religious group, Muslim Religious group, Adult, Child, Artist or Writer, Celebrity, Royalty and 'Other'. The frequencies were combined using the 'transform' function in SPSS.

2   To an extent, of course, this is entirely in keeping with the practical journalistic approach to objectivity: if a journalist includes criticisms of an individual, or a group, or a religion, then he/she should properly include a source to counter such criticism.

Chapter 10

1   This chapter implicitly acknowledges the diversity of portrayals in the mass media; however, due to limitations of space it can only refer to general trends.

2   Elaine Sciolino of the *New York Times* is a primary example.

3   The governments of Saudi Arabia, Kuwait and Egypt are considered allies.

4   CNN, 'You are either with us, or against us', <http://www.cnn.com/2001/

US/11/06/gen.attack.on.terror/> (6 November 2001); accessed: 18 August 2004.

5   Paraphrased and translated from a conference paper given by Antonius Rachad, cited in Briemberg (1992).

6   For sound historical assessments of this much-maligned group, see Farhad Daftary, *The Assassin Legends: Myths of the Isma'ilis* (London: I.B. Tauris, 1995) and Marshall G.S. Hodgson, *The Order of Assassins* (The Hague: Mouton & Co., 1955).

7   Prominent journalists like Laurence Zuckerman, associate editor of the *Columbia Journalism Review*, made the case to keep the press's spotlight continually focused on the Western hostages in Beirut. Laurence Zuckerman, 'The Dilemma of the Forgotten Hostages', *Columbia Journalism Review* (July/August 1986), pp. 30–4. Whereas numerous articles had appeared about the Western hostages, there was massive coverage of the release of Terry Waite on 19 November 1991 and that of Terry Anderson on 5 December 1991, including lead stories, editorials, columns, analyses and backgrounders. A survey by the International Institute of Communications of the news broadcasts of 87 television channels in 55 countries on 19 November 1991, reported in *The Economist* on 8 February 1992, indicated that the release of Thomas Sutherland and Terry Waite on consecutive days had dominated the air waves.

8   Kampfner presented a BBC programme in which the inside story about the 'rescue' and its staging by the Pentagon was revealed. This information seems to have come to light mainly because the communication official of the British military, the US's primary ally in the war, was upset by the overt tactics of American propagandists.

9   See, for example, Jerry Adler, 'The Rescue: Jessica's Liberation (cover story)', *Newsweek* (2003), 42–7.

Chapter 11

The author wishes to thank Michelle Feuerlicht for the background work undertaken for this article.

1   This is not to say many in the Muslim community in Sydney did not feel the sting of Australian involvement in the first Gulf War. A considerable literature has built up on the experiences of prejudice by Arabic, Muslim and others 'of Middle Eastern appearance' during this period (see Jakubowicz et al. 1994).

2   QSR International Pty Ltd produces the Non-numerical Unstructured Data Indexing, Searching and Theorizing (NU'DIST) qualitative data analysis software out of Melbourne, Australia.

3   One week later, having been caught out in Australia, there was a new Op-Ed piece, again promoting the book, but this time in the *New York Times*. But Manji had done the paper the honour of new thoughts.

Chapter 12

* This chapter was translated from Hebrew by Anat Schultz.

1   Despite their significance, Malka's accusations did not have an impact on the public and received scant coverage in the Israeli press. For an elaboration, see David Hirst, 'Don't Blame Arafat', *Guardian*, 17 July 2004.

2   See: Caspit Ben, 'Israel is not a state that has an army but an army with an affiliated state', *Ma'ariv*, 6 September 2002; *B'tselem* (the Israeli Information Center for Human Rights in the Occupied Territories), Information Sheet, *Illusion of Restraint*, December 2000.

3   See *B'tselem* (<http://www.btselem.org/>). Palestinian sources report higher numbers of casualties, see, for example, the data posted by the website of the Palestine Red Crescent Society (<http://www.palestinercs.org/>). The *B'tselem* data do not include Palestinians who died after medical treatment was delayed due to restrictions of movement.

4   *Yediot* is Israel's best selling newspaper. On weekends its circulation is higher than that of all the other Hebrew daily newspapers put together and is over 500,000 (Israel's population is 6.7 million). The circulation of *Haaretz* is close to 50,000 a day (Caspi and Limor 1999; Tokatly 2000).

5   In accordance with the already familiar pattern, after the assassination of A'tef Abayat on October 18, 2001, all three newspapers listed well-known attacks ascribed to him by IDF officials, indicating the precise dates and names of the casualties. The five Israeli casualties he was said to be directly involved in included the names of two soldiers, whose deaths had been previously attributed to Hussein Abayat (A'tef Abayat's cousin), assassinated by Israel nearly a year earlier.

6   Between the beginning of March and the Ashdod Port attack on 14 March 2004, the IDF had killed thirty-six Palestinians in various operations, at least nine of them civilians. Between the Ashdod attack and the killing of Sheikh Yassin on 22 March 2004, Israel assassinated two members of the Islamic Jihad in the Gaza Strip, twelve Palestinians were killed in IDF operations in Rafah and Absan (two were civilians), a girl was killed in Khan Yunis and an armed man was killed in the Balata refugee camp near Nablus.

7   Pages 6 and 7 were dedicated to the memory of Moran Vardi, the Marine Commando officer killed two years after his good friend Nir Krichman, the first Marine Commando casualty of the present intifada. Under the headline 'Through fire and water', the item, accompanied by photographs, brought the story of Nir and Moran 'who did everything together'. The article also lists the six Marine Commando casualties killed in the Territories from the start of the intifada and the circumstances in which they were killed (*Yediot* 7 July 2004).

8   *Haaretz* is the only Israeli newspaper that employs a journalist living in the West Bank and bringing first-hand accounts from the Territories.

Chapter 13

1   A version of this chapter appeared in *Global Dialogue*, 6, 1–2, Winter/Spring 2004, pp. 108–18.

2   This analysis excluded Iran. (Iran's Internet access was unclassified in the separate UNDP *Human Development Report 2001: Making New Techologies Work for Human Development* [<http://hdr.undp.org/reports/global/2001/en/>] (UNDP, 2001). See *AHDR 2002*, especially pp. 65–83. All URLs in this article correct at February 2004. Updates from Virtually Islamic: <www.virtuallyislamic.com>.

3   *Middle East Online*, 'ADSL in Iran', 9 January 2004, [<http://www.middle-east-online.com/english/>]. BBC, 'Doing business in the desert', 3 December 2003. BBC, 'Egyptians tackle taboos through net', 2 September 2003, <http://news.bbc.co.uk>.

4   SFGate.com, 'Stifled by clerics, Iranians escape', 16 November 2003, <http://www.sfgate.com>.

5   BBC, 'Postcards from Iran: Surfing the net', 13 February 2004, <http://news.bbc.co.uk>.

6   *Gulf News*, 'Internet chatting is becoming an addiction', 29 July 2003, <http://www.gulf-news.com>.

7   Awais Ahmad Khan Leghari, cited in *Associated Press*, 'Is the World Wide Web only for the West?', 19 December 2003, <http://msnbc.msn.com>.

8   A range of sites representing this diversity can be found on the writer's own Islamic Studies Pathways, <http://www.lamp.ac.uk/cis/pathways>.

9   Radio Free Europe/Radio Liberty, 'Analyst Speaks About "Globalization" Of Islam', 28 May 2003, <http://www.rferl.org/newsline/>.

10 *Associated Press*, 'Saudi Cleric's Followers Face Charges', 31 May 2003.

11 *Dar al-Hayat*, 'Young Saudis Volunteer To Preach In "Modern" Way', 27 May 2003, <http://english.daralhayat.com>.

12 *Asharq al-Awsat*, 'Sheikh Terra', 10 February 2004, <http://www.aawsat.com>.

13 *NewsForge*, 'Meet Saudi Arabia's most famous computer expert', 14 January 2004, <http://www.newsforge.com>.

14 *Daily Summit*, <http://dailysummit.net>.

15 *The Register*, 'US sponsors Anonymiser – if you live in Iran', 28 August 2003, <http://www.the register.co.uk>.

16 *Guardian*, 'Webwatch', 4 December 2003, <http://www.guardian.co.uk>, referring to Mohammed Ali Abtahi, <http://www.webnevesht.com>.

17 See the campaigning website Peacefire, <http://www.peacefire.org>, and the commercial Anonymizer, <http://anonymizer.com>, which has a free 'Privacy Toolbar'.

18 Ayatollah al-Sistani, <http://al-sistani.org>.

19 See Yusuf al-Qaradawi, <http://www.qaradawi.net>, and Islam Online, <http://www.islam-online.net>.

20   *SF Gate.com*, 'A Muslim calls for reform – and she's a lesbian', 19 January 2004, <http://www.sfgate.com>.
21   *Independent*, 'Saudi gays flaunt new freedoms', 20 February 2004, <http://news.independent.co.uk.
22   BBC, 'Iranians arrested for net dating', 3 March 2003, <http://news.bbc.co.uk>.
23   *Newsweek*/MSNBC – 'Serious Muslim Seeks Spouse – Online', 6 February 2004, <http://www.msnbc.msn.com>.
24   International Islamic Digital Library, <http://www.iidl.net>.
25   *The Star*, 'Harnessing technology to stay connected', 27 December 2003, <http://www.thestar.com.my>.
26   *Wired*, 'The Great Library of Amazonia', 23 October 2003, <http://www.wired.com/news>.

Chapter 14

1   Various studies have been conducted on the negative representation of Islam and Muslims in the media prior to September 11, see for example, Abbas (2000) and Poole (2002). These were supplemented by a number of other studies following September 11, for example, Allen & Nielson (2002) and the Runnymede Trust (2001).
2   Runnymede Trust 1997.
3   Data collected for doctoral research (Ahmed 2003). This consisted of eight semi-structured group interviews with a total of 27 young South Asian Muslims (who were asked to complete viewing diaries) and editors of five Muslim publications. It also comprised a survey distributed through Muslim publications.
4   Muslim press is defined here as any publication aimed mainly at a Muslim readership containing material of interest to them because of their religious affiliation, but dealing with a broad number of issues. Various media, including independent/satellite television channels, radio programmes, audio-visual material, new forms of electronic media, including the Internet, as well as an extensive range of books are other types of Muslim media that also exist in Britain.
5   For example, *Impact International* began in the early 1970s.
6   The majority of respondents were South Asian Muslims; therefore it is this section of the Muslim population that is the focus of this research whilst acknowledging the great ethnic diversity of British Muslims.
7   *Dawah* is the Arabic word for invitation to or propagation of Islam.
8   The Qur'an is the Holy Book of Islam.
9   *Hadith* literature relates to the sayings and practices of the Holy Prophet Muhammad (peace be upon him).
10   This data was collected from a Muslim media survey distributed through four publications; *Trends, Q-News, The Muslim News* and *Crescent International*.

Of a total of 1,500 surveys distributed, 77 were completed and returned.

11 See *After September 11th. TV News and Transnational Audiences.*, <http://www.afterseptember11.tv/>.

12 For example, statements by politicians, including the Prime Minister, in *The Muslim News*.

13 This is already happening to a degree, where journalists linked to Muslim publications are contributing to broadsheets such as the *Guardian* and the *Independent*. In some instances Muslim media is being reported on by mainstream press, see for example, Vallely 2000.

Chapter 16

1 An earlier version of this chapter was presented as a keynote address at the International Conference on Muslims and Islam in the 21st Century: Image and Reality, at the International Islamic University, Kuala Lumpur, Malaysia, August 2004.

2 Conversation with the author.

Chapter 17

1 An account of these is published elsewhere as *Bad News from Israel* (Pluto Press 2004).

References

Abbas, T. (2000). 'Images of Islam', *Index on Censorship* (29(5)): 64–8

ABC Online: <www.abc.net.au> contains 'Media Watch' and '7.30 Report'

Abdel-Fattah, R. (1997). 'Muslims and the Media', *Salam* (July–August, Lakemba, Sydney)

Abdelkhah, F. (1998). *Etre moderne en Iran* (Paris, Karthala)

Adler, J. (2003). 'The Rescue: Jessica's Liberation' (cover story), *Newsweek* (42–7)

Ahmed, A.S. (1992). *Postmodernism and Islam: Predicament and Promise* (London: Routledge)

Ahmed, S. T. (2003). 'Young British Muslims: Social Space and Active Identity', unpublished Ph.D. thesis (University of Leicester)

Al Shammari, S. (1999). *The Arab Nationalist Dimension in Al Jazeera Satellite Channel: A Case Study of the Opposite Direction* (Doha, Dar Al Sharq)

Alden, C. (2004). *Media Directory 2005* (London, Guardian Newspapers Ltd)

al-Khuri, R. (2001). 'The Day After: The Punishment of States', *Al-Anwar* (13 September 2001)

Allen, C. (2001). 'Islamophobia in the Media since September 11th', paper given at *Exploring Islamophobia* (University of Westminster, London, 29 September 2001)

Allen, C. and Nielsen, J. (2002). *Summary Report on Islamophobia in the EU after 11 September 2001* (Vienna, European Monitoring Centre on Racism and Xenophobia)

Altheide, D.L. (2003). 'Notes towards a politics of fear', *Journal for Crime, Conflict and the Media* (1(1): 37–54)

Amiraux, V. (2001). *Acteurs de l'islam entre Allemagne et Turquie: parcours militants et expériences religieuses* (Paris, L'Harmattan, 'Logiques politiques')

Amnesty International (2002). *Israel and the Occupied Territories: Shielded from Scrutiny: IDF Violations in Jenin and Nablus* (London, Amnesty International)

Anderson, B. (1983). *Imagined Communities: Reflections on the Origin and Spread of Nationalism* (London, Verso)

Ang, I., Brand, J.E., Noble, G. and Wilding, D. (2002). *Living Diversity: Australia's Multicultural Future* (Special Broadcasting Service (SBS). Artarmon, NSW)

Anthias, F. and Yuval-Davis, N. in association with Cain, H. (1992). *Racialized Boundaries: Race, Nation, Gender, Colour and Class and the Anti-Racist Struggle* (London, Routledge)

Anti-Discrimination Board of NSW (2003). *Race for the Headlines: Racism and Media Discourse* (Sydney)

Ashrawi, H. (2001). Image and reality: The role of the US in the Middle East, <http://www.miftah.org/Display.cfm?DocId=167&CategoryId=1> (28 December 2004)

Associated Press (2001). Congress Members Seek Officer's Dismissal, <http://www.nytimes.com/aponline/national/AP-Boykin-Investigation.html (2 September 2004)

Ata, A.W. (1984). 'Moslem-Arab portrayal in the Australian Press and in School Textbooks', *Australian Journal of Social Issues* (19(3): 207–18)

Athwal, H. (2004). 'Analysis: who are the terrorists?', *Institute of Race Relations*, <http://www.irr.org.uk/2004/august/ak000007.html,> (12 August 2004)

Atran, S. (2003). *Strategic Threat from Suicide Terror* (AEI-Brookings Joint Center for Regulatory Studies)

Ayish, M.I. (2002). 'Political Communication on Arab World Television: Evolving Patterns', *Political Communication* (19(2): 137–54)

Back, L., Keith, M., Khan, A., Shukra, K. and Solomos, J. (2002). 'New Labour's White Heart: Politics, Multiculturalism and the Return of Assimilation', *The Political Quarterly* (vol. 73(4): 445–54)

Bauman, Z. (2000). *Liquid Modernity* (Cambridge, Polity)

Bendle, M.F. (2002). 'Guest Editorial', *Australian Religious Studies Review* (15(1):5–9)

Benyon, J. and Solomos, J. (1987). *The Roots of Urban Unrest* (Oxford, Pergamon)

Berry, M. (2004). 'Reporting on Contested Territory: Television News Coverage of the Israel–Palestine Conflict', unpublished Ph.D. thesis (University of Glasgow)

Bin Laden, O. (2001). 'Statement to the Muslim People', *Journal of Palestine Studies* (7 October 2001, 31 (2): 133–4)

Bishara, M. (2004). 'Propaganda TV won't help the US', *International Herald Tribune* (23 February 2004)

Blair, T. (2001). 'We won't lose our nerve or falter, Blair tells doubters',

Guardian (31 October 2001)

Brasted, H.V. (1997). 'The Politics of Stereotyping: Western Images of Islam', *Manushi* (Issue 89), <www.indiatogether.org/manushi/issue98/islam.htm>

Brasted, H.V. (2001). 'Contested representations in historical perspective: images of Islam and the Australian Press, 1950–2000', in A. Saeed and S. Akbarzadeh, *Muslim Communities in Australia* (Sydney, University of New South Wales Press)

Briemberg, M. (1992). 'Sand in the Snow: Canadian High-brow Orientalism', in M. Briemberg (ed.), *It Was, It Was Not: Essays and Art on the War Against Iraq* (Vancouver, New Star Books)

Bright, M. (2001). 'Terror, security and the media', *Observer* (21 July 2001)

Brumberg, D. (2002). 'Arab public opinion and US foreign policy: A complex encounter', Committee on Government Reform, Subcommittee on National Security, Veterans Affairs, and International Relations. United States Congress, House of Representatives, <http://www.ceip.org/files/pdf/2002-10-08-BrumbergHilltestimony. pdf> (8 October 2002)

Bunglawala, I. (2002). 'British Muslims and the Media', in *The Quest for Sanity: Reflections on September 11 and the Aftermath* (London, MCB)

Bunt, G. (2000). *Virtually Islamic* (Cardiff, University of Wales Press)

Bunt, G. (2003). *Islam in the Digital Age* (London, Pluto Press)

Burke, J. and Bright, M. (2003). 'Britain faces fresh peril from the "clean-skinned" terrorists', *Observer* (12 January 2003)

Bush, G.W. (2001a). Address to a Joint Session of Congress and the American People (Washington, D.C., The White House)

Bush, G.W. (2001b). President Directs Humanitarian Aid to Afghanistan (Washington, D.C., The White House)

Bush, G.W. (2001c). 'Freedom itself was attacked this morning', <http://www.americanrhetoric.com/speeches/gwbush911barksdale.ht>

Bush, G.W. (2001d). 'We'll destroy them, says Bush', *Observer*, 16 September 2001, available at <http://observer.guardian.co.uk/international/story/0,,552727,00.html>

Bush, G.W. (2002a). 'Call for New Palestinian Leadership: Conflict or Peace', *Vital Speeches of the Day* (68(19): 578)

Bush, G.W. (2002b). President Bush, Secretary Powell Discuss Middle East, <http://www.whitehouse.gov/news/releases/2002/04/20020418-3.html> (18 April 2002)

Bush, G.W. (2004). Interview with President George W. Bush. at <http://www.msnbc.msn.com/id/4179618/> (8 February 2004)

Butler, J. (2004). *Precarious Life* (London, Verso)

Carroll, R. (2002). 'Marines seize al-Qaida caves as Afghan violence escalates', *Guardian* (9 April 2002)

Caspi, D. and Limor, Y. (1999). *The In/Outsiders: The Media in Israel* (Cresskill, N.J., Hampton Press)

Césari J. (1998). *Musulmans et républicains. Les jeunes, l'islam et la France* (Bruxelles, Complexe)

Chermak, S. (2003). 'Marketing fear: representing terrorism after September 11', *Journal for Crime, Conflict and the Media* (1(1): 5 -22)

Central Intelligence Agency (CIA) (2002). *The War on Terrorism: Terrorism FAQs*, at <http://www.cia.gov/terrorism/faqs.html>

Clark, P.M. and Mowlana, H. (1978). 'Iran's Perception of Western Europe: A Study in National and Foreign Policy Articulation', *International Interactions* (4(2): 99–123)

Cleland, B. (2001). 'The History of Muslims in Australia', in Saeed, A. and Akbarzadeh, S., *Muslim Communities in Australia* (Sydney, University of New South Wales Press)

CNN (2001). 'You are either with us, or against us', at <http://www.cnn.com/2001/US/11/06/gen.attack.on.terror> (6 November 2001)

Cohen, N. (2003). 'How to stitch up a terror suspect', *Observer* (12 January 2003)

Collins, J., Noble, G., Poynting, S. and Tabar, P. (2000). *Kebabs, Kids, Cops and Crime* (Sydney, Pluto Press)

Committee on Standards in Public Life (2004). *Survey of Public Attitudes Towards Conduct in Public Life*, at <http://www.public-standards.gov.uk/research/researchreport.pdf>

Cottle S. (ed.) (2000). *Ethnic Minorities and the Media. Changing Cultural Boundaries* (Buckingham, Open University Press)

Cottle, S. (2000). 'Rethinking News Access', *Journalism Studies* (1(3): 427–48)

Daftary, F. (1995). *The Assassin Legends: Myths of the Isma'ilis* (London, I.B. Tauris)

Dahlgren, P. and Chakrapani, S. (1982). 'The Third World on TV news: Western ways of seeing the "Other"', in W.C. Adams (ed.), *TV Coverage of International Affairs* (New Jersey, Ablex Publishing)

Day, J. (2002). 'US steps up global PR drive', *Guardian* (30 July 2002)

Dayan, D. (1998). 'Particularistic Media and Diasporic Communications', in Liebes, T. and Curran, J. (eds), *Media, Ritual and Identity* (London, Routledge)

Defence Committee (2001). *Second report*, Session 2001–2, 12 December 2001, at <www.publications.parliament.uk/pa/cm200102>

Dijk, T. van (1991). *Racism and the Press* (London, Routledge)

Dijk, T.A. van (1988). *News Analysis: Case Studies of International and National News in the Press* (Hillsdale, N.J., Lawrence Erlbaum)

Dijk, T.A. van (1998). 'Critical Discourse Analysis', at <http://www.let.uva.ul/~teun/cda.2>

Djerjian, E.P. (2003). *Changing Minds, Winning Peace: A New Strategic Direction for US Diplomacy in the Arab and Muslim World* (Washington, D.C., Advisory Group for Public Diplomacy for the Arab and Muslim World, Committee on Appropriations, US House of Representatives)

Dorril, S. (2000). *MI6: Inside the Covert World of Her Majesty's Secret Intelligence Service* (New York, The Free Press)

Drummond, J. (2001). 'Qatari broadcaster emerges as key channel of communication', *Financial Times* (9 October 2001)

Dunn, K.M. and Geeraert, P. (2003). 'The geography of "race" and racisms', *GeoDate* (16(3): 1–6)

Dunn, K.M., Forrest, J., Burnley, I. and McDonald, A. (2004). 'Constructing Racism in Australia', *Australian Journal of Social Issues* (39(4): 409–30)

Esposito, J.L. (1992). *The Islamic Threat: Myth or Reality?* (Oxford, Oxford University Press)

Farah, J. (2001). 'What does the Arab world really think about the Mideast conflict?', *WorldNetDaily.com* at <http://www.worldnetdaily.com/news/article.asp?ARTICLE_ID=23863> (1 August 2001)

Ferguson, R. (1998). *Representing 'Race'. Ideology, Identity and the Media* (London, Arnold)

Fisk, R. (1991). *Pity the Nation: Lebanon at War* (Oxford, Oxford Univerity Press)

Flanders, L. (2001). 'Arab CNN' first berated, then bombed by US, at <www.zmag.org/flandersarabcnn.htm> (14 November 2001)

Foot, P. (2000). 'The slow death of investigative journalism', in Glover, Stephen (ed.), *The Penguin Book of Journalism: Secrets of the Press* (London, Penguin)

Foreign Affairs Select Committee (2003). *Ninth Report The Decision to go to War in Iraq*, at <http://www.parliament.the-stationery-office.co.uk/pa/cm200203/cmselect/cmfaff/813/81308.htm> (7 July 2003)

Fortier, A.-M. (2005). 'Pride Politics and Multiculturalist Citizenship', *Ethnic and Racial Studies* (vol. 28(3))

Fowler, R. (1991). *Language in the News: Discourse and Ideology in the Press* (London, Routledge)

Francis, J. (2003). 'White Culture, Black Mark', *British Journalism Review* (14(3): 67–73)

Friedman, T. (2001). 'TV station beams beacon of freedom to Arab world', *Milwaukee Journal Sentinel* (28 February, 31A)

Frost, C. (2004). 'The Press Complaints Commission: a study of ten years of adjudications of press complaints', *Journalism Studies* (5(1): 101–14)

Gabriel, J. (1998). *Whitewash: Racialised Politics and the Media* (London, Routledge)

Gallup (2002). 'Poll of the Islamic World', *USA Today* (27 February 2002)

Galtung, J. and Ruge, M. (1965). 'The Structure of Foreign News', *Journal of Peace Research* (2: 74–91)

Gannon, K. (2001). 'Kabul Awakes to the Aftermath of Another Night's Heavy Bombing', *Guardian* (27 October 2001)

Geisser, V. (2003). *La nouvelle islamophobie* (Paris, La Découverte)

Ghanoonparvar, M. R. (1993). *In a Persian Mirror: Images of the West and Westerners in Iranian Fiction* (Austin, University of Texas)

Goldenberg, S. (2002). 'Long after the air raids, bomblets bring more death', *Guardian* (28 January 2002)

Göle, N. (1993). *Musulmanes et modernes. Voile et civilisation en Turquie* (Paris, La Découverte)

Gordon, N. (2004). 'Rationalising extra-judicial executions: the Israeli press and the legitimisation of abuse', *International Journal of Human Rights* (8(3): 1–20)

Granatt, M. (2003). Address to the 'Communicating the War on Terror' conference, the Royal Institution, London, (5 June 2003)

Guardian (2001a). 'The World at War' (8 October 2001)

Guardian (2001b). 'Blair Plays it Cooler' (31 October 2001)

Guardian (2001c). 'Tony Blair's Dilemma' (5 November 2001)

Guardian (2001d) 'Restraint Urged Over Prisoners' (24 November 2001)

Habermas, J. (1989). *The Structural Transformation of the Public Sphere* (Cambridge, MIT Press)

Haddad, S. and Khashan, H. (2002). 'Islam and Terrorism: Lebanese Muslim Views on September 11', *Journal of Conflict Resolution* (46(6): 812–28)

Haddad, Y.Y. (1996). 'Islamist Perceptions of US Policy in the Near East', in David W. Lesch (ed.), *The Middle East and the United States: A Historical and Political Reassessment* (Boulder, Westview Press)

Hafez, K. (2000). *Islam and the West in the Mass Media. Fragmented Images in a Globalizing World* (Cresskill, NJ, Hampton Press)

Hage, G. (1998). *White Nation: Fantasies of White Supremacy in a Multicultural Society* (Annandale, Australia, Pluto Press)

Hall, S. (1992). 'The Question of Cultural Identity', in S. Hall, D. Held and T. McGrew (eds), *Modernity and Its Futures* (Cambridge, Polity and

Open University Press)

Hall, S. and Jacques, M. (1983). 'Introduction', in S. Hall and M. Jacques, *The Politics of Thatcherism* (London, Lawrence and Wishart)

Hall, S., Critcher, C., Jefferson, T., Clarke, J. and Roberts, B. (1978). *Policing the Crisis: Mugging, the State, and Law and Order* (London, Macmillan)

Halliday, F. (1996). *Islam and the Myth of Confrontation* (London: I.B. Tauris)

Hammond, A. (2001). 'Moving the Masses', *The Jerusalem Report* (15 January 2001)

Hammond, P. (2000). 'Reporting "Humanitarian" Warfare: Propaganda, Moralism and NATO's Kosovo War', *Journalism Studies* (1(3): 365–86)

Hammond, P. (2003). 'The Media War on Terrorism', *Journal for Crime, Conflict and the Media* (1(1): 23–36)

Hartmann, P., Husband, C. and Clark, J. (1974). *Race as News: A Study in the Handling of Race in the British Press from 1963 to 1970* (Paris, UNESCO)

Hassan, R. (2002). 'On Being Religious: A study of Christian and Muslim piety in Australia', *Australian Religious Studies Review* (15(1): 87–114)

Herold, M. (2001). 'A Dossier on Civilian Victims of United States' Aerial Bombing of Afghanistan: A Comprehensive Accounting', at <www.medialens.org> (December 2001)

Herold, M. (2002a). 'Counting the Dead', *Guardian* (8 August 2002)

Herold, M. (2002b). 'Who Will Count the Dead?', in Roger Burbach and Ben Clarke (eds), *September 11 and the US war: Beyond the curtain of smoke* (San Francisco, City Light Books)

Hickey, N. (2002). 'Perspectives on War', *Columbia Journalism Review* at <http://www.cjr.org/issues/2002/2/war-hickey.asp>

Hodgson, M.G.S. (1955). *The Order of Assassins* (The Hague, Mouton & Co.)

Holohan, S. (2005). *The Search for Justice in a Media Age: Reading Stephen Lawrence and Louise Woodward* (Aldershot, Ashgate)

Holohan, S. and Poole, E. (2002). 'Race, Representation and Power: the Experience of British Muslims', *Intersections: The Journal of Global Communications and Culture* (2(3/4): 79–88)

Home Office (2002). *Secure Borders, Safe Haven: Integration with Diversity in Modern Britain* (London, Stationery Office)

House of Commons Culture, Media and Sport Committee (2003). *Privacy and Media Intrusion*, vol. 1 (London, The Stationery Office)

Human Rights and Equal Opportunity Commission (2004). 'Ismae-Listen: National Consultations on Eliminating Prejudice Against Arab and

Muslim Australians'

Human Rights Watch (2001a). 'Afghanistan: US Bombs Kill Twenty-Three Civilians', at <www.hrw.org> (26 October 2001)

Human Rights Watch (2001b). 'Afghanistan: New Civilian Deaths Due to US Bombing', at <www.hrw.org> (30 October 2001)

Human Rights Watch (2001c). 'Cluster Bombs in Afghanistan', at <www.hrw.org> (October 2001)

Human Rights Watch (2002a). *World Report 2002: Afghanistan*

Human Rights Watch (2002b). 'Afghanistan: Return of the warlords', at <www.hrw.org> (June 2002)

Hume, B. (2001). 'Special Report Roundtable', *Fox News* (16 October)

Hume, B. (2003). 'Text of Bush interview with Fox News', *Fox News*, available at <http://www.foxnews.com/story/0,2933,98006,00.html> (22 September 2003)

Husband, C. (2002). 'Diasporic Identities and Diasporic Economies: the Case of Minority Ethnic Media', in M. Martiniello and B. Piquard (eds), *Diversity in the City* (Bilbao, Universidad de Deusto)

Husband, C., Beattie, L. and Markelin, L. (2002). 'The Key Role of Minority Ethnic Media in Multiethnic Societies: Case Study, UK', Research Paper, International Media Working Group Against Racism and Xenophobia (IMRAX) and the International Federation of Journalists (IFJ) <www.ifj.org>

Illin, B., Thorn, L. and Burton, P.S. (2003). 'Nine Red Herrings: How the Western Left has Misread Iraq', at <http://www.marxist.org.uk/htm_docs/comm12.htm> (25 April 2003)

Independent Television Commission (2003). *The Public's View*

Jacobs, Ronald N. (2000). *Race, Media and the Crisis of Civil Society. From Watts to Rodney King* (Cambridge, Cambridge University Press)

Jacobson, J. (1998). *Islam in Transition. Religion and Identity among British Pakistani Youth* (London, Routledge)

Jakubowicz, A. (forthcoming 2006) 'Political Islam and the Future of Australian Multiculturalism', *Canadian Ethnic Studies*.

Jakubowicz, A., Goodall, H., Martin, J., Mitchell, T., Randall, L. and Seneviratne, K. (1994). *Racism, Ethnicity and the Media* (Sydney, Allen and Unwin)

Jempson, M. (2004). 'Time for a Culture Change', in Jempson et al. (eds), *Satisfaction Guaranteed?: Press Complaints Systems Under Scrutiny* (Bristol, MediaWise)

Journalism Training Forum (2002). *Journalists at Work* (Publishing NTO/Skillset)

Kampfner, J. (2003). 'The Truth about Jessica', *Guardian*, at

<http://www.guardian.co.uk/Iraq/Story/0,2763,956255,00.html>, (15 May 2003)

Kampmark, B. (2003). 'Islam, Women and Australia's Discourse of Terror', *Hecate* (29(1): 86–105)

Karim, K.H. (2003). *Islamic Peril: Media and Global Violence* (2nd edn) (Montreal, Black Rose)

Kassis, H. E. (1992). 'Christian Misconceptions of Islam', in M. Briemberg (ed.), *It Was, It Was Not: Essays and Art on the War Against Iraq* (Vancouver, New Star Books)

Khosrokhavar, F. (1997). *L'Islam des jeunes* (Paris: Flammarion, 'Essais')

Khouri, R. (2003). 'For the Full Story, Watch US and Arab TV', *Daily Star* (26 March 2003)

Kifner, J. (2001). 'The new power of Arab public opinion', *New York Times* (11 November 2001)

Klein, M. (2003). *The Jerusalem Problem: the Struggle for permanent Status* (Gainesville, University Press of Florida)

Kohut, A. (2003). *American Public Diplomacy in the Islamic World: Remarks of Andrew Kohut to the Senate Foreign Relations Committee* (Philadelphia, PA, Pew Center for the People and the Press)

Korn, A. (2004a). 'Israeli Press and the War Against Terrorism: the Construction of the "Liquidation Policy"', *Crime, Law & Social Change* (41(3): 209–34)

Korn, A. (2004b). 'Reporting Palestinian Casualties in the Israeli Press: the Case of *Haaretz* and the Intifada', *Journalism Studies* (5(2): 247–62)

Krugman, P. (2003). 'Matters of emphasis', *New York Times* (29 April 2003)

Krull, S. (2004). 'The Press and Public Misperceptions About the Iraq War', *Nieman Reports* (Summer: 64–66)

Kundnani, A. (2000). '"Stumbling on": Race, Class and England', *Race and Class* (vol. 41(4): 1–18)

Kundnani, A. (2001). 'From Oldham to Bradford: the Violence of the Violated', *Race and Class* (vol. 43(2): 105–31)

Kurtz, H. (2004). 'The Post on WMDs: an Inside Story. Prewar Articles Questioning Threat Often Didn't Make Front Page', *Washington Post* (12 August 2004)

Kymlicka, W. (1995). *Multicultural Citizenship: A Liberal Theory of Minority Rights* (Oxford, Clarendon Press)

Laor, Y. (2001). 'Tears of Zion', *New Left Review* (10: 47–60)

Laor, Y. (2004). 'In Hebron', *London Review of Books* (26(14): 32–3)

Leigh, D. (2000). 'Britain's Security Services and Journalists: the Secret Story', *British Journalism Review* (11(2): 21–6)

Lygo, I. (2004). *News Overboard: the tabloid Media, Race Politics and*

Islam (Narrogin, Western Australia, Southerly Change Media)

Lynch, M. (2003). 'Taking Arabs seriously', *Foreign Affairs* (82/6) at <http://www.foreignaffairs.org/20030901faessay82506/marc-lynch/taking-arabs-seriously.html>

Macpherson, Sir W. (1999). *The Stephen Lawrence Inquiry: Report of an Inquiry* (London, Stationery Office)

Makovsky, D. (2001). 'A Voice from the Heavens: Al Jazeera's Satellite Broadcasts Inflame Emotions Across the Arab World', *US News & World Report* (14 May, 26–8)

Malcolm, J. (1990). *The Journalist and the Murderer* (New York, Vintage Books)

Mandaville, P. (2001). *Transnational Muslim Politics: Reimagining the Umma* (London, Routledge)

Manning, P. (2003). 'Arabic and Muslim People in Sydney's Daily Newspapers, Before and After September 11', *Media International Australia, Incorporating Culture and Policy* (109: 50–70)

Manning, P. (2004a). *Dog Whistle Politics and Journalism: reporting Arabic and Muslim people in Sydney Newspapers* (Sydney, Australian Centre for Independent Journalism, University of Technology)

Manning, P. (2004b). 'A colonial state of mind', *Griffith Review* (Griffith University, Nathan, Queensland)

Marginson, S. (2004). *Survey of International Tertiary Students in Australia* (Melbourne, Monash Institute for the Study of Global Movements, Monash University)

McCarthy, R. (2002). 'Pashtuns Suffer in Brutal Raids by Rival Ethnic Groups', *Guardian* (3 April 2002)

Medialens (2002). 'Media Ignores the Mass Death of Civilians in Afghanistan', at <www.medialens.org/alerts/2002/020103_de_Afghanistan.html> (3 January 2002)

Meital, Y. (2004). *Peace in Tatters: Israel, Palestine and the Middle East* (Jerusalem, Carmel) [Hebrew]

Mernissi, F. (1992). *Islam and Democracy: Fear of the Modern World*, trans. Mary Jo Lakeland (New York, Addison Wesley)

Miller, D. (2003). '"They Were All Asylum Seekers": the Propaganda Campaign to Link Iraq to Terrorism at the Expense of Refugees', *Scoop*, art <http://www.scoop.co.nz/mason/stories/HL0303/S00262.htm> (27 March 2003)

Molotch, H. and Lester, M. (1974). 'News as Purposive Behaviour: on the Strategic Use of Routine Events, Accidents and Scandals', *American Sociological Review* (39: 101–12)

Monbiot, G. (2001). 'Gagging the Sceptics', *Guardian* (16 October 2001)

Morin, R. and Deane, C. (2002). 'The Poll That Didn't Add Up: Spin on Data Blurs Findings from Gallup's Muslim Survey', *Washington Post* (23 March 2002)

Mujani, S. and Liddle, R.W. (2004). 'Politics, Islam, and Public Opinion', *Journal of Democracy* (15(1): 109–23)

Muslim Council of Britain (2002). *The Quest for Sanity: Reflections on September 11 and the Aftermath* (London, Muslim Council of Britain)

New York Times (2004). 'The Times and Iraq' (26 May 2004)

Nisbet, E.C. et al. (2003). 'Public Diplomacy, Television News, and Muslim Opinion', *Harvard Journal of Press/Politics* (9 (2): 11–37)

Norton-Taylor, R. (2001). 'Strident about Trident', *Guardian* (7 December 2001)

Norton-Taylor, R. (2002a). 'A Quarter of US Bombs Missed Target in Afghan Conflict', *Guardian* (10 April 2002)

Norton-Taylor, R. (2002b). 'Afghanistan Littered with 14,000 Unexploded Bomblets, Says UN', *Guardian* (23 March 2002)

Oifi, M. (2003). 'Une opinion arabe est née', *Libération* (18 March 2003)

Oifi, M. (2005). 'Influence Without Power', in Mohamed Zayani (ed.), *The Al Jazeera Phenomenon: Critical Perspectives on New Arab Media* (London, Pluto Press)

Palestinian Red Crescent Society (2004). 'Total Daily Numbers of Deaths & Injuries – West Bank & Gaza', at <http://palestinercs.org/crisistables/table_of_figures.htm> (3 August 2004)

Pax, S. (2003). *The Baghdad Blog* (London, Guardian Books)

Petley, J. (1997). 'No Redress from the PCC', *British Journalism Review* (8(4): 66–73)

Petley, J. (2004). 'A Modern Day Circumlocution Office?', in Jempson et al. *Satisfaction Guaranteed?: Press Complaints Systems Under Scrutiny* (Bristol, Mediawise)

Pew (2002). *Public's News Habits Little Changed by Sept. 11: Americans Lack Background to Follow International News* (Washington, D.C., Pew Research Center for the People and the Press)

Pew (2003). *Views of a Changing World: The Pew Global Attitudes Project* (Washington, D.C., The Pew Research Center for the People and the Press)

Philo, G. (2004). 'Black Holes of History: Public Understanding and the Shaping of Our Past', in Miller, D. (ed.), *Tell Me Lies: Propaganda and Media Distortion in the Attack on Iraq* (London, Pluto Press)

Philo, G. (1995) (ed.). *Glasgow Media Group Reader* (vol. 2. London, Routledge)

Philo, G. and Berry, M. (2004). *Bad News from Israel* (London, Pluto Press)

Pilger, J. (2003). 'War on Truth', *New Statesman* (4 August 2003: 14–15)

Pintak, L. (2003). *Seeds of Hate: How America's Flawed Lebanon Policy Ignited the Jihad* (Sterling, VA, Pluto Press)

Pintak, L. (2006). *Reflections in a Bloodshot Lens: The Communications Gap Between America and the World's Muslims* (London and Ann Arbor, Pluto Books/University of Michigan Press)

Pollock, D. (1992). *The Arab Street? Public Opinion in the Arab World* (Washington, D.C., The Washington Institute for Near Eastern Policy)

Poniwozik, J. (2001). 'The Battle for Hearts and Minds: even before bin Laden's Tape, the US was Losing the Propaganda War in the Arab World', *Times Magazine* (22 October: 65)

Poole, E. (2002). *Reporting Islam: Media Representations of British Muslims* (London, I.B. Tauris)

Poynting, S. and Noble, G. (2003). '"Dog Whistle Journalism" and Muslim Australians Since 2001', *Media International Australia, Incorporating Culture and Policy* (109: 41–9)

Press Complaints Commission (2003). *Annual Review 2002* (London, Press Complaints Commission)

Press Complaints Commission (2004). *Annual Review 2003* (London, Press Complaints Commission)

Reagan, R. (1974). 'City Upon a Hill: the President at the First Annual CPAC Conference, at <www.presidentreagan.info/speeches/city_upon _a_hill.cfm, accessed>

Reinhart, T. (2002). *Israel/Palestine: How to End the War of 1948* (New York, Seven Stories Press)

Reynolds, H. (1999). *Why Weren't We Told?* (Melbourne, Penguin)

Richardson, J.E. (2001a). '"Now is the Time to Put an End to All This" Argumentative Discourse Theory and Letters to the Editor', *Discourse and Society* (12(2): 143–68)

Richardson, J.E. (2001b). 'British Muslims in the Broadsheet Press: a Challenge to Cultural Hegemony?', *Journalism Studies* (2(2): 221–42)

Richardson, J.E. (2004). *(Mis)Representing Islam: The Racism and Rhetoric of British Broadsheet Newspapers* (Amsterdam, John Benjamins)

Rigoni, I. (2001). *Mobilisations et enjeux des migrations de Turquie en Europe de l'Ouest* (Paris, L'Harmattan, 'Logiques sociales')

Rogers, P. (2001). 'There Was an Alternative', *Red Pepper* (December 2001)

Runnymede Trust (1997). *Islamophobia: a Challenge for Us All* (London, Runnymede Trust)

Runnymede Trust (2000). *The Future of Multi-Ethnic Britain* (London, Profile Books)

Runnymede Trust (2001). *Addressing Prejudice and Islamophobia. Resources, References and Guidance on the Internet* (London, Runnymede Trust)

Saad, L. (2002). 'Al Jazeera: Arabs Rate its Objectivity', *Gallup Poll Tuesday Briefing* (23 April 2002)

Sackur, S. (2002). *BBC 10 O'Clock News* (4 March 2002)

Said, E. (1987). 'The MESA Debate: the Scholars, the Media, and the Middle East', *Journal of Palestinian Studies* (16(2): 88–9)

Said, E.W. (1978). *Orientalism* (New York, Pantheon Books)

Said, E.W. (1981). *Covering Islam: How the Media and the Experts Determine How We See the Rest of the World* (New York, Pantheon Books)

Said, E.W. (1994). *Culture and Imperialism* (London, Vintage)

Said, E.W. (1995). *Orientalism* (London, Penguin)

Said, E.W. (1997). *Covering Islam* (London, Vintage)

Sanger, D. (2003). 'On High-Speed Trip, Bush Glimpses a Perception Gap', *New York Times* (25 October 2003)

Sardar, Z. and Davies, M.W. (2002) *Why Do People Hate America?* (Cambridge, Icon)

Schanzer, J. (2003). 'The Arab Street and the War: are Regimes in Control?', *Policywatch* (The Washington Institute for Near Eastern Policy, no. 729, at <http://www.washingtoninstitute.org/watch/policy watch/policywatch2003/729.htm> (21 March 2003)

Schleifer, S.A. (2003). *Satellite Television News: Up, Down, and Out in Doha, Dubai, and Abu Dhabi*, at <http://www.tbsjournal.com/Archives/ Spring03/satellite%20tv.html>

Shaheen, J. (1984). *The TV Arab* (Bowling Green, Ohio, Bowling Green State University Popular Press)

Shboul, A. (1988). 'Islam and the Australian Media', *Australian Religious Studies Review* (1(2): 18–23)

Shelah, O. (2003). *The Israeli Army: a Radical Proposal* (Or Yehuda, Kinneret, Zmora-Bitan, Dvir) [Hebrew]

Shlaim, A. (2000). *The Iron Wall: Israel and the Arab World* (London, Penguin Press)

Simon, R.S. (1989). *The Middle East in Crime Fiction: Mysteries, Spy Novels, and Thrillers From 1916 to the 1980s* (New York, Lilian Barber Press)

Society of Editors Training Committee (2004). *Diversity in the Newsroom – Employment of Minority Ethnic Journalists in Newspapers*

Spotbeam Communications (2002). 'Middle East Communications and Internet Via Satellite', at <http://www.mindbranch.com/page/catalog/ product/2e6a73703f706172746e65723d31303326636f64653d52313331

2d303038.html>

St John, R.B. (2004). 'High Time Bush Defines the Enemy, Foreign Policy in Focus', at <http://www.fpif.org/commentary/2004/0407enemy.html>

Steele, J. (2001). 'Fighting the Wrong War', *Guardian* (11 December 2001)

Steele, J. (2002). 'Forgotten victims', *Guardian* (20 May 2002)

Taylor, C. (1994). *Multiculturalism*, ed. A. Gutman (Princeton, Princeton University Press)

Telhami, S. (2002). 'Public Opinion Could Flare out of Control in Arab Nations', *San Jose Mercury News* at <http://www.brookings.edu/views/op-ed/telhami/20020407.htm> (7 April 2002)

Telhami, S. (2004). 'Double Blow to Mideast Democracy', *Washington Post* (1 May 2004)

Telhami, S. and Zogby, J. (2004). *Arab Attitudes Towards Political and Social Issues, Foreign Policy and the Media* at <http://www.bsos.umd.edu/sadat/pub/Arab%20Attitudes%20Towards%20Political%20and%20Social%20Issues,%20Foreign%20Policy%20and%20the%20Media.htm> (23 July 2004)

Tessler, M. (2003). 'Arab and Muslim Political Attitudes: Stereotypes and Evidence from Survey Research', *International Studies Perspectives* (4: 175–80)

Tessler, M. and Corstange, D. (2002). 'How Should Americans Understand Arab and Muslim Public Opinion Attitudes: Combating Stereotypes with Public Opinion Data from the Middle East', *Journal of Social Affairs* (19/76: 13–34)

Tester, K. (2001). *Compassion, Morality and the Media* (Buckingham, Open University Press)

Tokatly, Oren (2000). *Communication Policy in Israel* (Tel-Aviv, Open University of Israel) [Hebrew]

Troop, P. (2003). Address to 'Communicating the War on Terror Conference', the Royal Institution (London, 5 June 2003)

Troyna, B. (1981). *Public Awareness and the Media: a Study of Reporting on Race* (London, CRE)

Tuchman, G. (1972). 'Objectivity as Strategic Ritual: an Examination of Newsmen's Notions of Objectivity', *American Journal of Sociology* (77 (4): 660–79)

Turner, G. (2003). 'After Hybridity: Muslim-Australians and the Imagined Community', *Continuum: Journal of Media and Cultural Studies* (17(4): 411–18)

UNDP Arab Fund for Economic and Social Development (2003). *Arab Human Development Report: Building a Knowledge Society* (UNDP 2003 [*AHDR 2003*]: 63–5)

UNDP Arab Fund for Economic and Social Development (2002). *Arab Human Development Report: Creating Opportunities for Future Generations* (UNDP 2002) at <http://www.undp.org/rbas/ahdr/> (*AHDP 2002*: 75)

Vallely, P. (2000). 'It's Time to Say What's Good About Being a Muslim', *Independent* (31 October 2000)

Vertovec, S. (1998). 'Young Muslims in Keighley, West Yorkshire: Cultural Identity, Context and "Community"', in Vertovec, S. and Rogers, A. (eds), *Muslim European Youth. Reproducing Ethnicity, Religion and Culture* (Aldershot, Ashgate)

Walker, D. (1999). *Anxious Nation: Australia and the Rise of Asia, 1850–1939* (Brisbane, University of Queensland Press)

Weibel, N. (2000). *Par-delà le voile. Femmes d'islam en Europe* (Bruxelles, Complexe)

Werbner, P. (1994). 'Diaspora and the Millennium: British Pakistani Global–Local Fabulations of the Gulf War', in Ahmed, A. and Donnan, H. (eds), *Islam, Globalisation and Postmodernity* (London, Routledge)

Woodward, B. (2004). *Plan of Attack* (New York, Simon and Schuster)

Woollacott, M. (2001). 'A Military Response is Risky But Necessary for America, *Guardian* (21 September 2001)

Yavari-D'Hellencourt, N. (2000), '"Diabolisation" et "normalisation" de l'islam. Une analyse du discours télévisuel en France', in Brechon, Pierre and Willaime, Jean-Paul (eds), *Médias et religions en miroir* (Paris, PUF)

Zogby, J. (2003). 'Bush and the Middle East', in *Washingtonpost.com Live Online* at <http://discuss.washingtonpost.com/zforum/03/sp_world _zogby060403.htm> (4 June 2003)

Zogby, J. and Zogby, J.J. (2004). *Impressions of America 2004: How Arabs View America; How Arabs Learn About America* (Washington, D.C., The Arab American Institute/Zogby International)

Zuckerman, L. (1986). 'The Dilemma of the Forgotten Hostages', *Columbia Journalism Review* (July/August 30–4)

Index

Numbers in italics refer to information in tables and figures

233